PRACTICE
MAKES
PERFECT®

Basic English

PRACTICE MAKES PERFECT ®

Basic English

PREMIUM FOURTH EDITION

Julie Lachance

New York   Chicago   San Francisco   Athens   London   Madrid
Mexico City   Milan   New Delhi   Singapore   Sydney   Toronto

1 2 3 4 5 6 7 8 9   LHS   28 27 26 25 24 23

ISBN   978-1-265-38886-7
MHID   1-265-38886-5

e-ISBN   978-1-265-39104-1
e-MHID   1-265-39104-1

Interior design by Village Bookworks, Inc.

McGraw Hill products are available at special quantity discounts to use as premiums and sales promotions or for use in corporate training programs. To contact a representative, please visit the Contact Us pages at www.mhprofessional.com.

McGraw Hill is committed to making our products accessible to all learners. To learn more about the available support and accommodations we offer, please contact us at accessibility@mheducation.com. We also participate in the Access Text Network (www.accesstext.org), and ATN members may submit requests through ATN.

McGraw Hill Language Lab App

Recordings for 50 pronunciation exercises, listed in the appendix, are available as streaming audio via our unique Language Lab app, in addition to recordings of the answer key to numerous exercises throughout the book. Go to mhlanguagelab.com to access the online version of this application, or download the mobile version from the Apple App store (for iPhone and iPad), or the Google Play store (for Android devices). Note: Internet connection required.

This book is dedicated to my students because they have taught and given me so much over the years.

Contents

REVIEW EXERCISES

APPENDIX

Introduction

Congratulations on choosing *Practice Makes Perfect: Basic English* for your first year of English language learning.

There is really only one way to learn a new language, and that is to build your vocabulary, learn the verb tenses and the mechanics of that language, and then practice, practice, practice. This workbook was designed to help you do just that.

This workbook will help you to proficiently learn and effectively master the strategies and methods needed to provide you with a solid foundation in English. All the lessons are presented in a simple and progressive format designed to help you retain the knowledge and gain confidence by applying and reinforcing the skills acquired throughout the workbook.

You will learn the mechanics of English through user-friendly, interactive, and well-constructed grammar exercises. These exercises are loaded with everyday basic words intended to help you quickly and efficiently enrich your vocabulary and give you a firm understanding of the lesson before moving on to the next.

Ample space is provided in each lesson for you to record your new vocabulary words in a central location to allow you to study these words regularly and refer back to them quickly when necessary. Be sure to learn these words by heart as they are basic and useful English words.

The second section of *Practice Makes Perfect: Basic English* provides you with a variety of review exercises specially designed to allow you to measure your comprehension and retention of the concepts covered in the lessons of this workbook. Since these review exercises are directly related to the learning objectives of this workbook, they will allow you to recognize your achievements and highlight your progress. They will also provide you with the opportunity to strengthen your abilities by serving as extra practice for the material previously studied. To assure a fair and accurate self-evaluation of your progress, be sure to complete the entire workbook before attempting these review exercises.

This Premium Fourth Edition is enhanced by 50 pronunciation exercises, available as streaming audio through the McGraw Hill Language Lab app. These exercises provide extensive practice of the sounds that learners of English find particularly difficult—simply listen and repeat. The text of the thirty example sentences for each exercise is provided in the appendix of this book, as well as within the app. Additional audio practice is provided by the recordings of answers to selected exercises throughout the book; the app enables you to compare your responses to those of native speakers.

Learning a new language is an interesting and exciting journey that is enhanced when the learning material is presented in a stimulating and enjoyable manner that encourages a learner to keep moving forward.

We wish you much success and enjoyment throughout your learning process using this workbook, and we are confident that you will gain from it exactly what was intended: a solid comprehension of your first year of English language learning.

Good luck, and above all, have fun.

Basic English

To Be: Present Tense

The verb **to be** describes the identity, qualities, or condition of a person or object. Use the following to form the present tense of the verb **to be**.

I am	→	I am happy today.
you are	→	You are smart.
he is	→	He is my friend.
she is	→	She is busy.
it is	→	It is true.
we are	→	We are tired.
they are	→	They are here.

EXERCISE

1·1

Use your dictionary to find the meaning of the new vocabulary words needed for this exercise before you begin. Write the words in your language in the space provided.

flashlight	_____	happy	_____
kitchen	_____	sick	_____
girl	_____	flower	_____
vacuum	_____	tent	_____
counter	_____	toy	_____
basement	_____	ribbon	_____
closet	_____	dirty	_____
today	_____	pink	_____
nice	_____	pretty	_____
smart	_____	yellow	_____
microwave oven	_____	here	_____
busy	_____	ready	_____
small	_____	fridge	_____
floor	_____	hair	_____
tired	_____	twins	_____
true	_____	friend	_____

Rewrite the following sentences to create the present tense by choosing the correct form of the verb **to be** *in parentheses.*

1. The girl (am, is, are) pretty.

   _____

2. I (am, is, are) ready.

   _____

3. She (am, is, are) my friend.

   _____

4. They (am, is, are) twins.

   _____

5. The flowers (am, is, are) yellow.

   _____

6. The flashlight (am, is, are) in the tent.

   _____

7. The fridge and counter in the kitchen (am, is, are) dirty.

   _____

   _____

8. I (am, is, are) tired today.

   _____

9. We (am, is, are) busy.

   _____

10. The toys (am, is, are) in the basement.

    _____

11. The ribbons in my hair (am, is, are) pink.

    _____

12. The kitchen (am, is, are) very small.

    _____

13. The vacuum (am, is, are) in the closet.

    _____

14. He (am, is, are) nice.

    _____

15. The microwave oven (am, is, are) in the kitchen.

    _____

16. The toy (am, is, are) on the floor.

_____

17. I (am, is, are) sick today.

_____

_____

Use your dictionary to find the meaning of the new vocabulary words needed for this exercise before you begin. Write the words in your language in the space provided.

aunt	_____	cousin	_____
cloud	_____	uncle	_____
red	_____	bright	_____
window	_____	blue	_____
cold	_____	brother	_____
teacher	_____	class	_____
man	_____	tall	_____
news	_____	hot	_____
furniture	_____	upstairs	_____
moon	_____	green	_____
bug	_____	woman	_____
bald	_____	student	_____
open	_____	juice	_____
sad	_____	lawyer	_____
room	_____	grass	_____
old	_____	lazy	_____

Complete the following sentences using the correct form of the verb **to be**.

1. My aunt _____ nice.

2. The clouds _____ white.

3. Kathy _____ sick.

4. The ribbons _____ yellow.

5. We _____ twins.

6. The windows _____ open.

7. Colton and Cody _____ brothers.

8. We _____ teachers.

9. It _____ a French book.

10. You _____ very smart.

11. It _____ sad news.

12. She _____ my cousin.

13. You _____ tired.

14. The grass _____ green.

15. It _____ in my room.

16. They _____ lazy.

17. The flower _____ yellow.

18. The bug _____ on the counter.

19. I _____ tall.

20. The man _____ happy.

21. The vacuum _____ red.

22. The tent _____ blue.

23. The juice _____ cold.

24. She _____ a student.

25. They _____ in my class.

26. The woman _____ a lawyer.

27. She _____ upstairs.

28. The teacher _____ smart.

29. The ribbon _____ blue.

30. The water _____ hot.

31. My uncle _____ bald.

32. The furniture _____ old.

33. The fridge _____ in the kitchen.

34. The moon _____ bright.

To Be: Present Tense: Negative Form

Place **not** after the verb **to be** to create the negative form of the present tense.

I am	→	I am not	→	I am not ready.
you are	→	you are not	→	You are not busy.
he is	→	he is not	→	He is not my friend.
she is	→	she is not	→	She is not tall.
it is	→	it is not	→	It is not true.
we are	→	we are not	→	We are not tired.
they are	→	they are not	→	They are not pink.

The negative form of the present tense of the verb **to be** can also be expressed with the contraction **isn't** or **aren't**. There is no contraction for **am not**.

I am not	→	I am not	→	I am not sick.
you are not	→	you aren't	→	You aren't a teacher.
he is not	→	he isn't	→	He isn't a lawyer.
she is not	→	she isn't	→	She isn't ready.
it is not	→	it isn't	→	It isn't a toy.
we are not	→	we aren't	→	We aren't twins.
they are not	→	they aren't	→	They aren't yellow.

EXERCISE
2·1

Use your dictionary to find the meaning of the new vocabulary words needed for this exercise before you begin. Write the words in your language in the space provided.

table	_____	neighbor	_____
city	_____	cheese	_____
kid	_____	Italian	_____
sister	_____	early	_____
bus	_____	Spanish	_____
sister-in-law	_____	drawer	_____
sour	_____	empty	_____
lime	_____	pregnant	_____

Rewrite the following sentences to express the negative form. Write the sentence once using **am not**, **is not**, *or* **are not** *and once using the contraction* **isn't** *or* **aren't**.

1. The cheese is on the table.

   _____

   _____

2. She is my sister.

   _____

   _____

3. My neighbors are Spanish.

   _____

   _____

4. My sister-in-law is Italian.

   _____

   _____

5. Diane is pregnant.

   _____

   _____

6. The limes are sour.

   _____

   _____

7. The bus is empty.

   _____

   _____

8. The kids are early for class today.

   _____

   _____

9. The drawers are empty.

   _____

   _____

10. It is a nice city.

   _____

   _____

Use your dictionary to find the meaning of the new vocabulary words needed for this exercise before you begin. Write the words in your language in the space provided.

boss	_____	wife	_____
mall	_____	boy	_____
far	_____	dragonfly	_____
subway	_____	full	_____
road	_____	white	_____
eraser	_____	bowl	_____
fair	_____	black	_____
wide	_____	hand	_____
husband	_____	pen	_____
good	_____	expensive	_____
idea	_____	late	_____
store	_____	car	_____
key	_____	garbage can	_____
office	_____	garbage bag	_____
work	_____	shelf	_____
book	_____	pencil case	_____
school	_____	shoe	_____
ceiling	_____	doctor	_____

Use **am not** or the contraction **isn't** or **aren't** to complete the following negative sentences.

1. The subway _____ full.

2. The windows _____ dirty.

3. It _____ a dragonfly.

4. The keys _____ in the car.

5. The microwave oven _____ in the kitchen.

6. My boss _____ at the office.

7. The boys _____ in the tent.

8. We _____ busy at work.

9. My hands _____ dirty.

10. The eraser _____ in the pencil case.

11. She _____ a teacher in my school.

To Be: Present Tense: Negative Form   **7**

12. The ceiling _____ white.

13. The bowls _____ on the table.

14. The garbage bags _____ in the drawer.

15. The garbage can _____ full.

16. The store _____ far.

17. It _____ fair.

18. The roads in the city _____ wide.

19. My husband _____ a doctor.

20. The pens _____ black.

21. The books _____ on the shelf.

22. The vacuum _____ in the basement.

23. They _____ friends.

24. The ribbon _____ red.

25. She _____ late for class today.

26. It _____ true.

27. I _____ tired.

28. Barry _____ a good student.

29. The juice _____ cold.

30. My wife _____ at the mall.

31. The shoes _____ expensive.

32. The students _____ tired today

33. The woman _____ old.

34. It _____ a good idea.

To Be: Present Tense: Question Form

Place the verb **to be** before the subject to create the question form of the present tense.

I am	→	am I	→	Am I late?
you are	→	are you	→	Are you my new boss?
he is	→	is he	→	Is he your teacher?
she is	→	is she	→	Is she your neighbor?
it is	→	is it	→	Is it expensive?
we are	→	are we	→	Are we early?
they are	→	are they	→	Are they in the basement?

EXERCISE

3·1

Use your dictionary to find the meaning of the new vocabulary words needed for this exercise before you begin. Write the words in your language in the space provided.

wheel	_____	pond	_____
policeman	_____	bathroom	_____
goldfish	_____	outside	_____
sweet	_____	toothbrush	_____
meeting	_____	toothpaste	_____
serious	_____	bathing suit	_____
English	_____	desk	_____
orange	_____	coat	_____
sharpener	_____	cow	_____
clothesline	_____	box	_____
garage	_____	calf	_____
French	_____	frog	_____
brown	_____	poor	_____
downstairs	_____	very	_____

*Rewrite the following sentences to create questions by placing the verb **to be** before the subject.*
Don't forget to include a question mark (?) in your answer.

1. The wheels are in the garage.

   _____

2. The sharpener is on my desk.

   _____

3. The toothbrush and toothpaste are in the bathroom.

   _____

4. My bathing suit is on the clothesline.

   _____

5. I am in your English class.

   _____

6. It is cold outside.

   _____

7. He is a policeman in the city.

   _____

8. The coats are on the floor.

   _____

9. Johanne and Véronique are in a meeting.

   _____

10. The toys are in the box downstairs.

    _____

11. The cow and calf are brown.

    _____

12. The orange juice is sweet.

    _____

13. The frogs are in the pond.

    _____

14. The goldfish is in the bowl.

    _____

15. You are serious.

    _____

16. Marie is French.

    _____

Use your dictionary to find the meaning of the new vocabulary words needed for this exercise before you begin. Write the words in your language in the space provided.

knife	_____	gate	_____
dishwasher	_____	printer	_____
fork	_____	nail polish	_____
bill	_____	bird	_____
correct	_____	skunk	_____
living room	_____	pillow	_____
clean	_____	accountant	_____
real	_____	ink	_____
sharp	_____	fence	_____
lipstick	_____	thread	_____
oven	_____	curtain	_____
bed	_____	pen	_____
funny	_____	Mrs.	_____
pearl	_____	pot	_____
sheet	_____	birdhouse	_____
turkey	_____	pan	_____
Chinese	_____	pig	_____
Mr.	_____	garden	_____
Scottish	_____	again	_____
needle	_____	there	_____

Complete the following questions using the correct form of the verb **to be***.*

1. _____ it cold in Canada?

2. _____ the skunks in my garden again?

3. _____ the needle and thread in the drawer?

4. _____ he a good accountant?

5. _____ they in the living room?

6. _____ the ink in the printer?

7. _____ the pots and pans clean?

8. _____ she your sister-in-law?

9. _____ the forks in the dishwasher?

10. _____ we ready?

11. _____ it a black pen?

12. _____ I nice?

13. _____ you busy today?

14. _____ the gate open?

15. _____ the fridge empty?

16. _____ Mr. and Mrs. Yee Chinese?

17. _____ the pillows on the bed?

18. _____ the fence white?

19. _____ the books on the shelf?

20. _____ the sheets on the clothesline?

21. _____ the curtains blue?

22. _____ the nail polish purple?

23. _____ the pearls real?

24. _____ Mrs. McMahon Scottish?

25. _____ the turkey in the oven?

26. _____ the birds in the birdhouse?

27. _____ the pigs in the pen?

28. _____ the knife sharp?

29. _____ the bill correct?

30. _____ the lipstick red or pink?

31. _____ they there?

32. _____ I funny?

To Be: Past Tense

·4·

The past tense of the verb **to be** is created by using **was** or **were** in place of **am**, **is**, and **are**.

I am	→	I was	→	I was tired at school today.
you are	→	you were	→	You were downstairs.
he is	→	he was	→	He was funny.
she is	→	she was	→	She was at work.
it is	→	it was	→	It was on the shelf.
we are	→	we were	→	We were upstairs.
they are	→	they were	→	They were here.

EXERCISE

4·1

Use your dictionary to find the meaning of the new vocabulary words needed for this exercise before you begin. Write the words in your language in the space provided.

snake	_____	farm	_____
diaper	_____	minnow	_____
sorry	_____	crust	_____
beach	_____	grandmother	_____
pencil	_____	hairdresser	_____
bag	_____	exam	_____
roommate	_____	thick	_____
laundry room	_____	pool	_____
bucket	_____	washer	_____
pocket	_____	dryer	_____

Rewrite the following sentences to create the past tense by changing the present tense form of the verb **to be** *to the past tense form.*

1. He is my roommate.

   _____

2. It is in my pocket.

   _____

3. The snake is in the garden.

   _____

4. The diapers are in the bag.

   _____

5. Lisa is sick.

   _____

6. The kids are in the pool.

   _____

7. The bucket is full of minnows.

   _____

8. The washer and dryer are in the laundry room.

   _____

9. I am in my office.

   _____

10. The pencil is on the floor.

    _____

11. Sorry that I am late.

    _____

12. The flowers are for Jennifer.

    _____

13. My grandmother is in the hospital.

    _____

14. The exam is easy.

    _____

15. The crust is very thick.

    _____

16. The farm is very far.

    _____

Use your dictionary to find the meaning of the new vocabulary words needed for this exercise before you begin. Write the words in your language in the space provided.

huge	_____	cupboard	_____
ring	_____	asleep	_____
crib	_____	skating rink	_____
story	_____	slipper	_____
fresh	_____	wedding	_____
soft	_____	egg	_____
spicy	_____	shower	_____
baby	_____	awake	_____
with	_____	vase	_____
wine	_____	locker	_____
cellar	_____	soup	_____
rake	_____	whale	_____
downtown	_____	bedroom	_____
broken	_____	last night	_____
godmother	_____	couch	_____
yesterday	_____	both	_____
candle	_____	library	_____
nurse	_____	cafeteria	_____

Complete the following past tense sentences using **was** *or* **were***.*

1. The baby _____ in the crib.

2. The candles _____ on the table.

3. It _____ a good story.

4. They _____ awake.

5. My godmother _____ asleep on the couch.

6. The wine _____ in the cellar.

7. I _____ ready.

8. He _____ in the shower.

9. The bowls _____ in the cupboard.

10. The girls _____ at the skating rink.

11. The moon _____ bright last night.

12. The juice _____ fresh.

13. The eggs _____ on the counter.

14. My sister _____ outside.

15. The keys _____ in the car.

16. The ring _____ expensive.

17. You _____ at the wedding.

18. The soup _____ hot and spicy.

19. Both pillows _____ soft.

20. Annie _____ a nurse.

21. The flowers _____ in the vase.

22. The rake _____ in the garage.

23. My slippers _____ in the bedroom.

24. The whale _____ huge.

25. We _____ downtown yesterday.

26. Chris _____ in the cafeteria with Cory.

27. It _____ in my locker.

28. We _____ at the library.

29. The pool _____ small.

30. The printer _____ broken.

31. My pockets _____ full.

32. The teachers _____ in the office.

To Be: Past Tense: Negative Form

Place **not** after the past tense form of the verb **to be** to create a negative sentence.

I was	→	I was not	→	I was not sick yesterday.
you were	→	you were not	→	You were not at the beach.
he was	→	he was not	→	He was not at the meeting.
she was	→	she was not	→	She was not very nice.
it was	→	it was not	→	It was not on my desk.
we were	→	we were not	→	We were not late.
they were	→	they were not	→	They were not ready.

The negative form of the past tense of the verb **to be** can also be expressed with the contraction **wasn't** or **weren't**.

I was not	→	I wasn't	→	I wasn't tired last night.
you were not	→	you weren't	→	You weren't at work today.
he was not	→	he wasn't	→	He wasn't serious.
she was not	→	she wasn't	→	She wasn't here yesterday.
it was not	→	it wasn't	→	It wasn't true.
we were not	→	we weren't	→	We weren't at the library.
they were not	→	they weren't	→	They weren't busy last night.

EXERCISE

5·1

Use your dictionary to find the meaning of the new vocabulary words needed for this exercise before you begin. Write the words in your language in the space provided.

dress	_____	list	_____
purple	_____	year	_____
tree	_____	joke	_____
raccoon	_____	plate	_____
waitress	_____	play (n)	_____
fast	_____	name	_____

*Rewrite the following sentences to express the negative form. Write the sentence once using **was not** or **were not** and once using the contraction **wasn't** or **weren't**.*

1. The dress was blue.

   _____

   _____

2. The couch in the living room was dirty.

   _____

   _____

3. They were very fast.

   _____

   _____

4. It was a good joke.

   _____

   _____

5. The raccoons were in the tree.

   _____

   _____

6. The slippers were purple.

   _____

   _____

7. We were at the play last night.

   _____

   _____

8. The plates were in the dishwasher.

   _____

   _____

9. Karen was a waitress for three years.

   _____

   _____

10. My name was on the list.

   _____

   _____

Use your dictionary to find the meaning of the new vocabulary words needed for this exercise before you begin. Write the words in your language in the space provided.

phone	_____	stove	_____
quiet	_____	cat	_____
mark	_____	ugly	_____
clever	_____	slide	_____
landlord	_____	horn	_____
butter	_____	sock	_____
deep	_____	long	_____
loud	_____	big	_____
jam	_____	lake	_____
off	_____	toolbox	_____
binder	_____	ground	_____
shaver	_____	stroller	_____
nest	_____	rat	_____
right answer	_____	movie	_____
powder	_____	snowstorm	_____
stain	_____	light	_____
funeral	_____	hammer	_____
Greek	_____	bread	_____
polite	_____	museum	_____
vegetable	_____	on	_____

*Use the contraction **wasn't** or **weren't** to complete the following negative sentences.*

1. My marks _____ good at school last year.

2. It _____ a raccoon; it was a skunk.

3. The stain on the floor _____ big.

4. The vegetables _____ fresh.

5. You _____ very polite with the landlord.

6. It _____ the right answer.

7. The horn in my car _____ loud.

8. We _____ at the funeral.

9. The kids _____ quiet today in class.

10. The grass _____ long.

11. She _____ very clever.

12. The lake _____ deep.

13. The baby _____ in the stroller.

14. He _____ on the slide.

15. My socks _____ on the clothesline.

16. The shaver _____ in the bathroom.

17. The bread and butter _____ on the counter.

18. The museum _____ very big.

19. The rats _____ in the cellar.

20. The nest _____ on the ground.

21. I _____ on the phone.

22. It _____ a big snowstorm.

23. The binders _____ in my locker.

24. The man _____ Greek; he was Italian.

25. The jam _____ in the fridge.

26. It _____ a good movie.

27. The lights _____ on.

28. The stove _____ off.

29. It _____ ugly.

30. The cat _____ black.

31. The hammer _____ in the toolbox.

32. The powder _____ on the shelf.

To Be: Past Tense: Question Form

Place **was** or **were** before the subject to form questions in the past tense of the verb **to be**.

I was	→	was I	→	Was I funny?
you were	→	were you	→	Were you awake?
he was	→	was he	→	Was he very tall?
she was	→	was she	→	Was she downtown?
it was	→	was it	→	Was it on the floor?
we were	→	were we	→	Were we fast?
they were	→	were they	→	Were they asleep?

EXERCISE
6·1

Use your dictionary to find the meaning of the new vocabulary words needed for this exercise before you begin. Write the words in your language in the space provided.

recipe	_____	easy	_____
ship	_____	velvet	_____
free	_____	enough	_____
angry	_____	nail clippers	_____
low	_____	kindergarten	_____
door	_____	flight attendant	_____
lady	_____	tablecloth	_____
thin	_____	bitter	_____
young	_____	seasick	_____
crutches	_____	behind	_____
ashtray	_____	together	_____
sky	_____	airplane	_____

Rewrite the following sentences to create questions in the past tense by placing **was** *or* **were** *before the subject. Don't forget to include a question mark (?) in your answer.*

1. It was free.
   _____

2. The airplane was very low in the sky.
   _____

3. The mall was empty.
   _____

4. They were in kindergarten together.
   _____

5. It was bitter.
   _____

6. You were angry at Susan.
   _____

7. The recipe was easy.
   _____

8. The nail clippers were in the drawer.
   _____

9. The curtains were velvet.
   _____

10. The tablecloth was dirty.
    _____

11. It was enough.
    _____

12. She was a flight attendant when she was young.
    _____

13. The ashtrays were full.
    _____

14. The lady was thin.
    _____

15. Claude was seasick on the ship.
    _____

16. The crutches were behind the door.
    _____

Use your dictionary to find the meaning of the new vocabulary words needed for this exercise before you begin. Write the words in your language in the space provided.

plastic	_____	boring	_____
rotten	_____	water	_____
swan	_____	ripe	_____
teller	_____	on fire	_____
cashier	_____	driveway	_____
after	_____	parking lot	_____
jar	_____	laptop computer	_____
rib	_____	hardware store	_____
marker	_____	awful	_____
result	_____	snowflake	_____
snow	_____	every day	_____
iron	_____	instructions	_____
teddy bear	_____	new	_____
grocery store	_____	report card	_____
warm	_____	open	_____
high school	_____	pumpkin	_____
deodorant	_____	fruit	_____
bank	_____	high chair	_____
blanket	_____	president	_____
weather	_____	brush	_____

Complete the following sentences using **was** or **were** to form questions in the past tense.

1. _____ the weather awful?

2. _____ the snowflakes big?

3. _____ he at school every day?

4. _____ you a cashier at the grocery store?

5. _____ the movie boring?

6. _____ the vegetables fresh?

7. _____ your report card good?

8. _____ the jars on the shelf?

9. _____ the laptop computer new?

To Be: Past Tense: Question Form 23

10. _____ the teddy bear in the crib?

11. _____ the fruit in the bowl ripe?

12. _____ the baby in the high chair?

13. _____ you in my class in high school?

14. _____ the hardware store open?

15. _____ the ribs good?

16. _____ the swan white?

17. _____ the blankets warm?

18. _____ Sandra on the phone?

19. _____ they at the museum?

20. _____ the pumpkins rotten?

21. _____ the brush in the bathroom?

22. _____ the house on fire?

23. _____ the results good?

24. _____ the driveway full of snow?

25. _____ the iron hot?

26. _____ he the president?

27. _____ the water cold?

28. _____ the deodorant in the bathroom?

29. _____ Linda a teller at the bank?

30. _____ the parking lot full?

31. _____ the instructions in the plastic bag?

32. _____ the marker yellow?

33. _____ I fast enough?

34. _____ you at the funeral?

35. _____ they in the garden?

36. _____ she at the meeting?

37. _____ it expensive?

38. _____ we late for school yesterday?

39. _____ he at the beach with Mary?

Exceptional Uses with the Verb *To Be*

The following are common expressions that use the verb **to be**.

to be cold	to be hungry	to be twenty-five years old
to be hot	to be thirsty	to be scared/afraid
to be right	to be wrong	to be ashamed

EXERCISE

7·1

Use your dictionary to find the meaning of the new vocabulary words needed for this exercise before you begin. Write the words in your language in the space provided.

because	_____	thunder	_____
snowball	_____	please	_____
mother	_____	father	_____
behavior	_____	this morning	_____
spider	_____	race	_____
lightning	_____	son	_____
all the time	_____	size	_____
daughter	_____	guest	_____
birthday	_____	last	_____
breakfast	_____	dark	_____

Rewrite the following sentences using the correct form of the verb **to be.** *Use the information in parentheses at the end of each sentence to help you determine the correct tense and to know whether the sentence is affirmative or negative.*

1. My daughter (to be) afraid of the dark. (present tense, affirmative)

   _____

2. (To be) Jason right? (present tense, affirmative)

   _____

3. She (to be) hungry for breakfast this morning. (past tense, negative)

_____

_____

4. Please open the windows. I (to be) very hot. (present tense, affirmative)

_____

_____

5. I (to be) ashamed of the size of my shoes. (present tense, negative)

_____

_____

6. Cathy (to be) thirty-three years old on her last birthday. (past tense, affirmative)

_____

_____

7. We (to be) very thirsty after the race. (past tense, affirmative)

_____

8. You (to be) wrong again. (present tense, affirmative)

_____

9. I (to be) right all the time. (present tense, negative)

_____

10. (To be) you scared of thunder? (present tense, affirmative)

_____

11. He (to be) afraid of the lightning. (past tense, negative)

_____

12. I (to be) cold this morning. (past tense, affirmative)

_____

13. (To be) the guests hungry? (present tense, affirmative)

_____

14. My mother and father (to be) ashamed of my behavior. (past tense, affirmative)

_____

_____

15. (To be) your son scared of spiders? (present tense, affirmative)

_____

16. I (to be) eighteen years old. (present tense, negative)

_____

17. Bill is happy because he (to be) right. (present tense, affirmative)

_____

18. I (to be) cold because of the snowballs in my pocket. (present tense, affirmative)

_____

_____

_____

Use your dictionary to find the meaning of the new vocabulary words needed for this exercise before you begin. Write the words in your language in the space provided.

needle	_____	jellyfish	_____
never	_____	frequently	_____
crow	_____	summer	_____
shark	_____	usually	_____

Complete the following sentences using the correct form of the verb **to be**.

1. He _____ ashamed of you. (past tense, negative)

2. _____ they cold at the beach? (past tense, affirmative)

3. She _____ right. (present tense, negative)

4. We _____ wrong. (past tense, affirmative)

5. Sharon _____ twenty-two years old today. (present tense, affirmative)

6. It _____ hot last summer. (past tense, affirmative)

7. Mark _____ afraid of needles. (present tense, negative)

8. I _____ hungry all the time. (present tense, affirmative)

9. The baby _____ thirsty. (present tense, negative)

10. He _____ wrong. (present tense, affirmative)

11. _____ she right? (past tense, affirmative)

12. It _____ cold in Canada in the winter. (present tense, affirmative)

13. _____ you scared of sharks? (present tense, affirmative)

14. _____ it hot in your class yesterday? (past tense, affirmative)

15. _____ it cold outside? (past tense, affirmative)

16. They _____ wrong. (past tense, negative)

17. She _____ ashamed of her son. (present tense, negative)

18. _____ you cold? (past tense, affirmative)

Exceptional Uses with the Verb *To Be*   **27**

19. I _____ twenty-two years old. (past tense, negative)

20. They _____ ashamed of her. (present tense, negative)

21. Marcel _____ right. (present tense, affirmative)

22. _____ Ben thirsty? (past tense, affirmative)

23. The boys _____ hungry. (present tense, negative)

24. I _____ scared of jellyfish. (present tense, affirmative)

25. The girls _____ thirsty. (present tense, affirmative)

26. _____ they ashamed of me? (past tense, affirmative)

27. It _____ afraid of you. (past tense, negative)

28. Lucy _____ usually right. (present tense, affirmative)

29. He _____ scared of crows. (present tense, negative)

30. It _____ cold downstairs. (past tense, affirmative)

31. She _____ frequently wrong. (present tense, affirmative)

32. _____ Peter hungry? (present tense, affirmative)

33. I _____ afraid of the frog. (past tense, negative)

34. We _____ very hungry. (present tense, affirmative)

Adjectives

Adjectives are used to describe nouns. They are placed before the noun.

a *little* dog	a *clean* house	a *nice* neighbor	a *good* friend
a *pink* flower	a *busy* man	a *good* recipe	a *blue* bucket

Adjectives never take *-s* even if the noun is plural.

brown cows	*big* snowflakes	*expensive* cars	*clean* floors
young girls	*pretty* ribbons	*dirty* shoes	*soft* pillows

EXERCISE
8·1

Use your dictionary to find the meaning of the following verbs and vocabulary words needed for this exercise before you begin. Write the words in your language in the space provided.

to drink	_____	to see	_____
to want	_____	to look	_____
hard	_____	leather	_____
little	_____	hairy	_____
test	_____	for sale	_____
cute	_____	beautiful	_____
prune	_____	country	_____
handsome	_____	windy	_____

Rewrite the following sentences, and include the adjective(s) in the correct place in each sentence.

1. The house is for sale. (cute, little)

   _____

2. It is a knife. (very, sharp)

   _____

3. He is a man. (tall, handsome)

_____

4. It was a day yesterday. (cold, windy)

_____

5. I want a jacket. (black, leather)

_____

6. They drink juice every morning. (prune)

_____

7. The bug is in my shoe. (big, green)

_____

8. Elizabeth is a teacher. (French)

_____

9. The spider is in the kitchen. (ugly, hairy)

_____

10. Canada is a country. (big, beautiful)

_____

11. The test was hard. (English)

_____

12. He was a policeman. (nice)

_____

13. Look at the snow. (beautiful, white)

_____

14. The frog is in the pond. (little, green)

_____

15. It was a whale. (huge)

_____

Use your dictionary to find the meaning of the following verbs and vocabulary words needed for this exercise before you begin. Write the words in your language in the space provided.

to make	_____	to wear	_____
to hate	_____	to need	_____
to like	_____	to watch	_____
to love	_____	to draw	_____
pie	_____	right	_____
silver	_____	cake	_____
star	_____	BBQ	_____
watch	_____	knee	_____
junk	_____	wealthy	_____
sore	_____	dessert	_____
food	_____	swollen	_____
balloon	_____	left	_____
rhubarb	_____	strawberry	_____
Mexican	_____	yogurt	_____
picture	_____	round	_____
identical	_____	chocolate	_____

Rewrite the following sentences and include the adjective(s) in the correct place in the sentence.

1. It was a winter. (long, hard)

   _____

2. I need a watch. (new, silver)

   _____

3. My hand is sore. (right)

   _____

4. I want the balloons. (round)

   _____

5. We like to watch movies. (old)

   _____

6. Look at the stars in the sky. (bright)

   _____

7. I like chips. (BBQ)

   _____

8. They want cake for dessert. (chocolate)

   _____

9. I love food. (Mexican)

   _____

10. He is a lawyer. (wealthy)

    _____

11. You draw pictures. (funny)

    _____

12. It was a meeting. (long, boring)

    _____

13. My knee is swollen. (left)

    _____

14. The kids like food. (junk)

    _____

15. We like to make pies. (rhubarb)

    _____

16. I hate yogurt. (strawberry)

    _____

17. We wear shoes to school. (white)

    _____

18. They are twins. (identical)

    _____

To Have: Present Tense

Use the following to express the present tense of the verb **to have**.

I have	→	I have a red sharpener.
you have	→	You have a beautiful living room.
he has	→	He has a nice wife.
she has	→	She has a blue toothbrush.
it has	→	It has a small baby.
we have	→	We have a swimming pool.
they have	→	They have a new car.

EXERCISE

9·1

Use your dictionary to find the meaning of the new vocabulary words needed for this exercise before you begin. Write the words in your language in the space provided.

skill	_____	week	_____
bad	_____	attitude	_____
roof	_____	terrible	_____
skirt	_____	smile	_____
headache	_____	milk	_____
dandruff	_____	short	_____
sandwich	_____	next	_____
day off	_____	taste	_____
eye shadow	_____	paw	_____
tail	_____	sleeping bag	_____
lunch	_____	housekeeper	_____
weird	_____	peanut butter	_____

*Rewrite the following sentences using **has** or **have** to form the present tense of the verb **to have**.*

1. He (have, has) a bad attitude.

   _____

2. The cat (have, has) white paws.

   _____

3. I (have, has) a peanut butter sandwich for lunch today.

   _____

4. Maria (have, has) a red velvet skirt.

   _____

5. We (have, has) a nice landlord.

   _____

6. Jessica (have, has) a terrible headache.

   _____

7. We (have, has) a good housekeeper.

   _____

8. She (have, has) a lot of dandruff.

   _____

9. Tony (have, has) very good skills.

   _____

10. The milk (have, has) a weird taste.

    _____

11. The house (have, has) a green roof.

    _____

12. It (have, has) a short tail.

    _____

13. We (have, has) a day off next week.

    _____

14. I (have, has) a warm sleeping bag.

    _____

15. My sister (have, has) purple eye shadow.

    _____

16. You (have, has) a nice smile.

    _____

Use your dictionary to find the meaning of the new vocabulary words needed for this exercise before you begin. Write the words in your language in the space provided.

moose	_____	motorcycle	_____
heartburn	_____	shorts	_____
nail	_____	puppy	_____
education	_____	monkey	_____
kitten	_____	kettle	_____
mailman	_____	licorice	_____
same	_____	seat	_____
banana	_____	bedroom	_____
antlers	_____	cold (n)	_____
letter	_____	rocking chair	_____
parakeet	_____	skate	_____
scary	_____	girlfriend	_____
duck	_____	duckling	_____
helmet	_____	luggage	_____
area code	_____	braid	_____
purse	_____	mirror	_____
sunflower	_____	clock radio	_____
boyfriend	_____	skipping rope	_____

Complete the following sentences using **has** *or* **have** *to form the present tense of the verb* **to have**.

1. I _____ heartburn.

2. He _____ a black helmet.

3. Karina _____ long braids.

4. We _____ rats in the basement.

5. The monkey _____ a banana.

6. I _____ a mirror in my purse.

7. Jay _____ a fast motorcycle.

8. My cat _____ two orange kittens.

9. My sister _____ a boyfriend.

10. I _____ a clock radio in my bedroom.

11. It _____ leather seats.

12. My aunt _____ a cold.

13. Naomi _____ a skipping rope.

14. Derek and Joe _____ black licorice.

15. We _____ a white fridge.

16. He _____ a bad report card this year.

17. The moose _____ big antlers.

18. Billy _____ blue shorts.

19. We _____ sunflowers in the garden.

20. I _____ a new kettle.

21. The mailman _____ a letter for you.

22. They _____ a new puppy.

23. She _____ white skates.

24. You _____ long nails.

25. The duck _____ seven ducklings.

26. We _____ the same area code.

27. My brother _____ a new girlfriend.

28. She _____ a lot of luggage.

29. He _____ a good education.

30. I _____ a rocking chair in my living room.

31. Nathan _____ a scary movie.

32. Jason _____ a blue parakeet.

To Have: Present Tense: Negative Form

Place **do not** or **does not** before the verb **to have** to create a negative sentence. It is important to note that **have** is always used in the negative form and never **has**.

I have	→	I do not have	→	I do not have a dishwasher.
you have	→	you do not have	→	You do not have a pool.
he has	→	he does not have	→	He does not have a helmet.
she has	→	she does not have	→	She does not have braids.
it has	→	it does not have	→	It does not have white paws.
we have	→	we do not have	→	We do not have milk.
they have	→	they do not have	→	They do not have a daughter.

The negative form of the present tense of the verb **to have** can also be expressed with the contraction **don't** or **doesn't**.

I do not have	→	I don't have	→	I don't have a headache.
you do not have	→	you don't have	→	You don't have a flashlight.
he does not have	→	he doesn't have	→	He doesn't have a pen.
she does not have	→	she doesn't have	→	She doesn't have a lawyer.
it does not have	→	it doesn't have	→	It doesn't have a tail.
we do not have	→	we don't have	→	We don't have a garage.
they do not have	→	they don't have	→	They don't have a computer.

EXERCISE
10·1

Use your dictionary to find the meaning of the new vocabulary words needed for this exercise before you begin. Write the words in your language in the space provided.

surprise	_____	clown	_____
bangs	_____	antique	_____
straight	_____	nose	_____
jewelry	_____	about	_____
few	_____	brother-in-law	_____
flea	_____	satellite dish	_____
fantastic	_____	screwdriver	_____
customer	_____	snowmobile	_____

Rewrite the following sentences to create the negative form of the verb **to have**. *Write the sentence once using* **do not** *or* **does not** *and once using the contraction* **don't** *or* **doesn't**.

1. My cat has fleas.

   _____

   _____

2. We have a satellite dish on the roof.

   _____

   _____

3. I have a surprise for you.

   _____

   _____

4. Jimmy has a fast snowmobile.

   _____

   _____

5. We have many good books about antique jewelry.

   _____

   _____

6. She has a lot of customers.

   _____

   _____

7. My brother-in-law has a screwdriver.

   _____

   _____

8. The clown has a big red nose.

   _____

   _____

9. I have long straight hair and bangs.

   _____

   _____

10. She has fantastic news.

   _____

   _____

Use your dictionary to find the meaning of the new vocabulary words needed for this exercise before you begin. Write the words in your language in the space provided.

beard	_____	doll	_____
mean	_____	treadmill	_____
office	_____	bookmark	_____
shower	_____	nail file	_____
landlady	_____	coat	_____
whisker	_____	backyard	_____
fur	_____	curly	_____
glass	_____	ham	_____
horse	_____	pet	_____
ghost	_____	trunk	_____
cell phone	_____	soft	_____
job	_____	diamond	_____
saddle	_____	filing cabinet	_____
firecracker	_____	dandelion	_____
mouse	_____	keyboard	_____
relative	_____	German shepherd	_____

*Complete the following sentences using the contraction **don't** or **doesn't** to create the negative form of the verb **to have** in the present tense.*

1. You _____ have curly hair.

2. My aunt _____ have a diamond ring.

3. Jennifer _____ have a doll.

4. He _____ have a ham sandwich.

5. I _____ have a new saddle for my horse.

6. Glenn _____ have a boring job.

7. The boys _____ have firecrackers.

8. We _____ have a big back yard.

9. I _____ have a cell phone.

10. The cat _____ have soft fur.

11. We _____ have relatives in New York.

12. The mouse _____ have long whiskers.

13. Samuel _____ have a new keyboard.

14. I _____ have three pets.

15. Richard _____ have a German shepherd.

16. My car _____ have a big trunk.

17. You _____ have a vacuum.

18. She _____ have a question.

19. I _____ have a nail file in my purse.

20. My boss _____ have a filing cabinet.

21. We _____ have a mean landlady.

22. Derrick _____ have a beard.

23. She _____ have a bookmark for the book.

24. They _____ have a shower in the bathroom.

25. He _____ have a cold.

26. They _____ have a wealthy uncle.

27. I _____ have a fur coat.

28. We _____ have many dandelions in the yard.

29. You _____ have a treadmill in the basement.

30. The teachers _____ have a meeting today.

31. I _____ have a glass of red wine.

32. We _____ have a ghost in the attic.

33. Jason _____ have a car.

34. Sharon _____ have a toothbrush.

To Have: Present Tense: Question Form

Place **do** or **does** before the subject to create questions with the verb **to have**. As with the negative form, **have** is used for all persons and never **has**.

I have	→	do I have	→	Do I have good skills for the job?
you have	→	do you have	→	Do you have a headache?
he has	→	does he have	→	Does he have a good report card?
she has	→	does she have	→	Does she have a red binder?
it has	→	does it have	→	Does it have a long tail?
we have	→	do we have	→	Do we have a meeting?
they have	→	do they have	→	Do they have relatives in Montreal?

EXERCISE

11·1

Use your dictionary to find the meaning of the new vocabulary words needed for this exercise before you begin. Write the words in your language in the space provided.

scarf	_____	project	_____
dove	_____	meat loaf	_____
lease	_____	same	_____
rights	_____	deadline	_____
tight	_____	wing	_____
until	_____	celebration	_____
flip-flops	_____	Thanksgiving	_____
important	_____	Christmas Eve	_____
everything	_____	phone number	_____
appointment	_____	virtual reality headset	_____

41

*Rewrite the following sentences to create questions by placing **do** or **does** before the subject. Don't forget to include a question mark (?) in your answer.*

1. You have a pink eraser.

   _____

2. He has my phone number.

   _____

3. They have everything they need.

   _____

4. We have the same scarf.

   _____

5. I have rights.

   _____

6. Marissa has green flip-flops.

   _____

7. You have a huge turkey for Thanksgiving.

   _____

8. They have a lease until next year.

   _____

9. It has a funny taste.

   _____

10. You have two important appointments today.

    _____

11. The dove has white wings.

    _____

12. We have a day off next week.

    _____

13. David has a virtual reality headset.

    _____

14. Juanita has a good recipe for meat loaf.

    _____

15. We have a tight deadline for the project.

    _____

16. They have a big celebration on Christmas Eve.

    _____

Use your dictionary to find the meaning of the new vocabulary words needed for this exercise before you begin. Write the words in your language in the space provided.

mud	_____	receipt	_____
tire	_____	noodle	_____
gold	_____	tie	_____
claw	_____	show	_____
glasses	_____	time	_____
manager	_____	dictionary	_____
leg	_____	tooth	_____
flat	_____	ant	_____
wrong	_____	bruise	_____
Germany	_____	eye	_____
map	_____	poodle	_____
better	_____	membership	_____
marshmallow	_____	fax machine	_____
e-mail address	_____	cousin	_____
bathrobe	_____	binoculars	_____
ladybug	_____	gym	_____
necklace	_____	beaver	_____
bib	_____	silk	_____
shirt	_____	polka dot	_____
mattress	_____	scar	_____

*Complete the following questions with **do** or **does** to create the question form in the present tense with the verb **to have**.*

1. _____ I have lipstick on my tooth?

2. _____ you have a new mattress?

3. _____ Mike have a black tie?

4. _____ the kids have a bag of marshmallows?

5. _____ he have the wrong answer?

6. _____ I have a bruise on my arm?

7. _____ he have a membership for the gym?

8. _____ we have binoculars for the show?

9. _____ the soup have a lot of noodles?

10. _____ it have green eyes?

11. _____ you have a better map of the city?

12. _____ they have a poodle?

13. _____ Carlos have my e-mail address?

14. _____ we have winter tires?

15. _____ the horse have a saddle?

16. _____ it have pink polka dots?

17. _____ she have a silk bathrobe?

18. _____ the beaver have a flat tail?

19. _____ I have a scar on my leg?

20. _____ we have a new manager today?

21. _____ she have a cousin in Germany?

22. _____ you have the receipt in the bag?

23. _____ Shaun have new glasses?

24. _____ I have a ladybug on my shirt?

25. _____ Samantha have a gold necklace?

26. _____ we have ants in the basement?

27. _____ I have mud on my shoes?

28. _____ you have a dictionary?

29. _____ they have a fax machine?

30. _____ you have a bib for the baby?

31. _____ I have the right time?

32. _____ the cat have sharp claws?

The Simple Present Tense

The simple present tense is used when stating general facts or true statements that have no time. Add **-s** to the verb for **he**, **she**, and **it**.

I need	→	I need a new computer.
you need	→	You need a good lawyer.
he needs	→	He needs a roommate.
she needs	→	She needs a blanket.
it needs	→	It needs a lot of work.
we need	→	We need a flashlight.
they need	→	They need a new fridge.

Add **-es** to verbs when using **he**, **she**, and **it** if the verb:

ends with z, s, x, ss, ch, or sh	ends with o	ends with y preceded by a consonant—change the y to i before adding -es
I wash the car.	I go to school.	I try very hard.
You wash the car.	You go to school.	You try very hard.
He washes the car.	He goes to school.	He tries very hard.
She washes the car.	She goes to school.	She tries very hard.
It washes the car.	It goes to school.	It tries very hard.
We wash the car.	We go to school.	We try very hard.
They wash the car.	They go to school.	They try very hard.

EXERCISE 12·1

Use your dictionary to find the meaning of the following verbs and vocabulary words needed for this exercise before you begin. Write the words in your language in the space provided.

to amaze	_____	to help	_____
to cry	_____	to see	_____
to guard	_____	to kiss	_____
to jump	_____	to go	_____
to blush	_____	to flush	_____
to smoke	_____	to scratch	_____

village	_____	American	_____
toilet	_____	kingdom	_____
knight	_____	castle	_____
cigarette	_____	apple	_____
king	_____	caramel	_____
every	_____	people	_____

Rewrite the following sentences with the correct form of the simple present tense using the verb in parentheses.

1. He (to smoke) American cigarettes.

   _____

2. Karen (to blush) when she (to see) that boy.

   _____

3. I (to love) caramel apple cake.

   _____

4. He (to cry) like a baby.

   _____

5. It (to amaze) me.

   _____

6. It (to jump) very high.

   _____

7. He (to kiss) all the girls in school.

   _____

8. My cats (to scratch) the furniture.

   _____

9. They (to help) many people in the village.

   _____

10. The knights (to guard) the king and castle in the kingdom.

    _____

    _____

11. He never (to flush) the toilet.

    _____

Use your dictionary to find the meaning of the following verbs and vocabulary words needed for this exercise before you begin. Write the words in your language in the space provided.

to crush	_____	to make	_____
to spoil	_____	to push	_____
to explain	_____	to drive	_____
to manage	_____	to melt	_____
to dream	_____	to buy	_____
to own	_____	to eat	_____
to do	_____	to fear	_____
to follow	_____	to owe	_____
to whisper	_____	to earn	_____
to carry	_____	to obey	_____
paramedic	_____	patient	_____
lemon	_____	rule	_____
money	_____	cottage	_____
stretcher	_____	tea	_____
carriage	_____	laundry	_____
perfume	_____	child	_____
raw	_____	onion	_____
bank	_____	grape	_____
spring	_____	housework	_____
local	_____	restaurant	_____
everywhere	_____	waterfalls	_____
Laundromat	_____	nothing	_____

Complete the following sentences with the correct form of the simple present tense using the verb in parentheses.

1. My teacher _____ (to explain) everything.

2. We _____ (to whisper) in class.

3. He _____ (to crush) grapes to make wine.

4. Lisa _____ (to buy) a lot of perfume.

5. I _____ (to do) the housework for my mother.

6. They _____ (to earn) a lot of money.

7. Linda _____ (to work) downtown.

8. My uncle _____ (to manage) a restaurant.

9. The paramedics _____ (to carry) the patient on a stretcher.

10. You _____ (to owe) me money.

11. My grandmother _____ (to eat) raw onions.

12. He _____ (to fear) nothing.

13. They _____ (to follow) me everywhere.

14. I _____ (to work) in the local bank.

15. She _____ (to drink) tea with lemon.

16. Jessica _____ (to push) the baby in a carriage.

17. He _____ (to spoil) his child.

18. Connie _____ (to dream) about waterfalls.

19. Leo _____ (to drive) to work.

20. My husband _____ (to do) the laundry.

21. She _____ (to go) to the Laundromat every week.

22. We _____ (to own) a cottage in the country.

23. The boys _____ (to obey) the rules in class.

24. The snow _____ (to melt) in the spring.

The Simple Present Tense: Negative Form

Place **do not** or **does not** before the verb to create the negative form of the simple present tense. The simple form of the verb is always used. Never add *-s* to **he**, **she**, and **it** in the negative form of the simple present tense.

I wear	→	I do not wear	→	I do not wear orange.
you wear	→	you do not wear	→	You do not wear perfume.
he wears	→	he does not wear	→	He does not wear diapers.
she wears	→	she does not wear	→	She does not wear a watch.
it wears	→	it does not wear	→	It does not wear shoes.
we wear	→	we do not wear	→	We do not wear slippers.
they wear	→	they do not wear	→	They do not wear nail polish.

The negative form of the simple present tense can also be expressed with the contraction **don't** or **doesn't**.

I do not drink	→	I don't drink	→	I don't drink apple juice.
you do not drink	→	you don't drink	→	You don't drink wine.
he does not drink	→	he doesn't drink	→	He doesn't drink lemon juice.
she does not drink	→	she doesn't drink	→	She doesn't drink milk.
it does not drink	→	it doesn't drink	→	It doesn't drink water.
we do not drink	→	we don't drink	→	We don't drink or smoke.
they do not drink	→	they don't drink	→	They don't drink and drive.

EXERCISE 13·1

Use your dictionary to find the meaning of the following verbs and vocabulary words needed for this exercise before you begin. Write the words in your language in the space provided.

to sell	_____	to trust	_____
to yell	_____	to dislike	_____
to collect	_____	to believe	_____
to snore	_____	to swear	_____

meat	_____	fish	_____
giant	_____	several	_____
language	_____	sewing machine	_____
coin	_____	foreign	_____

Rewrite the following sentences to express the negative form of the simple present tense. Write the sentence once using **do not** *or* **does not** *and once using the contraction* **don't** *or* **doesn't**.

1. My husband snores every night.

   _____

   _____

2. I believe your story about the giant monkeys.

   _____

   _____

3. Nancy and Yvan collect coins.

   _____

   _____

4. She speaks several foreign languages.

   _____

   _____

5. It dislikes fish.

   _____

   _____

6. Ron swears and yells in class.

   _____

   _____

7. Sara sells sewing machines.

   _____

   _____

8. I trust you.

   _____

   _____

9. We eat meat.

   _____

   _____

Use your dictionary to find the meaning of the following verbs and vocabulary words needed for this exercise before you begin. Write the words in your language in the space provided.

to bother	_____	to study	_____
to gossip	_____	to travel	_____
to live	_____	to listen	_____
to smell	_____	to cook	_____
to learn	_____	to cough	_____
to know	_____	to laugh	_____
to hurt	_____	to belong	_____
to iron	_____	to forgive	_____
to deserve	_____	to feed	_____
to sneeze	_____	to write	_____
stray	_____	office	_____
coffee	_____	ponytail	_____
hard	_____	clothes	_____
towel	_____	alone	_____
well	_____	cotton candy	_____
pancake	_____	cockroach	_____

*Complete the following sentences using the contraction **don't** or **doesn't** to create the negative form of the simple present tense.*

1. It _____ work well.

2. We _____ feed the stray cats.

3. I _____ dream a lot.

4. Mark _____ want pancakes for breakfast.

5. I _____ iron my clothes.

6. It _____ bother me.

7. She _____ write to Bob.

8. I _____ cook every night.

9. He _____ listen to me.

10. I _____ travel alone.

11. She _____ know you.

12. It _____ hurt.

13. You _____ deserve that.

14. They _____ like cockroaches.

15. Roger _____ want cotton candy.

16. I _____ owe you money.

17. She _____ sneeze all the time.

18. You _____ drink coffee.

19. It _____ smell good.

20. He _____ cough at night.

21. My dog _____ snore.

22. You _____ laugh a lot.

23. He _____ study very hard.

24. Betty _____ gossip in the office.

25. I _____ forgive you.

26. They _____ learn a lot in class.

27. Glenn _____ live here.

28. It _____ belong to you.

29. I _____ need a towel.

30. Latonya _____ want a ponytail in her hair.

The Simple Present Tense: Question Form

Place **do** or **does** before the subject to create questions in the simple present tense. The simple form of the verb is used when creating questions in the simple present tense.

I dream	→	do I dream	→	Do I dream a lot?
you work	→	do you work	→	Do you work well?
he sees	→	does he see	→	Does he see the clock?
she wears	→	does she wear	→	Does she wear flip-flops?
it hates	→	does it hate	→	Does it hate milk?
we want	→	do we want	→	Do we want a dog?
they own	→	do they own	→	Do they own the house?

EXERCISE
14·1

Use your dictionary to find the meaning of the following verbs and vocabulary words needed for this exercise before you begin. Write the words in your language in the space provided.

to touch	_____	to read	_____
to scream	_____	to boil	_____
to skate	_____	to put	_____
to cost	_____	to play	_____
mortgage	_____	train	_____
on time	_____	soldier	_____
afternoon	_____	dough	_____
pepper	_____	crown	_____
newspaper	_____	hobby	_____
everything	_____	fox	_____
night	_____	horror	_____
salt	_____	woods	_____

*Rewrite the following sentences to create the question form of the simple present tense. Place **do** or **does** before the subject and use the simple form of the verb. Don't forget to include a question mark (?) in your answer.*

1. She skates in the morning.

   _____

2. They boil the vegetables.

   _____

3. He sleeps in the afternoon.

   _____

4. The boys play chess at night.

   _____

5. You pay the mortgage on time.

   _____

6. She reads the English newspaper.

   _____

7. They drive to work together.

   _____

8. It costs $20 to travel by train to the city.

   _____

9. She screams when she watches horror movies.

   _____

10. She wants a new hobby.

    _____

11. The king wears a red velvet crown.

    _____

12. Bobby plays with toy soldiers.

    _____

13. You put salt and pepper in the dough.

    _____

14. Jackie touches everything in my office.

    _____

15. You see the fox in the woods.

    _____

Use your dictionary to find the meaning of the following verbs and vocabulary words needed for this exercise before you begin. Write the words in your language in the space provided.

to agree	_____	to rent	_____
to annoy	_____	to fish	_____
to increase	_____	to feel	_____
to disturb	_____	to walk	_____
to interest	_____	to mix	_____
to participate	_____	to dye	_____
to chase	_____	to snow	_____
to weigh	_____	to park	_____
credit card	_____	children	_____
piggy bank	_____	facecloth	_____
cigar	_____	change	_____
lobster	_____	worm	_____
house	_____	coupon	_____
noise	_____	sick	_____
minimum wage	_____	driveway	_____
smoke	_____	pound	_____
truth	_____	glove	_____
pea	_____	mushroom	_____

*Complete the following sentences using **do** or **does** to create questions in the simple present tense.*

1. _____ he annoy you?

2. _____ you pay with your credit card?

3. _____ it snow in your country?

4. _____ you need change?

5. _____ we agree?

6. _____ the minimum wage increase every year?

7. _____ you need a facecloth?

8. _____ he know the truth?

9. _____ you see the smoke?

10. _____ Chris and Jim rent a house?

11. _____ Joan have black gloves?

12. _____ you feel sick?

13. _____ he park in the driveway?

14. _____ it interest you?

15. _____ they want the coupons?

16. _____ she mix the eggs with the milk?

17. _____ the noise disturb you?

18. _____ the children like peas?

19. _____ they walk to school?

20. _____ your dog chase cats?

21. _____ it weigh twenty pounds?

22. _____ you eat lobster?

23. _____ she have a piggy bank?

24. _____ you fish with worms?

25. _____ Jerry smoke cigars?

26. _____ you dye your hair?

27. _____ they like mushrooms?

28. _____ Leslie participate at school?

Possessive Adjectives

Possessive adjectives are used to show ownership or possession of someone or something. They are placed before the noun.

I	→	my	→	I drink my coffee.
you	→	your	→	You drive your car.
he	→	his	→	He needs his screwdriver.
she	→	her	→	She wears her slippers.
it	→	its	→	It chases its tail.
we	→	our	→	We want our money.
they	→	their	→	They help their kids.

EXERCISE

15·1

Use your dictionary to find the meaning of the following verbs and vocabulary words needed for this exercise before you begin. Write the words in your language in the space provided.

to dress	_____	to burn	_____
to open	_____	to visit	_____
to keep	_____	to bite	_____
to lick	_____	to wipe	_____
to take	_____	to hide	_____
to wash	_____	to forget	_____
master	_____	sleeve	_____
sponge	_____	sailor	_____
under	_____	jewel	_____
homework	_____	apartment	_____
submarine	_____	stair	_____
mail	_____	carpet	_____

Rewrite the following sentences by choosing the correct possessive adjective indicated in parentheses that refers back to the subject pronoun.

1. She visits (their, her) relatives every summer.

   _____

2. We hide (our, your) money under the carpet in the master bedroom.

   _____

   _____

3. They keep (his, their) jewels in a jewelry box.

   _____

   _____

4. I wash (your, my) stairs with a sponge.

   _____

5. He passes all (our, his) exams.

   _____

6. She dresses (her, his) dolls in pink.

   _____

7. I open (my, your) mail after breakfast.

   _____

8. He bites (my, his) nails.

   _____

9. We rent (my, our) apartment.

   _____

10. It licks (its, their) paws.

    _____

11. I burn (your, my) marshmallows.

    _____

12. Jeff takes (his, our) pills in the morning.

    _____

13. The boys forget (my, their) homework every day.

    _____

    _____

14. He wipes (his, her) nose on (my, his) sleeve.

    _____

15. She dyes (her, your) hair.

    _____

16. The sailors believe (their, my) new submarine is better.

_____

_____

Use your dictionary to find the meaning of the following verbs and vocabulary words needed for this exercise before you begin. Write the words in your language in the space provided.

to ride	_____	to curl	_____
to fry	_____	to leave	_____
to sail	_____	to argue	_____
to sell	_____	to cut	_____
to fly	_____	to hang	_____
to greet	_____	to lace	_____
to give	_____	to use	_____
to protect	_____	to demand	_____
world	_____	day care	_____
boat	_____	footprint	_____
sand	_____	fireman	_____
market	_____	kite	_____
around	_____	week	_____
water	_____	skim	_____
bike	_____	diary	_____
field	_____	boot	_____
head	_____	curling iron	_____
skate	_____	sunglasses	_____
lawn mower	_____	arena	_____
freedom	_____	fireplace	_____

Complete the sentences using the correct possessive adjective according to the subject.

1. They sail _____ boat around the world.

2. She fries _____ eggs in butter.

3. We give _____ old clothes to Peter.

4. I ride _____ bike to school.

5. She curls _____ hair with a curling iron.

6. You need _____ dark sunglasses.

7. I lace _____ skates at the arena.

8. It drinks _____ water.

9. We sell _____ vegetables at the market.

10. The fireman wears _____ black boots.

11. The twins love and protect _____ brother.

12. I greet _____ guests.

13. They argue with _____ neighbors.

14. He needs _____ lawyer.

15. We demand _____ rights.

16. He uses _____ lawn mower to cut the grass.

17. I scratch _____ head.

18. She hangs _____ clothes on the clothesline.

19. They clean _____ fireplace every week.

20. I drink _____ tea with skim milk.

21. Laura loves _____ husband.

22. You want _____ freedom.

23. We leave _____ kids at the day care.

24. She writes in _____ diary.

25. He flies _____ kite in the field.

26. I see _____ footprints in the sand.

The Simple Past Tense $\cdot 16 \cdot$

The simple past is used to describe an action that happened in the recent past. Follow these rules to create the simple past tense with regular verbs.

Add -ed to the simple form of the verb.

to visit

I visited
you visited
he visited
she visited
it visited
we visited
they visited

When -ed is added to verbs that end in d, pronounce the last syllable separately.

to need

I need-ed
you need-ed
he need-ed
she need-ed
it need-ed
we need-ed
they need-ed

Add only -d if the verb ends in e.

to believe

I believed
you believed
he believed
she believed
it believed
we believed
they believed

When -ed is added to verbs that end in t, pronounce the last syllable separately.

to want

I want-ed
you want-ed
he want-ed
she want-ed
it want-ed
we want-ed
they want-ed

Delete y and add -ied to the simple form of the verb if the verb ends in y preceded by a consonant.

to cry

I cried
you cried
he cried
she cried
it cried
we cried
they cried

The ending of all other regular verbs is pronounced as one syllable when -ed is added.

to open

I opened
you opened
he opened
she opened
it opened
we opened
they opened

Use your dictionary to find the meaning of the following verbs and vocabulary words needed for this exercise before you begin. Write the words in your language in the space provided.

to answer	_____	to reward	_____
to increase	_____	to notice	_____
to share	_____	to land	_____
to kill	_____	to dry	_____
to try	_____	to sign	_____
to lie	_____	to challenge	_____
hair dryer	_____	ditch	_____
upside down	_____	inside out	_____
snack	_____	another	_____
lease	_____	eel	_____
age	_____	toad	_____
sweater	_____	building	_____

Rewrite the following sentences in the simple past tense by adding **-ed** *or* **-ied** *to the simple form of the verb in parentheses.*

1. I (to use) my hair dryer to dry my hair.

   _____

2. We (to try) a new recipe last night.

   _____

3. Thomas (to answer) the phone.

   _____

4. I (to notice) that your sweater was inside out.

   _____

5. The car (to land) upside down in the ditch.

   _____

6. She (to share) her snack with her friends at school yesterday.

   _____

   _____

7. The minimum wage (to increase) last year.

_____

8. Suzanne (to lie) about her age.

_____

9. My company (to sign) the lease for our building for another three years.

_____

_____

10. The teacher (to challenge) her students and (to reward) them for their hard work.

_____

_____

11. The eel (to kill) the toad.

_____

Use your dictionary to find the meaning of the following verbs and vocabulary words needed for this exercise before you begin. Write the words in your language in the space provided.

to destroy	_____	to please	_____
to describe	_____	to expect	_____
to rain	_____	to serve	_____
to knock	_____	to deny	_____
to borrow	_____	to accept	_____
to avoid	_____	to marry	_____
to move	_____	to arrest	_____
to tidy	_____	to prove	_____
to decide	_____	to join	_____
to obtain	_____	to paint	_____
in-line skates	_____	in detail	_____
contract	_____	someone	_____
lawn	_____	weekend	_____
accident	_____	terms	_____
everybody	_____	audience	_____

innocent	_____	conditions	_____
plain	_____	passport	_____
army	_____	court	_____
door	_____	alert	_____
makeup	_____	appetizer	_____
collision	_____	singer	_____
doctor	_____	police	_____

*Complete the sentences using the simple past tense by adding **-ed** or **-ied** to the simple form of these regular verbs.*

1. We _____ (to accept) the terms and conditions of the contract.

2. My brother _____ (to join) the army.

3. My neighbors _____ (to move) to Vancouver.

4. Someone _____ (to knock) on the door.

5. He _____ (to describe) the accident in detail.

6. I _____ (to prove) that I was innocent in court.

7. The man _____ (to deny) everything.

8. Tina _____ (to borrow) my in-line skates.

9. They _____ (to watch) the kids in the pool.

10. She _____ (to use) my makeup.

11. I _____ (to tidy) the house for my mother.

12. It _____ (to rain) all day.

13. My husband _____ (to paint) the bathroom on the weekend.

14. I was alert and I _____ (to avoid) the collision.

15. We _____ (to push) the baby in the carriage.

16. My cousin _____ (to marry) a doctor.

17. The singer _____ (to please) the audience.

18. Your dog _____ (to destroy) my lawn.

19. We _____ (to serve) appetizers to our guests.

20. Mike _____ (to obtain) his passport.

21. The police _____ (to arrest) everybody.

22. We _____ (to order) a plain pizza last night.

23. I _____ (to decide) to learn English.

24. We _____ (to expect) to see you there.

The Simple Past Tense with Irregular Verbs: 1

Some verbs do not use the *-ed* ending to express the past tense. These are irregular verbs, and they have unique past tense forms. They have the same form for all persons in the past tense, and they must be memorized.

to hide (hid)	to drink (drank)	to wear (wore)	to go (went)
I hid	I drank	I wore	I went
you hid	you drank	you wore	you went
he hid	he drank	he wore	he went
she hid	she drank	she wore	she went
it hid	it drank	it wore	it went
we hid	we drank	we wore	we went
they hid	they drank	they wore	they went

EXERCISE 17·1

Use your dictionary to find the meaning of the following irregular verbs and vocabulary words needed for this exercise before you begin. Write the words in your language in the space provided.

to feel	→ felt	_____	to do	→ did	_____
to bite	→ bit	_____	to find	→ found	_____
to blow	→ blew	_____	to fall	→ fell	_____
to shake	→ shook	_____	to cut	→ cut	_____
to tear	→ tore	_____	to break	→ broke	_____
to slide	→ slid	_____	to buy	→ bought	_____
to spend	→ spent	_____	to take	→ took	_____
to teach	→ taught	_____			

honeymoon	_____	dishes	_____
earthquake	_____	saw	_____
grandparent	_____	cup	_____
toboggan	_____	overseas	_____
Ireland	_____	down	_____
finger	_____	favorite	_____
mountain	_____	high school	_____
when	_____	after	_____
pants	_____	gift	_____
math	_____	ankle	_____

*Rewrite the following sentences in the simple **past tense** using the irregular past tense form of the verb in parentheses.*

1. She (to blow) on her soup because it was hot.

   _____

   _____

2. The house (to shake) a lot during the earthquake.

   _____

   _____

3. They (to take) the plane and (to spend) their honeymoon overseas.

   _____

   _____

4. I always (to feel) sick when I was pregnant.

   _____

   _____

5. He (to tear) his pants when he (to fall).

   _____

6. We (to buy) a nice gift for our grandparents in Ireland.

   _____

   _____

7. The kids (to slide) down the mountain on their new toboggan.

   _____

   _____

8. I (to do) the dishes after supper.

   _____

9. I (to cut) my finger on the sharp saw.

_____

10. You (to break) my favorite cup.

_____

11. Your dog (to bite) my ankle.

_____

12. Karen (to find) a purse at the beach.

_____

13. I (to teach) math at the high school last year.

_____

_____

EXERCISE 17·2

Use your dictionary to find the meaning of the following irregular verbs and vocabulary words needed for this exercise before you begin. Write the words in your language in the space provided.

to speak	→ spoke	_____	to draw	→ drew	_____
to hold	→ held	_____	to leave	→ left	_____
to pay	→ paid	_____	to swear	→ swore	_____
to steal	→ stole	_____	to sit	→ sat	_____
to hang	→ hung	_____	to hear	→ heard	_____
to shoot	→ shot	_____	to see	→ saw	_____
to begin	→ began	_____	to give	→ gave	_____
to dig	→ dug	_____			

niece	_____	plastic	_____
front	_____	broom	_____
store	_____	great	_____
whistle	_____	swing	_____
thing	_____	speech	_____
pantry	_____	calculator	_____
bored	_____	problem	_____
witch	_____	tunnel	_____

midnight _____	crossing guard _____
party _____	pink flamingo _____
stop sign _____	nephew _____
shoplifter _____	underground _____

Complete the following sentences in the simple past tense using the irregular past tense form of the verb indicated in parentheses.

1. The teachers _____ (to speak) about the computer problems in detail.

2. I _____ (to begin) my homework after school.

3. He _____ (to give) money to his niece and nephew for their birthdays.

4. She _____ (to hang) the whistle around her neck.

5. I _____ (to see) the shoplifter in the store.

6. We _____ (to sit) on the swings and talked about many things.

7. Somebody _____ (to steal) my calculator and pencils at school.

8. I _____ (to pay) a lot of money for the plastic pink flamingos on my front lawn.

9. Cheyenne _____ (to draw) a nice picture of a witch on a broom.

10. David _____ (to swear) in class today.

11. The workers _____ (to dig) a big underground tunnel.

12. The crossing guard _____ (to hold) the stop sign in her left hand.

13. The police _____ (to shoot) the man in the leg.

14. We _____ (to hear) your speech last night, and it was great.

15. They _____ (to leave) the party at midnight because they were bored.

16. We _____ (to see) a mouse in the pantry last night.

The Simple Past Tense with Irregular Verbs: 2

·18·

Some verbs do not use the *-ed* ending to express the past tense. These are irregular verbs, and they have unique past tense forms. They have the same form for all persons in the past tense, and they must be memorized.

EXERCISE
18·1

Use your dictionary to find the meaning of the following irregular verbs and vocabulary words needed for this exercise before you begin. Write the words in your language in the space provided.

to lend	→	lent	_____
to have	→	had	_____
to drive	→	drove	_____
to come	→	came	_____
to wake	→	woke	_____
to build	→	built	_____
to forget	→	forgot	_____
to freeze	→	froze	_____
to catch	→	caught	_____
to beat	→	beat	_____
to ride	→	rode	_____
to bend	→	bent	_____
to sleep	→	slept	_____
to understand	→	understood	_____
to withdraw	→	withdrew	_____

bacon	_____	cheese	_____	enough	_____
stamp	_____	bullfrog	_____	tadpole	_____
rifle	_____	hanger	_____	envelope	_____
sheep	_____	hunter	_____	post office	_____
hay	_____	lamb	_____	sand castle	_____
first	_____	bagel	_____	warehouse	_____
lunch	_____	month	_____	inventory	_____
barn	_____	whole	_____	lettuce	_____

Rewrite the following sentences in the simple past tense using the irregular past tense form of the verb in parentheses.

1. We (to withdraw) enough money for the whole month.

   _____

   _____

2. I (to catch) a bullfrog and four tadpoles in the pond.

   _____

   _____

3. Salina (to ride) a horse for the first time yesterday.

   _____

   _____

4. Robert, Claire, and Daniel (to build) a huge sand castle on the beach.

   _____

   _____

5. Brandon (to bend) the hanger to open the car door.

   _____

   _____

6. I (to drive) to the post office to buy some stamps and envelopes.

   _____

   _____

7. The hunter (to forget) his rifle in the woods.

   _____

   _____

8. You (to wake) your grandmother when you knocked on the window.

   _____

   _____

9. The sheep and lamb (to sleep) on the hay in the barn.

_____

_____

10. I (to have) a bagel with bacon, tomato, cheese, and lettuce for lunch.

_____

_____

11. Camilie (to understand) what the teacher taught in class today.

_____

_____

12. My mother (to freeze) the vegetables for the winter.

_____

_____

13. Dimitri (to lend) the shovel to his neighbor.

_____

14. The red team (to beat) the blue team.

_____

15. Laurent (to come) to help us with the inventory in the warehouse.

_____

_____

EXERCISE
18·2

Use your dictionary to find the meaning of the following irregular verbs and vocabulary words needed for this exercise before you begin. Write the words in your language in the space provided.

to shut	→ shut	_____	to keep	→ kept	_____
to bring	→ brought	_____	to rise	→ rose	_____
to win	→ won	_____	to mean	→ meant	_____
to send	→ sent	_____	to hurt	→ hurt	_____
to choose	→ chose	_____	to put	→ put	_____
to grow	→ grew	_____	to lose	→ lost	_____
to cost	→ cost	_____	to think	→ thought	_____
to forgive	→ forgave	_____			

package	_____	bride	_____
cookie	_____	gardener	_____
early	_____	hearing aid	_____
toe	_____	deaf	_____
cauliflower	_____	hand	_____
gorgeous	_____	airmail	_____
joke	_____	umbrella	_____
park	_____	blind	_____
nail	_____	groom	_____
screw	_____	gift certificate	_____
weed	_____	even though	_____
cabbage	_____	as	_____

Complete the following sentences in the simple past tense using the irregular past tense form of the verb indicated in parentheses.

1. I _____ (to bring) my umbrella when we went for a walk in the park.

2. It _____ (to cost) a lot, but it was gorgeous and we loved it.

3. The sun _____ (to rise) early this morning.

4. He _____ (to win) a gift certificate at the Christmas party.

5. We _____ (to grow) cabbages, cauliflowers, and pumpkins in our garden last summer.

6. The gardener _____ (to put) the weeds in the garbage can.

7. I _____ (to mean) that as a joke.

8. Jasmin _____ (to shut) the door on her toe.

9. The bride and groom _____ (to choose) a beautiful wedding cake.

10. Even though he lied, she _____ (to forgive) him.

11. I _____ (to think) you liked peas.

12. Sharon is blind and deaf, and she _____ (to lose) her hearing aid.

13. It _____ (to hurt) when the cat scratched my hand.

14. My father _____ (to keep) the nails and screws in jars in the garage.

15. He _____ (to send) the package by airmail.

16. We _____ (to drink) milk with our cookies.

The Simple Past Tense with Irregular Verbs: 3

Some verbs do not use the *-ed* ending to express the past tense. These are irregular verbs, and they have unique past tense forms. They have the same form for all persons in the past tense, and they must be memorized.

EXERCISE

19·1

Use your dictionary to find the meaning of the following irregular verbs and vocabulary words needed for this exercise before you begin. Write the words in your language in the space provided.

to meet	→	met	to spin	→	spun
to sing	→	sang	to feed	→	fed
to ring	→	rang	to fight	→	fought
to throw	→	threw	to light	→	lit
to run	→	ran	to eat	→	ate
to get	→	got	to fit	→	fit
to know	→	knew	to read	→	read
to sell	→	sold			

fire		Monday	
too		Tuesday	
ice		Wednesday	
guilty		Thursday	
crime		Friday	
paper		Saturday	
noisy		Sunday	
parrot		raise (n)	
middle		evening	
icing		liquor store	

power failure   _____   concert   _____

out of control   _____   phone   _____

Rewrite the following sentences in the simple past tense using the irregular past tense form of the verb in parentheses.

1. She (to sing) on Monday, Wednesday, and Friday at the concert in Montreal.

   _____

   _____

2. The house was dark because of the power failure, so we (to light) the candles.

   _____

   _____

3. The car (to spin) out of control on the ice.

   _____

4. I (to read) the newspaper in the evening on Saturday and Sunday.

   _____

   _____

5. My son (to fight) at school on Tuesday and Thursday last week.

   _____

   _____

6. The phone (to ring) in the middle of the night.

   _____

7. I (to know) that he was guilty of the crime.

   _____

8. She (to meet) Sara at the liquor store.

   _____

9. Sorry, but I (to eat) all the icing on your cake when you went to the bathroom.

   _____

   _____

10. I (to get) a big raise at work last month.

    _____

11. We (to sell) our parrot because he was too noisy.

    _____

    _____

12. Alexandre (to throw) the papers in the fire.

    _____

13. My pants (to fit) me last year.

_____

14. Carmen (to run) and hid under the bed.

_____

15. We (to feed) meat to the fox.

_____

Use your dictionary to find the meaning of the following verbs and vocabulary words needed for this exercise before you begin. Write the words in your language in the space provided.

to swim	→	swam	_____	to write	→ wrote	_____
to say	→	said	_____	to sweep	→ swept	_____
to tell	→	told	_____	to stand	→ stood	_____
to hit	→	hit	_____	to deal	→ dealt	_____
to stick	→	stuck	_____	to make	→ made	_____
to lead	→	led	_____	to quit	→ quit	_____
to fly	→	flew	_____	to become	→ became	_____
to weep	→	wept	_____	to wear	→ wore	_____

sidewalk	_____	glue	_____
dentures	_____	dolphin	_____
wall	_____	issue (n)	_____
date	_____	truth	_____
snowman	_____	stream	_____
minute	_____	princess	_____
corner	_____	jury	_____
chalk	_____	drink (n)	_____
piece	_____	housecoat	_____
blackboard	_____	on vacation	_____

Complete the following sentences in the simple past tense using the irregular past tense form of the verb indicated in parentheses.

1. He _____ (to deal) with many issues at work yesterday.

2. I thought you _____ (to say) it was free.

3. Liliane _____ (to sweep) the sidewalk with her new broom.

4. The kindergarten class _____ (to make) a snowman this morning.

5. I _____ (to stick) the pieces of wood together with glue.

6. I _____ (to hit) my head on the wall when I fell down the stairs.

7. My father _____ (to become) angry when I _____ (to quit) school last year.

8. My grandmother _____ (to wear) her dentures for her date with Mr. Olsen.

9. I _____ (to lead) my horse to the stream for a drink of cold water.

10. We _____ (to fly) the kite in the field all day.

11. The teacher _____ (to write) on the blackboard with pink chalk.

12. Emy and Meghan _____ (to swim) with dolphins when they were on vacation in Florida.

13. The princess _____ (to weep) alone in her room.

14. She says that she _____ (to tell) the truth to the jury.

15. I _____ (to stand) on the corner in the rain and waited for you for twenty minutes.

16. He _____ (to give) me a housecoat and a puppy for my birthday.

The Simple Past Tense: Negative Form

·20·

Place **did not** after the subject and use the simple form of the verb to create the negative form of the simple past tense for regular and irregular verbs.

I did not	→	I did not break	→	I did not break the cup.
you did not	→	you did not answer	→	You did not answer me.
he did not	→	he did not believe	→	He did not believe you.
she did not	→	she did not pass	→	She did not pass her test.
it did not	→	it did not jump	→	It did not jump on me.
we did not	→	we did not sell	→	We did not sell our house.
they did not	→	they did not touch	→	They did not touch it.

The negative form of the simple past tense can also be expressed with the contraction **didn't**.

I did not boil	→	I didn't boil	→	I didn't boil the eggs.
you did not build	→	you didn't build	→	You didn't build your house.
he did not want	→	he didn't want	→	He didn't want coffee.
she did not do	→	she didn't do	→	She didn't do her homework.
it did not cost	→	it didn't cost	→	It didn't cost a lot.
we did not sign	→	we didn't sign	→	We didn't sign it.
they did not find	→	they didn't find	→	They didn't find their cat.

EXERCISE

20·1

Use your dictionary to find the meaning of the following verbs and vocabulary words needed for this exercise before you begin. Write the words in your language in the space provided.

to shave	_____	to apologize	_____
to waste	_____	to report	_____
bottle	_____	medicine	_____
screen	_____	valuable	_____
skin	_____	mussels	_____
income	_____	clam	_____

Rewrite the following sentences to express the negative form of the simple past tense. Write the sentence once using **did not** *and once using the contraction* **didn't**.

1. They watched the hockey game on their new big-screen TV.

   _____

   _____

2. I forgot to tell him.

   _____

   _____

3. She wasted my valuable time.

   _____

   _____

4. Marcia reported her income.

   _____

   _____

5. I shook the bottle of medicine.

   _____

   _____

6. My uncle shaved his head.

   _____

   _____

7. He apologized to his friend.

   _____

   _____

8. We found clams and mussels in the sand on the beach.

   _____

   _____

9. The police read the man his rights.

   _____

   _____

10. It scratched my skin.

   _____

   _____

Use your dictionary to find the meaning of the following verbs and vocabulary words needed for this exercise before you begin. Write the words in your language in the space provided.

to translate	_____	to prevent	_____
to deposit	_____	to express	_____
to gain	_____	to brush	_____
to last	_____	to save	_____
inch	_____	opinion	_____
wallet	_____	mitten	_____
hat	_____	antenna	_____
shower	_____	pipe	_____
upstairs	_____	grandson	_____
pay	_____	granddaughter	_____
trip	_____	savings account	_____
litter box	_____	pantyhose	_____
Greece	_____	horoscope	_____
leftovers	_____	plumber	_____

Rewrite the following sentences in the negative form using the contraction **didn't** *and the simple form of the verb.*

1. He prevented the accident.

   _____

2. She expressed her opinion.

   _____

3. The movie lasted three hours.

   _____

4. They went to see their granddaughter and grandson.

   _____

   _____

5. They saved a lot of money for their trip to Greece.

   _____

   _____

6. Patricia lost her mittens, scarf, and hat at school.

_____

_____

7. Sonia translated the letter.

_____

8. I bought a gift for her.

_____

9. Mario found a black leather wallet in the snow.

_____

_____

10. We put the leftovers in plastic bags.

_____

11. I tore my pantyhose.

_____

12. I knew you were there.

_____

13. He deposited his pay in his savings account.

_____

_____

14. The plumber fixed the pipes, shower, and toilet in the bathroom upstairs.

_____

_____

15. I cleaned the litter box and brushed the cat this morning.

_____

_____

16. I read my horoscope today.

_____

17. The wind bent the antenna.

_____

18. Laura grew two inches and gained ten pounds last year.

_____

_____

The Simple Past Tense: Question Form

·21·

Place **did** before the subject to create questions in the simple past tense. The simple form of the verb is always used when creating questions in the simple past tense with regular and irregular verbs.

I ate	→	did I eat	→	Did I eat your sandwich?
you ate	→	did you eat	→	Did you eat my last cookie?
he ate	→	did he eat	→	Did he eat his dessert?
she ate	→	did she eat	→	Did she eat the vegetables?
it ate	→	did it eat	→	Did it eat the egg?
we ate	→	did we eat	→	Did we eat everything?
they ate	→	did they eat	→	Did they eat the meat?

EXERCISE

21·1

Use your dictionary to find the meaning of the following verbs and vocabulary words needed for this exercise before you begin. Write the words in your language in the space provided.

to weigh	_____	to cheat	_____
to elect	_____	to offend	_____
to escape	_____	to indicate	_____
to change	_____	to remain	_____
cards	_____	prison	_____
salad	_____	peanut	_____
deer	_____	scale	_____
garlic	_____	mind	_____
fight	_____	starfish	_____
argument	_____	remote control	_____
squirrel	_____	overtime	_____
rainbow	_____	timesheet	_____

*Rewrite the following sentences to create questions in the simple past tense by placing **did** before the subject and using the simple form of the verb. Don't forget to include a question mark (?) in your answer.*

1. You saw the beautiful rainbow.

   _____

2. He offended you when he said that.

   _____

3. Jessica found a starfish on the beach.

   _____

4. The squirrel ate the peanuts.

   _____

5. He shot a deer last weekend.

   _____

6. I indicated my overtime hours on my timesheet.

   _____

   _____

7. They remained friends after the argument.

   _____

8. Luke broke the remote control for the TV.

   _____

9. She changed her mind.

   _____

10. Brandon cheated when we played cards.

    _____

11. They weighed the fish on the scale.

    _____

12. You put garlic in the salad.

    _____

13. The people elected a new president.

    _____

14. He escaped from prison.

    _____

15. It slept under your bed.

    _____

Use your dictionary to find the meaning of the following verbs and vocabulary words needed for this exercise before you begin. Write the words in your language in the space provided.

to load	_____	to appear	_____
to lock	_____	to attend	_____
to pick	_____	to convince	_____
to ask	_____	to climb	_____
sunset	_____	diver	_____
comb	_____	seafood	_____
arm	_____	maid	_____
apron	_____	tree	_____
true	_____	bubble	_____
thief	_____	wagon	_____
safe	_____	handcuffs	_____
earring	_____	roller-coaster	_____
chipmunk	_____	ice-cream cone	_____
rattlesnake	_____	treasure chest	_____

Rewrite the following sentences using **did** *and the simple form of the verb to create questions in the simple past tense. Don't forget to include a question mark (?) in your answer.*

1. You took a picture of the sunset.

   _____

2. She locked the safe.

   _____

3. They attended the funeral.

   _____

4. Barry ordered seafood.

   _____

5. The chipmunk climbed the tree.

   _____

6. They rode the roller-coaster.

   _____

7. She made the earrings.

_____

8. The divers found a treasure chest.

_____

9. The baby blew bubbles in the bath.

_____

10. They loaded the wagon.

_____

11. The rattlesnake bit his arm.

_____

12. The policeman put handcuffs on the thief.

_____

13. She convinced you.

_____

14. You picked a flower for me.

_____

15. It appeared to be true.

_____

16. You asked a question.

_____

17. The maid ironed my apron.

_____

18. The dog licked my ice-cream cone.

_____

19. She drew a picture of a mermaid.

_____

20. Ravi lost his comb.

_____

Prepositions: *In* and *On*

Use *in* as a preposition to indicate:

the position or location

The towels are <u>in the dryer</u>.

the months and seasons

My flower garden is beautiful
   <u>in the summer</u>.
It's my birthday <u>in April</u>.

the year of occurrence

We married <u>in 2003</u>.

points of the day

He left <u>in the afternoon</u>.
   (exception: <u>at night</u>)

location within countries, cities, states, and provinces

She goes to school <u>in Montreal</u>.
He lives <u>in Ohio</u>.

We had fun <u>in Mexico</u>.
I met him <u>in British Columbia</u>.

Use *on* as a preposition to indicate:

**an object supported by a
top surface**

The cup is <u>on the table</u>.

a time of occurrence

I worked <u>on the weekend</u>.
She was sick <u>on Friday</u>.

the means of expression

We talked <u>on the phone</u> for two hours.
They played the song <u>on the radio</u>.
I watched it <u>on TV</u> last week.

**the directional position
of something**

It's the first door <u>on the left</u>.

a method of transportation

I felt sick <u>on the plane</u>.
   (exception: <u>in the car</u>)

the subject of study

I have a good book <u>on horses</u>.

EXERCISE
22·1

*Rewrite the following sentences correctly by choosing **in** or **on**.*

1. The garbage can is (in, on) the garage.

   _____

2. Do you see signs of life (in, on) the moon?

   _____

3. We will talk about it (in, on) the morning.

_____

4. Mark moved here (in, on) 1997.

_____

5. Don't throw your empty bottle (in, on) the ground.

_____

_____

6. We spent five days (in, on) Paris.

_____

7. All the kids start school (in, on) September.

_____

8. I will see you (in, on) Saturday.

_____

9. They advertised it (in, on) the radio (in, on) California.

_____

_____

10. What do you have (in, on) your mouth?

_____

11. I saw your picture (in, on) the newspaper (in, on) Ontario.

_____

_____

12. It's my birthday (in, on) Tuesday.

_____

13. The bathroom is (in, on) the left.

_____

14. We went for a ride (in, on) his motorcycle (in, on) the country.

_____

_____

15. She presented her project (in, on) trees.

_____

Use your dictionary to find the meaning of the new vocabulary words needed for this exercise before you begin. Write the words in your language in the space provided.

economy   _____   eyelash   _____

blister   _____   filling   _____

wart   _____   affairs   _____

lid   _____   switch   _____

*Complete the following sentences with **in** or **on**.*

1. They saw you _____ TV last night.

2. My aunt died _____ August.

3. She lives _____ the city.

4. I wrote an article _____ whales.

5. The people are _____ the ship.

6. We skate _____ the winter.

7. She has a wart _____ her nose.

8. We slept _____ the bus.

9. They divorced _____ 2001.

10. Turn the switch _____ the left.

11. Put the tablecloth _____ the table.

12. It's garbage day _____ Thursday.

13. Do you live _____ Michigan?

14. He became the president _____ 2005.

15. Your breakfast is _____ the tray.

16. I have a little eyelash _____ my eye.

17. The answer is _____ the book.

18. I want to change the carpet _____ my room.

19. The twins were born _____ Alberta.

20. We will buy a new car _____ the spring.

21. The flashlight is _____ the fridge.

22. We like to walk _____ the evening.

23. Who is the man _____ your right?

24. I have a filling _____ my back tooth.

25. Put the lid _____ the jar.

26. It is the best hotel _____ the world.

27. She gave a presentation _____ the economy.

28. We arrived _____ the morning.

29. I have a blister _____ my toe.

30. They work _____ the United States.

31. We have a day off _____ Monday.

32. His report was _____ world affairs.

33. Look at all the snow _____ the roof.

34. She screamed _____ the middle of the night.

35. The fly is _____ the ceiling.

36. She lives _____ Washington.

37. Paul wasn't with me _____ Wednesday.

38. I had lunch _____ the train.

39. Celine will have her baby _____ January.

40. We bought our house _____ 1995.

There Is and *There Are:*
Present Tense

·23·

Use **there is** and **there are** to show that something exists. Use **there is** with singular nouns and **there are** with plural nouns.

Singular

There is a gift for you on the table.

There is a sand castle on the beach.

There is a dove on the fence.

There is a button on the floor.

Plural

→   There are two gifts for you on the table.

→   There are a lot of sand castles on the beach.

→   There are many doves on the fence.

→   There are three buttons on the floor.

EXERCISE

23·1

Use your dictionary to find the meaning of the new vocabulary words needed for this exercise before you begin. Write the words in your language in the space provided.

colt	_____	meatball	_____
sink	_____	gigantic	_____
rock	_____	peppers	_____
street	_____	seagull	_____
piglet	_____	quilt	_____
stallion	_____	sauce	_____
caterpillar	_____	fire hydrant	_____
whiteboard	_____	signature	_____

Rewrite the following sentences by choosing **there is** *or* **there are** *depending on whether the noun is singular or plural.*

1. (There is, There are) many meatballs and red peppers in the sauce.

   _____

   _____

2. (There is, There are) a whiteboard in my classroom.

   _____

3. (There is, There are) rocks in my boot.

_____

4. (There is, There are) a signature on the letter.

_____

5. (There is, There are) gigantic footprints in the snow.

_____

_____

6. (There is, There are) a fire hydrant at the corner of my street.

_____

_____

7. (There is, There are) many caterpillars on the tree.

_____

8. (There is, There are) a black stallion in the field.

_____

9. (There is, There are) four piglets and three colts in the barn.

_____

_____

10. (There is, There are) a quilt on my bed.

_____

11. (There is, There are) many seagulls on the beach.

_____

12. (There is, There are) a new keyboard in the box.

_____

13. (There is, There are) two sponges in the bucket.

_____

14. (There is, There are) many dirty plates in the sink.

_____

_____

15. (There is, There are) six diamonds on my ring.

_____

16. (There is, There are) a few gray squirrels in the tree.

_____

_____

Use your dictionary to find the meaning of the new vocabulary words needed for this exercise before you begin. Write the words in your language in the space provided.

tow truck	_____	proof	_____
airport	_____	near	_____
shoulder	_____	cave	_____
dressing	_____	bat	_____
beehive	_____	check	_____
ear	_____	gun	_____
oil	_____	muffin	_____
sugar	_____	snack	_____
paper clip	_____	bullet	_____
toothpick	_____	wrinkle	_____
chin	_____	dustpan	_____
mosquito	_____	raisin	_____
pen	_____	over there	_____
downtown	_____	polka dot	_____
tablespoon	_____	long-distance call	_____
several	_____	teaspoon	_____
reward	_____	freckle	_____
forehead	_____	fire extinguisher	_____

Complete the following sentences with **is** or **are** depending on whether the noun directly following the verb is singular or plural.

1. There _____ many stars in the sky.

2. There _____ a beehive in the garage.

3. There _____ enough proof.

4. There _____ a big roller-coaster over there.

5. There _____ several tow trucks downtown.

6. There _____ a small airport outside the city.

7. There _____ a check for you in the mail.

8. There _____ a teaspoon of sugar in my tea.

9. There _____ many bats in the cave.

10. There _____ a box of paper clips in the drawer.

11. There _____ bullets in the gun.

12. There _____ a dustpan in the closet.

13. There _____ spaghetti sauce on your chin.

14. There _____ many wrinkles on your forehead.

15. There _____ a parking lot at the corner.

16. There _____ a long-distance call for you.

17. There _____ three freckles on my nose.

18. There _____ a fire extinguisher in the kitchen.

19. There _____ hunters in the woods.

20. There _____ a dog pen in the backyard.

21. There _____ snacks for everybody.

22. There _____ a big reward for you.

23. There _____ pink polka dots on my dress.

24. There _____ a hardware store near the mall.

25. There _____ many raisins in my muffin.

26. There _____ a mosquito on your shoulder.

27. There _____ a scar on my knee.

28. There _____ two tablespoons of oil in the salad dressing.

29. There _____ a gold earring in his left ear.

30. There _____ a lot of toothpicks in the jar.

There Is and *There Are:* Present Tense: Negative Form

·24·

Place *not* after *there is* and *there are* to create a negative sentence.

there is	→	there is not	→	There is not a rocking chair downstairs.
there are	→	there are not	→	There are not many blankets on my bed.

The negative form of *there is* and *there are* can also be expressed with the contractions *there isn't* and *there aren't*.

there is not	→	there isn't	→	There isn't a bug in the house.
there are not	→	there aren't	→	There aren't many leftovers.

EXERCISE

24·1

Use your dictionary to find the meaning of the new vocabulary words needed for this exercise before you begin. Write the words in your language in the space provided.

folder	_____	rabbit	_____
shade	_____	tricycle	_____
log	_____	penny	_____
button	_____	dime	_____
turtle	_____	thermometer	_____
nickel	_____	wishing well	_____
cage	_____	scarecrow	_____
quarter	_____	angel	_____

*Rewrite the following sentences to express the negative form of **there is** and **there are**. Write the sentence once using **is not** or **are not** and once using the contraction **isn't** or **aren't**.*

1. There is a lot of shade in the backyard.

   _____

   _____

2. There are three gold buttons on my coat.

_____

_____

3. There are two yellow folders on my desk.

_____

_____

4. There is a tricycle on the sidewalk.

_____

_____

5. There is a thermometer in the bathroom.

_____

_____

6. There are three white rabbits in the cage.

_____

_____

7. There is a turtle on the log.

_____

_____

8. There are many angels in the picture.

_____

_____

9. There is a scarecrow in the field.

_____

_____

10. There are many dimes and nickels in the wishing well.

_____

_____

11. There are five quarters and a penny in my back pocket.

_____

_____

Use your dictionary to find the meaning of the new vocabulary words needed for this exercise before you begin. Write the words in your language in the space provided.

yearbook	_____	wrist	_____
alarm clock	_____	hollow	_____
wall	_____	woodpecker	_____
ferry	_____	face	_____
region	_____	cemetery	_____
phone booth	_____	grasshopper	_____
knot	_____	flour	_____
rubber	_____	rag	_____
satin	_____	dresser	_____
flight	_____	church	_____
tiny	_____	valley	_____
theater	_____	row	_____
feather	_____	butterfly	_____
dip	_____	cushion	_____
bracelet	_____	hole	_____
pay phone	_____	across	_____
passenger	_____	price tag	_____
lock	_____	dirt	_____
ice cube	_____	oar	_____
sandbox	_____		

Use the contraction **isn't** or **aren't** to complete the following negative sentences.

1. There _____ enough time.

2. There _____ a pay phone in my school.

3. There _____ many grasshoppers in the valley.

4. There _____ a phone booth at the corner.

5. There _____ several chairs in the basement.

6. There _____ a lock on the door.

7. There _____ a skunk in the hollow log.

8. There _____ a cemetery in my town.

9. There _____ many ice cubes in my drink.

There Is and *There Are*: Present Tense: Negative Form   **95**

10. There _____ a sandbox in the park.

11. There _____ a hole in my pocket.

12. There _____ many rags in the bucket.

13. There _____ a satin cushion on the floor.

14. There _____ two alarm clocks on my dresser.

15. There _____ a butterfly on the flower.

16. There _____ enough noodles in my soup.

17. There _____ a tiny spider on the wall.

18. There _____ many rows in the theater.

19. There _____ dirt on my face.

20. There _____ a knot in the gold necklace.

21. There _____ a price tag on the sweater.

22. There _____ many passengers on this flight.

23. There _____ enough flour for this recipe.

24. There _____ many woodpeckers in my region.

25. There _____ enough dip for the vegetables.

26. There _____ many cars on the ferry.

27. There _____ a bracelet on her wrist.

28. There _____ a church across the street.

29. There _____ many feathers in the pillow.

30. There _____ a picture of you in my yearbook.

31. There _____ oars in the rubber boat.

There Is and *There Are:* Present Tense: Question Form

Place *is* or *are* before ***there*** to create questions in the present tense.

| there is | → | is there | → | Is there a kitten outside? |
| there are | → | are there | → | Are there ducks in the pond? |

EXERCISE
25·1

Use your dictionary to find the meaning of the new vocabulary words needed for this exercise before you begin. Write the words in your language in the space provided.

owl	_____	handle	_____
alien	_____	catfish	_____
germ	_____	suitcase	_____
ruler	_____	UFO	_____
vending machine	_____	skyscraper	_____
measuring cup	_____	diving board	_____
place mat	_____	lifeguard	_____
candy cane	_____	life jacket	_____

Rewrite the following sentences to create questions by placing **is** *or* **are** *before* **there**. *Don't forget to include a question mark (?) in your answer.*

1. There is a vending machine in the cafeteria.

    _____

    _____

2. There are enough life jackets in the boat.

    _____

    _____

3. There are many skyscrapers in the city.

    _____

4. There is a lifeguard at the pool.

_____

5. There are two owls in the tree.

_____

6. There is a diving board at the public pool.

_____

_____

7. There are germs on my hands.

_____

8. There is a handle on my suitcase.

_____

9. There is a UFO in the sky.

_____

10. There are aliens in the UFO.

_____

11. There are candy canes on the Christmas tree.

_____

_____

12. There is a ruler on my desk.

_____

13. There are enough place mats on the table.

_____

_____

14. There is a measuring cup in the cupboard.

_____

_____

15. There is a catfish in the pail.

_____

16. There are many hangers in the closet.

_____

17. There is a mirror in your purse.

_____

Use your dictionary to find the meaning of the new vocabulary words needed for this exercise before you begin. Write the words in your language in the space provided.

fishing rod	_____	blister	_____
neighborhood	_____	spinach	_____
spare	_____	fingerprint	_____
corkscrew	_____	heel	_____
playroom	_____	rooster	_____
hitchhiker	_____	kennel	_____
blood	_____	flyswatter	_____
porcupine	_____	stew	_____
pool table	_____	marble	_____
traffic light	_____	jail	_____
walnut	_____	butcher	_____
pushpin	_____	elevator	_____
can opener	_____	rolling pin	_____
trunk	_____	tire	_____

Complete the following questions with **is** or **are** depending on whether the noun directly referring to the verb is singular or plural.

1. _____ there fingerprints on the gun?

2. _____ there a pool table in the playroom?

3. _____ there a porcupine in the yard?

4. _____ there many marbles in the jar?

5. _____ there a rolling pin in the drawer?

6. _____ there a rooster on your farm?

7. _____ there many traffic lights in the city?

8. _____ there a hitchhiker on the road?

9. _____ there a spare tire in the trunk?

10. _____ there two blisters on my heel?

11. _____ there many fishing rods in the boat?

12. _____ there enough marshmallows for me?

13. _____ there a mouse in the house?

14. _____ there blood on your shirt?

15. _____ there three elevators in this building?

16. _____ there a lot of dandelions in the yard?

17. _____ there a fireman at the door?

18. _____ there a can opener on the counter?

19. _____ there meatballs in the stew?

20. _____ there a pushpin on the floor?

21. _____ there clean socks in the drawer?

22. _____ there many dogs in the kennel?

23. _____ there a corkscrew in the drawer?

24. _____ there many parking lots in Montreal?

25. _____ there a signature on the document?

26. _____ there walnuts in the spinach salad?

27. _____ there a jail in your neighborhood?

28. _____ there icing on the cake?

29. _____ there a fire hydrant near your house?

30. _____ there enough plates for everybody?

31. _____ there baby squirrels in the nest?

32. _____ there a flyswatter in the kitchen?

33. _____ there a broom in the garage?

34. _____ there are many good butchers in the city?

There Is and *There Are:* Past Tense

The past tense of the singular *there is* is *there was*, and the past tense of the plural *there are* is *there were*. Use *there was* and *there were* to show that something existed in the past.

there is	→	there was	→	There was a loud noise downstairs last night.
there are	→	there were	→	There were dark clouds in the sky.

EXERCISE
26·1

Use your dictionary to find the meaning of the new vocabulary words needed for this exercise before you begin. Write the words in your language in the space provided.

circle	_____	gravy	_____
west	_____	alley	_____
rust	_____	east	_____
straw	_____	wet	_____
square	_____	cork	_____
south	_____	north	_____
hurricane	_____	speed bump	_____
stray	_____	belly button	_____
triangle	_____	magnifying glass	_____
fireworks	_____	mashed potatoes	_____

Rewrite the following past tense sentences by choosing **was** *or* **were** *depending on whether the noun directly following the verb is singular or plural.*

1. There (was, were) rust on the knife.

   _____

2. There (was, were) rules to follow.

   _____

3. There (was, were) a big sale at the mall, so I bought a scarf and shoes.

_____

_____

4. There (was, were) many speed bumps on the road.

_____

_____

5. There (was, were) wet towels on the floor after he took his shower.

_____

_____

6. There (was, were) a hurricane in the southeast last week.

_____

_____

7. There (was, were) many stray cats in the alley.

_____

_____

8. There (was, were) beautiful fireworks in the sky last night.

_____

_____

9. There (was, were) a magnifying glass on the table.

_____

_____

10. There (was, were) two circles, three squares, and four triangles in the picture.

_____

_____

11. There (was, were) a diamond in her belly button.

_____

_____

12. There (was, were) a cork in the bottle of wine.

_____

_____

13. There (was, were) many straws in the cup on the counter in the kitchen.

_____

_____

14. There (was, were) a good story about you in the newspaper this morning.

_____

_____

15. There (was, were) a lot of dirty pots and pans in the sink.

_____

_____

16. There (was, were) many dimes, nickels, and quarters in my piggy bank.

_____

_____

17. There (was, were) gravy on my mashed potatoes but not on my meat.

_____

_____

18. There (was, were) a snowstorm in the northwest last night.

_____

_____

EXERCISE
26·2

Use your dictionary to find the meaning of the new vocabulary words needed for this exercise before you begin. Write the words in your language in the space provided.

lily pad	_____	cheek	_____
tear	_____	reason	_____
wax	_____	spiderweb	_____
stranger	_____	commercial	_____
priest	_____	teapot	_____
guy	_____	dance	_____
pear	_____	windmill	_____
wooden	_____	dew	_____
calendar	_____	France	_____
in line	_____	pole	_____
flag	_____	online	_____
teabag	_____	decision	_____

ladder _____   Mother's Day _____

clothespin _____   knitting needle _____

*Complete the following past tense sentences using **was** or **were** depending on whether the noun directly following the verb is singular or plural.*

1. There _____ a new priest in my church today.

2. There _____ a lot of clothespins in the bag.

3. There _____ many houses for sale last year.

4. There _____ a spiderweb in my truck.

5. There _____ good reasons for his decision.

6. There _____ a wooden ladder in the garage.

7. There _____ many pears in the tree.

8. There _____ a flag on the pole.

9. There _____ three knitting needles in the basket.

10. There _____ a rainbow after the storm.

11. There _____ dew on the grass this morning.

12. There _____ a parade on Mother's Day.

13. There _____ many people online.

14. There _____ four rubber ducks in the bath.

15. There _____ a stranger at the door.

16. There _____ many tourists in France last year.

17. There _____ a calendar on my desk.

18. There _____ two teabags in the teapot.

19. There _____ a car in the ditch.

20. There _____ tears on her cheek.

21. There _____ frogs on the lily pads.

22. There _____ a ghost in the attic.

23. There _____ wax on the table.

24. There _____ someone in the phone booth.

25. There _____ a good commercial on TV.

26. There _____ windmills in the field.

27. There _____ a mosquito in the tent.

28. There _____ many tall guys at the dance.

29. There _____ only one waitress yesterday.

30. There _____ many people in line.

31. There _____ a lot of weeds in the garden.

32. There _____ many accidents this morning.

33. There _____ a power failure last night.

34. There _____ a hockey game on TV last night.

There Is and *There Are:* Past Tense: Negative Form

Place **not** after **there was** and **there were** to create a negative sentence.

| there was | → | there was not | → | There was not a doll on the chair. |
| there were | → | there were not | → | There were not many kids in the pool. |

The negative form of **there was** and **there were** can also be expressed with the contractions **there wasn't** and **there weren't**.

| there was not | → | there wasn't | → | There wasn't a bruise on his arm. |
| there were not | → | there weren't | → | There weren't many fish in the lake. |

EXERCISE
27·1

Use your dictionary to find the meaning of the new vocabulary words needed for this exercise before you begin. Write the words in your language in the space provided.

wreath	_____	desert	_____
stone	_____	beaver	_____
dam	_____	crack	_____
hall	_____	shell	_____
bridge	_____	windshield	_____
octopus	_____	wheelchair	_____
game	_____	peach	_____
camel	_____	heavy	_____

*Rewrite the following sentences to express the negative form. Write the sentence once using **was not** or **were not** and once using the contraction **wasn't** or **weren't**.*

1. There was a crack in my windshield.

    _____

    _____

2. There were many shells and stones in the sand on the beach.

3. There were a lot of big heavy trucks on the bridge this morning.

4. There was a peach in my lunch box.

5. There were two staplers on my desk in my office.

6. There was a big brown beaver near the dam.

7. There were many wheelchairs in the hall in the hospital.

8. There was a wreath on the door.

9. There were many camels in the desert.

10. There was a huge octopus in the boat.

11. There were many fun games to play.

Use your dictionary to find the meaning of the new vocabulary words needed for this exercise before you begin. Write the words in your language in the space provided.

wicker	_____	scrambled eggs	_____
wiener	_____	wallpaper	_____
zoo	_____	mouthwash	_____
breeze	_____	hamburger	_____
sign	_____	poison ivy	_____
cool	_____	bank account	_____
plenty	_____	sheet of paper	_____
stable	_____	glove compartment	_____
ash	_____	live concert	_____
gorilla	_____	bus strike	_____
cub	_____	traffic jam	_____
lock	_____	hot dog bun	_____
rope	_____	crowd	_____
pickle	_____	chapter	_____
polar bear	_____	cinnamon	_____
stuffing	_____	forest	_____
crumb	_____	tuna	_____
stripe	_____	shadow	_____

Use the contraction **wasn't** *or* **weren't** *to complete the following negative sentences.*

1. There _____ a bottle of mouthwash on the shelf in the bathroom.

2. There _____ many chapters in the book.

3. There _____ a rope in the boat.

4. There _____ scrambled eggs for breakfast.

5. There _____ wallpaper on the wall.

6. There _____ a traffic jam on the highway.

7. There _____ stripes on his shirt.

8. There _____ a tuna sandwich for you.

9. There _____ many signs on the road.

10. There _____ a shadow on the wall.

11. There _____ a map in the glove compartment.

12. There _____ many sheets of paper.

13. There _____ crumbs on the plate.

14. There _____ ink in the printer.

15. There _____ enough pickles on my hamburger.

16. There _____ a bus strike in the city.

17. There _____ a lot of money in her bank account.

18. There _____ plenty of time.

19. There _____ three polar bear cubs.

20. There _____ a teaspoon of cinnamon in the jar.

21. There _____ gorillas at the zoo.

22. There _____ many wicker chairs in the store.

23. There _____ enough wieners for the hot dog buns.

24. There _____ ashes in the fireplace.

25. There _____ a big crowd outside.

26. There _____ stuffing in the turkey.

27. There _____ many horses in the stable.

28. There _____ a live concert on TV last night.

29. There _____ poison ivy in the forest.

30. There _____ a cool breeze last night.

31. There _____ a big ship in the lock.

32. There _____ hunters in the woods.

There Is and *There Are:* Past Tense: Question Form

Place **was** or **were** before **there** to create questions in the past tense.

there was	→	was there	→	Was there a cushion on the chair?
there were	→	were there	→	Were there enough snacks for the kids?

EXERCISE
28·1

Use your dictionary to find the meaning of the new vocabulary words needed for this exercise before you begin. Write the words in your language in the space provided.

splinter	_____	bone	_____
rose	_____	skull	_____
rude	_____	dice	_____
thumb	_____	bow	_____
room	_____	thorn	_____
locksmith	_____	rearview mirror	_____
outhouse	_____	cigarette butt	_____
entrance	_____	Canada goose	_____
fuzzy	_____	garage sale	_____
without	_____	blind spot	_____

*Rewrite the following sentences to create questions by placing **was** or **were** before **there**. Don't forget to include a question mark (?) in your answer.*

1. There were many knights to guard the castle in the kingdom.

   _____

   _____

2. There was a wooden outhouse behind our cottage in the country.

   _____

   _____

3. There was a picture of a skull and bones on the bottle.

_____

_____

4. There were many cigarette butts in the ashtray.

_____

_____

5. There was a car in my blind spot.

_____

6. There were pink fuzzy dice on his rearview mirror.

_____

_____

7. There was a splinter in his thumb.

_____

8. There was enough room on the bus for everybody.

_____

_____

9. There was a rude boy in your class last year.

_____

_____

10. There were two pretty blue bows in her hair.

_____

_____

11. There was a Canada goose near the lake.

_____

_____

12. There was a green carpet on the floor in the entrance.

_____

_____

13. There was a lot of garlic in the butter.

_____

14. There were many people without a passport at the airport.

_____

_____

15. There were many thorns on the rose.

   _____

16. There was a garage sale last weekend.

   _____

17. There were many people on the roller-coaster.

   _____

   _____

18. There was a locksmith in the mall.

   _____

Use your dictionary to find the meaning of the new vocabulary words needed for this exercise before you begin. Write the words in your language in the space provided.

ocean	_____	playpen	_____
walrus	_____	playground	_____
tusk	_____	anchor	_____
blind	_____	fly	_____
dime	_____	rusty	_____
oatmeal	_____	dinosaur	_____
axe	_____	dimple	_____
olive	_____	prize	_____
password	_____	bench	_____
factory	_____	lane	_____
ketchup	_____	bus stop	_____
penny	_____	pillowcase	_____
Earth	_____	cardboard	_____
fog	_____	raft	_____

*Complete the following past tense questions with **was** or **were** depending on whether the noun directly referring to the verb is singular or plural.*

1. _____ there dinosaurs on Earth?

2. _____ there a cardboard box in the bedroom?

3. _____ there a lock on the door?

4. _____ there a manager in the restaurant?

5. _____ there a blind on the window?

6. _____ there a bench in the playground?

7. _____ there a rusty axe in the barn?

8. _____ there many pennies in the jar?

9. _____ there toys in the playpen for the baby?

10. _____ there a fly in the spiderweb?

11. _____ there a motorcycle in the parking lot?

12. _____ there a dime in your pocket?

13. _____ there two olives in your drink?

14. _____ there a pillowcase on the pillow?

15. _____ there a raft on the river?

16. _____ there stars in the sky that night?

17. _____ there enough hangers in the closet?

18. _____ there a prize for me?

19. _____ there many lanes on the highway?

20. _____ there a bus stop at the corner?

21. _____ there many workers in the factory?

22. _____ there a password on your computer?

23. _____ there fog on the lake?

24. _____ there a broken tusk on the walrus?

25. _____ there a satellite dish in the yard?

26. _____ there cute dimples on her cheeks?

27. _____ there a silver earring in his left ear?

28. _____ there a huge anchor on the beach?

29. _____ there many divers in the ocean?

30. _____ there ketchup in the recipe?

31. _____ there a hair dryer in your luggage?

32. _____ there a goldfish in the bowl?

33. _____ there oatmeal cookies in the oven?

34. _____ there tea in the teapot?

Prepositions: *To and At*

Use *to* as a preposition to describe a movement or an action toward a person, place, or thing.

> I walk to school.   She goes to the bank every week.

Use *at* as a preposition to describe an action performed when a person or thing arrives at a location.

> We learn a lot at school.   I hurt my knee at the playground.

Use *at* as a preposition to refer to time.

> We have a meeting at three o'clock.   He eats breakfast at 7:30 A.M.

EXERCISE 29·1

Use your dictionary to find the meaning of the new vocabulary words needed for this exercise before you begin. Write the words in your language in the space provided.

daily	_____	opponent	_____
muzzle	_____	bonfire	_____
press	_____	Spain	_____
core	_____	England	_____

Rewrite the following sentences correctly by choosing **to** *or* **at**.

1. Please explain this (to, at) me.

   _____

2. The girls ate cake (to, at) the birthday party.

   _____

   _____

3. We saw Tony and his brother (to, at) the restaurant.

   _____

   _____

4. I sold my car (to, at) Mike.

_____

5. I bought a muzzle for my dog (to, at) the pet store.

_____

_____

6. The funeral was (to, at) four o'clock.

_____

7. We fed the apple cores (to, at) the raccoons.

_____

_____

8. I go (to, at) the gym daily.

_____

9. We made a bonfire (to, at) the beach.

_____

10. They drive (to, at) the city.

_____

11. The elevator went (to, at) the basement.

_____

12. We noticed that there was a policeman (to, at) the door.

_____

_____

13. He talked (to, at) the press after the meeting.

_____

_____

14. They gave the prize (to, at) my opponent.

_____

_____

15. Call me (to, at) 6:30 P.M.

_____

16. We went (to, at) England and Spain last year.

_____

_____

Use your dictionary to find the meaning of the new vocabulary words needed for this exercise before you begin. Write the words in your language in the space provided.

winner	_____	player	_____
dizzy	_____	cliff	_____
edge	_____	silk	_____
nearby	_____	loan	_____
auction	_____	shore	_____
outfit	_____	emerald	_____
race	_____	detention	_____
congratulations	_____	work of art	_____
Australia	_____	left-handed	_____
one-way ticket	_____	troublemaker	_____

Complete the following sentences with **to** *or* **at**.

1. I forgot my homework _____ my house.

2. They signed the contract _____ the courthouse.

3. He sent a gift certificate _____ his mother.

4. I felt dizzy _____ school today.

5. We met Bob _____ the airport.

6. Throw it _____ me.

7. The teacher sent the class troublemaker _____ the office.

8. Wait for me _____ the bus stop.

9. Meet me _____ the mall _____ one o'clock.

10. He bought a one-way ticket _____ Australia.

11. We walked _____ the edge of the cliff.

12. The kids jumped off the boat and swam _____ the shore.

13. They stayed _____ a nearby hotel.

14. Congratulations _____ the winner.

15. I lent my silk pants _____ Sylvie.

16. I think she is _____ work.

17. Go _____ bed.

18. She had a detention _____ school yesterday.

19. Linda gave her pink sharpener _____ me.

20. My appointment is _____ 3:30 P.M.

21. Talk _____ me.

22. They bought it _____ the garage sale.

23. The teacher read a story _____ the students.

24. I gave the black glove _____ the left-handed player.

25. She forgot her sweater _____ the day care.

26. They went _____ the bank for a loan.

27. I bought a work of art _____ the auction.

28. We lost a lot of money _____ the horse race.

29. She wore her white outfit _____ the party last night.

30. Mylene left her emerald ring _____ my house.

31. He returned _____ his apartment.

32. Ronald studied _____ McGill University.

33. It starts _____ six o'clock.

34. Happy birthday _____ you!

The Present Progressive (Continuous) Tense

The present progressive is used to describe an activity that is presently in progress. It is formed using the verb **to be** and by adding **-ing** to the simple form of the verb.

I drink	→	I am drinking	→	I am drinking my milk with a straw.
you drink	→	you are drinking	→	You are drinking my wine.
he drinks	→	he is drinking	→	He is drinking a cold beer.
she drinks	→	she is drinking	→	She is drinking a cup of tea.
it drinks	→	it is drinking	→	It is drinking the water in the toilet.
we drink	→	we are drinking	→	We are drinking orange juice.
they drink	→	they are drinking	→	They are drinking grape juice.

EXERCISE

30·1

Use your dictionary to find the meaning of the following verbs and vocabulary words needed for this exercise before you begin. Write the words in your language in the space provided.

to sue	_____	to cross	_____
to pour	_____	to howl	_____
to sew	_____	to worry	_____
to bark	_____	to discuss	_____
to shiver	_____	to growl	_____
to repair	_____	to knit	_____

wolf	_____	hiccup	_____
mayor	_____	pothole	_____
Big Dipper	_____	Little Dipper	_____
soft drink	_____	stepfather	_____
enormous	_____	goose bump	_____
groundhog	_____	bulletproof vest	_____
bleachers	_____	retirement home	_____
canoe	_____	stadium	_____

Rewrite the following sentences in the present progressive tense. Use the correct form of the verb **to be***, and add* **-ing** *to the simple form of the verb in parentheses.*

1. The wolf (to howl) at the moon.

   _____

2. Sheila (to worry) now because her daughter is late.

   _____

   _____

3. It is cold. We (to shiver) and we have goose bumps.

   _____

   _____

4. They (to cross) the lake in a canoe.

   _____

5. The mayor (to discuss) the enormous potholes on the roads.

   _____

   _____

6. She (to pour) a soft drink for you.

   _____

7. The nuns (to sew) clothes and (to knit) slippers for the children.

   _____

   _____

8. The policeman (to wear) his bulletproof vest.

   _____

   _____

9. My great-grandfather (to live) in a retirement home.

   _____

   _____

10. They (to sue) the city.

    _____

11. We (to look) at the Big Dipper and the Little Dipper with our binoculars.

    _____

    _____

12. Rollande (to drink) water because she has the hiccups.

    _____

    _____

13. My stepfather (to repair) the bleachers in the stadium.

_____

_____

14. It (to snow) again.

_____

15. The dog (to bark) and (to growl) at the groundhog outside.

_____

_____

EXERCISE
30·2

Use your dictionary to find the meaning of the following verbs and vocabulary words needed for this exercise before you begin. Write the words in your language in the space provided.

to overflow	_____	to chew	_____
to juggle	_____	to rattle	_____
to wave	_____	to tickle	_____
to surround	_____	to tease	_____
to rub	_____	to rewind	_____
to drool	_____	to deliver	_____
dentist	_____	flyer	_____
high heels	_____	poverty	_____
back	_____	filling	_____
law	_____	ball	_____
queen	_____	godfather	_____
postcard	_____	treat	_____

Complete the following sentences to form the present progressive tense. Use the correct form of the verb **to be,** *and add* **-ing** *to the simple form of the verb in parentheses.*

1. She _____ (to dress) the baby in the bedroom.

2. You _____ (to cough) a lot.

3. She _____ (to tickle) me.

4. I _____ (to rewind) the movie.

5. The queen _____ (to wave) at the crowd.

6. He _____ (to rub) my back.

7. The baby _____ (to drool) again.

8. They _____ (to sit) in the dining room.

9. Many people _____ (to live) in poverty.

10. Robin _____ (to deliver) flyers to the houses.

11. They _____ (to write) on their desks.

12. She _____ (to whisper) in my ear.

13. You _____ (to break) the law.

14. Someone _____ (to ring) the bell.

15. My team _____ (to win).

16. The windows _____ (to rattle).

17. He _____ (to tease) the dog.

18. You _____ (to annoy) me.

19. Karen _____ (to curl) her hair.

20. You _____ (to waste) my time.

21. The clown _____ (to juggle) the balls.

22. The toilet upstairs _____ (to overflow).

23. Your dog _____ (to chew) on your high heels.

24. The dentist _____ (to put) a filling in my tooth.

25. I _____ (to send) a postcard to my godfather.

26. The police _____ (to surround) the building.

27. I _____ (to leave) now.

28. Randy _____ (to draw) a picture for his friend.

29. The ice cubes _____ (to melt) in my glass.

30. I _____ (to give) the dog a treat.

The Present Progressive (Continuous) Tense: Negative Form

Place **not** after the verb **to be** to create the negative form of the present progressive tense.

I am following	→ I am not following	→	I am not following you.
you are following	→ you are not following	→	You are not following him.
he is following	→ he is not following	→	He is not following a recipe.
she is following	→ she is not following	→	She is not following the rules.
it is following	→ it is not following	→	It is not following me.
we are following	→ we are not following	→	We are not following the car.
they are following	→ they are not following	→	They are not following us.

The negative form of the present progressive tense can also be expressed with the contraction **isn't** or **aren't**. There is no contraction for **am not**.

I am not washing	→	→	I am not washing the floor.
you are not washing	→ you aren't washing	→	You aren't washing your hair.
he is not washing	→ he isn't washing	→	He isn't washing his hands.
she is not washing	→ she isn't washing	→	She isn't washing the dishes.
it is not washing	→ it isn't washing	→	It isn't washing its baby.
we are not washing	→ we aren't washing	→	We aren't washing our car.
they are not washing	→ they aren't washing	→	They aren't washing the dog.

EXERCISE
31·1

Use your dictionary to find the meaning of the following verbs and vocabulary words needed for this exercise before you begin. Write the words in your language in the space provided.

to plant	_____	to sink	_____
to shout	_____	to wait	_____
to stir	_____	to clap	_____
to bury	_____	to cheer	_____
seat belt	_____	seed	_____
elementary	_____	paintbrush	_____

*Rewrite the following sentences to create the negative form of the present progressive tense. Write your answer once with **am not**, **is not**, or **are not** and once with the contraction **isn't** or **aren't**.*

1. He is shouting at you.

   _____

   _____

2. They are waiting downstairs for us.

   _____

   _____

3. The ship is sinking.

   _____

   _____

4. The dog is burying the bone in the sand.

   _____

   _____

5. We are planting the seeds in the garden.

   _____

   _____

6. I am teaching in the elementary school this year.

   _____

   _____

7. Mike is stirring the paint with the paintbrush.

   _____

   _____

8. You are wearing your seat belt.

   _____

   _____

9. The crowd is clapping and cheering.

   _____

   _____

Use your dictionary to find the meaning of the following verbs and vocabulary words needed for this exercise before you begin. Write the words in your language in the space provided.

to separate	_____	to stare	_____
to wiggle	_____	to bore	_____
to joke	_____	to sharpen	_____
to invite	_____	to drip	_____
to surrender	_____	to star	_____
to solve	_____	to wrap	_____
to end	_____	to correct	_____
to wink	_____	to free	_____
to swallow	_____	to complain	_____
to pray	_____	to dance	_____
coleslaw	_____	real estate agent	_____
puzzle	_____	egg white	_____
thief	_____	cabbage roll	_____
scissors	_____	tap	_____
horseshoe	_____	present	_____
hostage	_____	yolk	_____
grapefruit	_____	buffalo	_____
relationship	_____	puddle	_____

*Use **am not** or the contraction **isn't** or **aren't** to complete the following sentences in the negative present progressive form. Add **-ing** to the simple form of the verb in parentheses.*

1. She _____ (to joke) about that.

2. They _____ (to pray) in the church.

3. We _____ (to dance) together.

4. I _____ (to make) cabbage rolls and coleslaw.

5. He _____ (to put) horseshoes on his horse.

6. The taps _____ (to drip) in the bathroom.

7. It _____ (to wiggle) in the box.

8. We _____ (to walk) in the puddle.

9. My mother _____ (to squeeze) the grapefruit.

10. I _____ (to separate) the yolk and egg white.

11. We _____ (to end) our relationship.

12. The teacher _____ (to correct) the exams.

13. We _____ (to complain).

14. It _____ (to bore) me.

15. He _____ (to aim) his rifle at the buffalo.

16. Ronald and Lee _____ (to solve) the puzzle.

17. My real estate agent _____ (to work) hard.

18. I _____ (to star) in a movie.

19. He _____ (to wink) at you.

20. They _____ (to free) the hostages.

21. The thief _____ (to surrender) to the police.

22. We _____ (to wrap) the presents.

23. The woman _____ (to swallow) the medicine.

24. He _____ (to sharpen) the scissors.

25. The secretary _____ (to type) a letter.

26. We _____ (to invite) the neighbors.

The Present Progressive (Continuous) Tense: Question Form

Place the verb **to be** before the subject to create questions in the present progressive tense.

I am watching	→	am I watching	→	Am I watching you?
you are watching	→	are you watching	→	Are you watching the game?
he is watching	→	is he watching	→	Is he watching the news?
she is watching	→	is she watching	→	Is she watching the time?
it is watching	→	is it watching	→	Is it watching me?
we are watching	→	are we watching	→	Are we watching them?
they are watching	→	are they watching	→	Are they watching the kids?

EXERCISE 32·1

Use your dictionary to find the meaning of the following verbs and vocabulary words needed for this exercise before you begin. Write the words in your language in the space provided.

to enjoy	_____	to slice	_____
to sweat	_____	to rock	_____
to talk	_____	to add	_____
to bleed	_____	to offer	_____
saleslady	_____	deal	_____
newborn	_____	bow	_____
suburb	_____	lip	_____
compass	_____	arrow	_____
backward	_____	business trip	_____
gas station	_____	employee	_____
sunrise	_____	pineapple	_____
expense	_____	forward	_____

*Rewrite the following sentences to create the question form of the present progressive tense by placing the verb **to be** before the subject. Don't forget to include a question mark (?) in your answer.*

1. They are talking about the newborn baby.

   _____

   _____

2. He is hunting with a bow and arrow.

   _____

3. The saleslady is offering you a good deal.

   _____

   _____

4. It is walking backward or forward.

   _____

5. The employees are adding their expenses for the business trip.

   _____

   _____

6. Mrs. Smith is living in the suburbs.

   _____

7. Mr. Jones is working in a gas station.

   _____

8. He is slicing the pineapple.

   _____

9. I am rocking the boat.

   _____

10. She is sweating a lot.

    _____

11. My lip is bleeding.

    _____

12. You are bringing your compass when we go in the woods.

    _____

    _____

13. Bob and Tina are on the beach enjoying the sunrise.

    _____

    _____

14. I am eating your muffin.

_____

15. Rosa is making a cake for the surprise birthday party.

_____

_____

_____

Use your dictionary to find the meaning of the following verbs and vocabulary words needed for this exercise before you begin. Write the words in your language in the space provided.

to crawl	_____	to burst	_____
to shuffle	_____	to fail	_____
to spy	_____	to grate	_____
to sob	_____	to kid	_____
to wag	_____	to suffer	_____
to show	_____	to throw up	_____
grater	_____	science	_____
leaf	_____	bagpipes	_____
wave	_____	maple	_____
snail	_____	seal	_____
wheelbarrow	_____	crusty bread	_____
breadboard	_____	water wings	_____

Rewrite the following sentences to create questions in the present progressive tense by placing the verb **to be** _before the subject._

1. Tom is spying on us.

_____

2. He is pushing the kids in the wheelbarrow.

_____

3. The patient is suffering a lot.

_____

4. She is cutting the crusty bread on the breadboard.

_____

_____

5. Jimmy is throwing up in the bathroom.

_____

_____

6. I am failing my science class.

_____

7. Roger is playing the bagpipes.

_____

8. The children are bursting the balloons.

_____

_____

9. The little boy is showing me something.

_____

_____

10. The snail is crawling on the tree.

_____

11. Shane is drawing a maple leaf.

_____

12. The seals are playing in the waves.

_____

13. They are swimming in the pool with their water wings.

_____

_____

14. Chris is grating the cheese with the grater.

_____

_____

15. They are kidding.

_____

16. He is shuffling the cards.

_____

17. Grace is sobbing in her bedroom.

_____

18. The dog is wagging its tail.

_____

The Present Progressive (Continuous) Tense: Question Form **129**

The Past Progressive (Continuous) Tense

The past progressive is used to describe an activity that happened and continued for a period of time in the past. It is formed using the past tense of the verb **to be** and by adding **-ing** to the simple form of the verb.

I am using	→	I was using	→	I was using the stove.
you are using	→	you were using	→	You were using my stapler.
he is using	→	he was using	→	He was using my car.
she is using	→	she was using	→	She was using my makeup.
it is using	→	it was using	→	It was using its paws.
we are using	→	we were using	→	We were using the glue.
they are using	→	they were using	→	They were using the laptop.

EXERCISE
33·1

Use your dictionary to find the meaning of the following verbs and vocabulary words needed for this exercise before you begin. Write the words in your language in the space provided.

to enter	_____	to cover	_____
to lower	_____	to change	_____
to test	_____	to divide	_____
to drop	_____	to place	_____
to roll	_____	to talk	_____
to ram	_____	to glow	_____
shock	_____	tollbooth	_____
tour	_____	distance	_____
wig	_____	disease	_____
lightbulb	_____	christening	_____
snowshoe	_____	up-to-date	_____
headphones	_____	laboratory	_____
Grand Canyon	_____	music	_____
during	_____	leukemia	_____

Rewrite the following sentences to form the past progressive tense. Use the correct past tense form of the verb **to be**, *and add* **-ing** *to the simple form of the verb in parentheses.*

1. The laboratory (to test) the blood for leukemia and other diseases.

   _____

   _____

2. We (to walk) in the snow with our snowshoes.

   _____

   _____

3. The mechanic (to lower) the car when it fell.

   _____

   _____

4. The girls (to talk) on the phone for two hours.

   _____

   _____

5. I (to change) the lightbulb when I got a shock.

   _____

   _____

6. The kids (to roll) down the mountain.

   _____

7. She (to place) a wig on her head when I entered.

   _____

   _____

8. George (to listen) to music with his headphones.

   _____

   _____

9. Vance (to cover) his answers during the test.

   _____

   _____

10. We (to buy) a gift for the christening.

    _____

11. I (to drop) a quarter in the tollbooth when he rammed the back of my car.

    _____

    _____

12. My daughter (to blow) her nose.

_____

13. The lights (to glow) in the distance.

_____

14. They (to struggle) to keep the files up-to-date.

_____

15. We (to divide) our time between the Grand Canyon and the casinos.

_____

_____

EXERCISE
33·2

Use your dictionary to find the meaning of the following verbs and vocabulary words needed for this exercise before you begin. Write the words in your language in the space provided.

to weave	_____	to scold	_____
to welcome	_____	to grieve	_____
to comb	_____	to crush	_____
to hatch	_____	to act	_____
to warn	_____	to bloom	_____
to gamble	_____	to reach	_____
janitor	_____	can	_____
parlor	_____	raincoat	_____
pork	_____	widower	_____
label	_____	memo	_____
hostess	_____	spoon	_____
railroad	_____	mask	_____
widow	_____	goal	_____
strange	_____	nuts	_____
drops	_____	bean	_____
tights	_____	spark	_____
recess	_____	bulletin board	_____
tablet	_____	everywhere	_____

Complete the following sentences to form the past progressive tense. Use the correct past tense form of the verb **to be**, *and add* **-ing** *to the simple form of the verb in parentheses.*

1. The flowers _____ (to bloom) in the garden.

2. Réal _____ (to eat) pork and beans.

3. Sam _____ (to crush) the tablets with a spoon.

4. The old man _____ (to warn) us.

5. The hostess _____ (to welcome) our guests.

6. I _____ (to put) the memo on the bulletin board.

7. We _____ (to wear) our raincoats.

8. The kids _____ (to play) ball during recess.

9. The squirrels _____ (to hide) the nuts in the backyard.

10. I _____ (to read) the label on the can.

11. Manon _____ (to wear) white tights.

12. I _____ (to talk) to my boss in his office.

13. They _____ (to cry) at school today.

14. The widow _____ (to grieve) for a long time.

15. They _____ (to weave) baskets.

16. I _____ (to comb) my hair.

17. She _____ (to scold) her children.

18. My father _____ (to work) on the railroad.

19. You _____ (to frighten) the kids with that scary mask on your face.

20. My uncle _____ (to gamble) all night.

21. The sparks _____ (to fly) everywhere.

22. The widower _____ (to act) strange at the funeral parlor.

23. We _____ (to reach) our goals.

24. Suzanne _____ (to sweep) the sidewalk.

25. The eggs _____ (to hatch).

26. I _____ (to put) drops in my eyes.

The Past Progressive (Continuous) Tense: Negative Form

Place **not** after the past tense form of the verb **to be** to create the negative form of the past progressive tense.

I was moving	→ I was not moving	→ I was not moving my leg.
you were moving	→ you were not moving	→ You were not moving it.
he was moving	→ he was not moving	→ He was not moving his pen.
she was moving	→ she was not moving	→ She was not moving her lips.
it was moving	→ it was not moving	→ It was not moving its tail.
we were moving	→ we were not moving	→ We were not moving our car.
they were moving	→ they were not moving	→ They were not moving it.

The negative form of the past progressive tense can also be expressed with the contraction **wasn't** or **weren't**.

I was not helping	→ I wasn't helping	→ I wasn't helping him.
you were not helping	→ you weren't helping	→ You weren't helping me.
he was not helping	→ he wasn't helping	→ He wasn't helping his aunt.
she was not helping	→ she wasn't helping	→ She wasn't helping the nurse.
it was not helping	→ it wasn't helping	→ It wasn't helping us.
we were not helping	→ we weren't helping	→ We weren't helping her.
they were not helping	→ they weren't helping	→ They weren't helping them.

EXERCISE
34·1

Use your dictionary to find the meaning of the following verbs and vocabulary words needed for this exercise before you begin. Write the words in your language in the space provided.

to nip	_____	to choke	_____
to smile	_____	to succeed	_____
side	_____	cancer	_____
collar	_____	stomach	_____
lung	_____	chemotherapy	_____
course	_____	treatment	_____

*Rewrite the following sentences to create the negative form of the past progressive tense. Write your answer once with **was not** or **were not** and once with the contraction **wasn't** or **weren't**.*

1. She was getting chemotherapy treatments for lung cancer.

   _____

   _____

2. My stomach was growling in class this morning.

   _____

   _____

3. We were driving on the wrong side of the road.

   _____

   _____

4. He was smiling at you.

   _____

   _____

5. It was nipping my ankle.

   _____

   _____

6. The collar was choking the dog.

   _____

   _____

7. Tania was succeeding in her course and she quit.

   _____

   _____

8. The guests were eating the potato salad.

   _____

   _____

9. They were joking.

   _____

   _____

Use your dictionary to find the meaning of the following verbs and vocabulary words needed for this exercise before you begin. Write the words in your language in the space provided.

to count	_____	to pet	_____
to taste	_____	to overdo	_____
to snip	_____	to hover	_____
to flap	_____	to slur	_____
to cope	_____	to rot	_____
to breathe	_____	to dive	_____
to drip	_____	to carve	_____
to distract	_____	to rely	_____
officer	_____	speech	_____
word	_____	donkey	_____
teeth	_____	lampshade	_____
shotgun	_____	chick	_____
dock	_____	underwear	_____
grease	_____	escalator	_____
wing	_____	dental floss	_____
wire	_____	helicopter	_____
artist	_____	undercover	_____
welfare	_____	gingerbread	_____

Complete the following sentences using the contraction **wasn't** or **weren't** to complete the following sentences in the negative past progressive form. Add **-ing** to the simple form of the verb in parentheses.

1. He _____ (to snip) the black wire.

2. The officer _____ (to work) undercover.

3. You _____ (to overdo) it.

4. The man _____ (to rely) on welfare.

5. The hunter _____ (to carry) a shotgun.

6. We _____ (to make) a gingerbread house.

7. The artist _____ (to carve) the wood.

8. She _____ (to cope) with it very well.

9. He _____ (to slur) his words.

10. They _____ (to dive) in your pool.

11. I _____ (to taste) your dessert.

12. We _____ (to feed) the ducks.

13. I _____ (to clean) my teeth with dental floss.

14. The bird _____ (to flap) its wings.

15. You _____ (to distract) me during my speech.

16. The grease _____ (to drip) on the floor.

17. He _____ (to wear) a lampshade on his head.

18. We _____ (to sit) on the dock.

19. They _____ (to jump) on the escalator.

20. The apples _____ (to rot) on the ground.

21. The helicopter _____ (to hover) over my house.

22. The little girl _____ (to pet) the donkey.

23. We _____ (to count) the baby chicks.

24. He _____ (to wear) clean underwear.

25. She _____ (to breathe).

26. They _____ (to laugh).

The Past Progressive (Continuous) Tense: Question Form

Place the past tense form of the verb *to be* before the subject to create questions in the past progressive tense.

I was swimming	→ was I swimming	→ Was I swimming well?
you were swimming	→ were you swimming	→ Were you swimming alone?
he was swimming	→ was he swimming	→ Was he swimming with you?
she was swimming	→ was she swimming	→ Was she swimming at night?
it was swimming	→ was it swimming	→ Was it swimming in the bath?
we were swimming	→ were we swimming	→ Were we swimming better?
they were swimming	→ were they swimming	→ Were they swimming fast?

EXERCISE 35·1

Use your dictionary to find the meaning of the following verbs and vocabulary words needed for this exercise before you begin. Write the words in your language in the space provided.

to drift	_____	to crack	_____
to heal	_____	to attract	_____
to thaw	_____	to guide	_____
to hope	_____	to stop	_____
to rehearse	_____	to grab	_____
to dust	_____	to float	_____
bull	_____	vitamin	_____
snorkel	_____	attention	_____
wound	_____	nightgown	_____
body	_____	pregnancy	_____
peacock	_____	watermelon	_____
goggles	_____	corn on the cob	_____
horn	_____	actor	_____
sea	_____	match	_____

*Rewrite the following sentences to create the question form of the past progressive tense by placing **was** or **were** before the subject. Don't forget to include a question mark (?) in your answer.*

1. The police were stopping everyone at the corner.

   _____

   _____

2. My yellow rubber duck was floating in the bath.

   _____

   _____

3. The meat was thawing on the counter.

   _____

4. The wounds on his body were healing.

   _____

5. She was hoping for a new nightgown for Christmas.

   _____

   _____

6. The ice was cracking on the lake.

   _____

7. The beautiful peacock was attracting a lot of attention.

   _____

   _____

8. She was buying watermelon and corn on the cob for the picnic.

   _____

   _____

9. The actors were rehearsing for the play.

   _____

10. It was drifting on the sea.

   _____

11. They were using matches to light the candles on the cake.

   _____

   _____

12. You were swimming with goggles and a snorkel.

   _____

   _____

13. Réal was grabbing the bull by the horns.

   _____

14. She was taking vitamins during her pregnancy.

   _____

   _____

15. The housekeeper was dusting the furniture.

   _____

Use your dictionary to find the meaning of the following verbs and vocabulary words needed for this exercise before you begin. Write the words in your language in the space provided.

to measure	_____	to pretend	_____
to investigate	_____	to close	_____
to rip	_____	to start	_____
to omit	_____	to beg	_____
to dare	_____	to spit	_____
to pant	_____	to raise	_____
crime	_____	detail	_____
barefoot	_____	detective	_____
ox	_____	pebble	_____
waist	_____	hip	_____
cart	_____	goat	_____
elbow	_____	ape	_____

Rewrite the following sentences to create questions in the past progressive tense by placing **was** *or* **were** *before the subject. Don't forget to include a question mark (?) in your answer.*

1. She was starting her car.

   _____

2. They were begging us to stay for supper.

   _____

3. We were closing the store early.

   _____

4. They were walking barefoot on the pebbles.

_____

_____

5. The dog was panting.

_____

6. You were scratching your elbow.

_____

7. She was measuring her waist and hips.

_____

8. Danny was daring me to jump in the lake.

_____

9. It was eating my peanut butter sandwich.

_____

10. You were ripping my sweater.

_____

11. Gary was omitting the details.

_____

12. It was following me.

_____

13. The detectives were investigating the crime.

_____

_____

14. He was spitting on the sidewalk.

_____

15. They were raising goats.

_____

16. You were pretending to be a big ape.

_____

17. I was reading the right letter.

_____

18. The ox was pulling the cart.

_____

_____

Prepositions: From and Of

Use *from* as a preposition to:

indicate a starting point of a movement

We drove <u>from Montreal to Toronto</u>.

measure between points

I work <u>from 8:00 A.M. to 4:00 P.M.</u>

indicate a starting point of an action

My husband called me <u>from work</u>.

indicate the source

She got the information <u>from John</u>.

Use *of* as a preposition to:

indicate the cause or reason of an action

He died <u>of a heart attack</u>.

indicate belonging

I met the <u>queen of England</u>.

indicate the contents

I drank two <u>cups of coffee</u> this morning.

describe a characteristic of a person

He is a <u>man of great courage</u>.

EXERCISE

36·1

Use your dictionary to find the meaning of the new vocabulary words needed for this exercise before you begin. Write the words in your language in the space provided.

talent	_____	beyond	_____
bouquet	_____	value	_____

*Rewrite the following sentences correctly by choosing **from** or **of**.*

1. We gave her a beautiful bouquet (from, of) flowers.

   _____

   _____

2. I got a toothbrush (from, of) my dentist.

   _____

   _____

3. He is a member (from, of) the hockey hall (from, of) fame.

_____

_____

4. She sent me a postcard (from, of) Canada.

_____

_____

5. Peter is a man (from, of) many talents.

_____

6. We heard voices (from, of) beyond the bushes.

_____

_____

7. He called me (from, of) a pay phone.

_____

8. I need a cup (from, of) sugar for this recipe.

_____

_____

9. Is that guy (from, of) Mexico?

_____

10. I work (from, of) Monday to Thursday. I don't work Friday.

_____

_____

11. Do you want a glass (from, of) beer?

_____

12. She is a woman (from, of) value in our company.

_____

_____

13. The cat jumped (from, of) the couch to the window.

_____

_____

14. Open the gift (from, of) me.

_____

Use your dictionary to find the meaning of the new vocabulary words needed for this exercise before you begin. Write the words in your language in the space provided.

monthly	_____	decade	_____
mouthful	_____	spoonful	_____
herd	_____	popcorn	_____
seventy	_____	litter	_____
odor	_____	theater	_____
century	_____	catalog	_____

*Complete the following sentences with **from** or **of**.*

1. She brought a basket _____ fruit for us.

2. He is a man _____ experience.

3. We receive checks monthly _____ the insurance company.

4. The little girl has a mouthful _____ milk.

5. Are you _____ Montreal?

6. Put this box _____ books in the basement.

7. Do you want a cup _____ tea?

8. The odor is coming _____ the fridge.

9. I have a picture _____ you.

10. Take out a sheet _____ paper _____ your binder.

11. Do you want to play a game _____ cards?

12. My cat had a litter _____ kittens last night.

13. We get vitamins _____ food.

14. I bought a bag _____ popcorn at the theater.

15. She counted _____ one to seventy in French.

16. I borrowed it _____ my cousin.

17. What is the special _____ the day?

18. My uncle died _____ cancer.

19. I have a closet full _____ old shoes.

20. I just got home _____ school.

21. Who is the woman _____ the decade?

22. She moved _____ her apartment to a retirement home.

23. We just came back _____ Italy.

24. She works _____ her home office.

25. I ate a bowl _____ chicken soup for lunch.

26. We got a call _____ your teacher.

27. I need a spoonful _____ honey.

28. You have a message _____ Tom.

29. We picked fresh tomatoes _____ our garden.

30. Thank you for the box _____ chocolates.

31. There is a herd _____ horses in the field.

32. The gorilla escaped _____ the zoo.

33. Where is the jar _____ pickles?

34. I received a long e-mail _____ my aunt.

35. We drank a bottle _____ wine with dinner.

36. She ordered it _____ the new catalog.

37. Who is the person _____ the century?

38. I got the results _____ my doctor.

Will: Future Tense

Use *will* to create the future tense for all persons. The simple form of the verb always follows *will*.

I will	→	I will hold	→	I will hold your books.
you will	→	you will hold	→	You will hold the baby.
he will	→	he will hold	→	He will hold my hand.
she will	→	she will hold	→	She will hold her doll.
it will	→	it will hold	→	It will hold the ball.
we will	→	we will hold	→	We will hold our fishing rods.
they will	→	they will hold	→	They will hold the ladder.

EXERCISE

37·1

Use your dictionary to find the meaning of the following verbs and vocabulary words needed for this exercise before you begin. Write the words in your language in the space provided.

to flip	_____	to reduce	_____
to ship	_____	to enlarge	_____
to hug	_____	to become	_____
to ban	_____	to pamper	_____
to introduce	_____	to envy	_____
to gather	_____	to grant	_____
fairy	_____	author	_____
top	_____	famous	_____
tax	_____	cherry	_____
brain	_____	several	_____
rich	_____	blueberry	_____
government	_____	raspberry	_____
lighthouse	_____	tobacco	_____
swordfish	_____	friendship	_____

*Rewrite the following sentences in the future tense by using **will** and the simple form of the verb in parentheses.*

1. I (to climb) to the top of the lighthouse to see the ships.

   _____

   _____

2. You (to become) a rich and famous author.

   _____

   _____

3. The government (to reduce) taxes next year.

   _____

   _____

4. The fairy (to grant) you several wishes.

   _____

5. My mother (to make) a cherry pie.

   _____

6. We (to study) the brain in my science class.

   _____

   _____

7. They (to enlarge) the picture of the swordfish that they caught.

   _____

   _____

8. We (to gather) blueberries, strawberries, and raspberries to make jam.

   _____

   _____

9. He (to hug) and kiss you when he sees you.

   _____

   _____

10. Brad (to introduce) me to his parents tomorrow night.

    _____

    _____

11. We (to ship) the package to you this afternoon.

    _____

    _____

12. Mary (to envy) your friendship with Paul.

_____

13. The government (to ban) tobacco in all public places.

_____

_____

14. She (to pamper) her new baby.

_____

15. I (to flip) the pancakes now.

_____

_____

Use your dictionary to find the meaning of the following verbs and vocabulary words needed for this exercise before you begin. Write the words in your language in the space provided.

to donate	_____	to concentrate	_____
to inform	_____	to stimulate	_____
to tame	_____	to postpone	_____
to wonder	_____	to nod	_____
to cause	_____	to last	_____
to develop	_____	to miss	_____
to continue	_____	to calculate	_____
to balance	_____	to bake	_____
budget	_____	muscle	_____
bake sale	_____	career	_____
music	_____	pay	_____
organ	_____	drum	_____
speeding	_____	once	_____
taste bud	_____	outcome	_____
wonderful	_____	public transportation	_____
fine (n)	_____	circus	_____
only	_____	twice	_____
lion	_____	why	_____

*Complete the sentences using **will** and the simple form of the verb in parentheses to create the future tense.*

1. Brian _____ (to calculate) his pay.

2. We _____ (to balance) our budget.

3. Denis _____ (to develop) his muscles at the gym.

4. They _____ (to concentrate) on their careers.

5. It _____ (to last) a long time.

6. We _____ (to postpone) the meeting.

7. He _____ (to learn) to play the drums.

8. They _____ (to tame) the lions for the circus.

9. I _____ (to tell) you only once.

10. They _____ (to wonder) why we left.

11. We _____ (to order) a pizza for supper.

12. The neighbors _____ (to move) next month.

13. I _____ (to miss) you.

14. She _____ (to bake) cookies for the bake sale.

15. Ricky Martin _____ (to continue) to make wonderful music.

16. It _____ (to be) cold tomorrow.

17. He _____ (to nod) his head twice.

18. We _____ (to use) public transportation.

19. You _____ (to get) a fine for speeding.

20. It _____ (to stimulate) your taste buds.

21. You _____ (to cause) a serious accident.

22. She _____ (to donate) her organs.

23. He _____ (to inform) us of the outcome.

24. Jim and Scott _____ (to share) the expenses.

Will: Future Tense: Negative Form

Place **not** after **will** to create the negative form of the future tense. The simple form of the verb always follows **will not**.

I will	→	I will not	→	I will not be there.
you will	→	you will not	→	You will not say that.
he will	→	he will not	→	He will not pay me.
she will	→	she will not	→	She will not see you.
it will	→	it will not	→	It will not eat.
we will	→	we will not	→	We will not borrow money.
they will	→	they will not	→	They will not drive to New York.

The negative form of the future tense with **will** can be expressed with the contraction **won't**.

I will not	→	I won't	→	I won't go.
you will not	→	you won't	→	You won't convince her.
he will not	→	he won't	→	He won't know.
she will not	→	she won't	→	She won't sleep late.
it will not	→	it won't	→	It won't bite you.
we will not	→	we won't	→	We won't spend a lot.
they will not	→	they won't	→	They won't help us.

EXERCISE
38·1

Use your dictionary to find the meaning of the following verbs and vocabulary words needed for this exercise before you begin. Write the words in your language in the space provided.

to recognize	_____	to allow	_____
to celebrate	_____	to pawn	_____
to confess	_____	to declare	_____
to trim	_____	to stay	_____
sideburns	_____	overnight	_____
blind date	_____	murder	_____
bankruptcy	_____	New Year's Eve	_____
guitar	_____	bush	_____

Rewrite the following sentences to create the negative form of the future tense. Write your answer once with **will not** *and once with the contraction* **won't**.

1. He will declare bankruptcy.

   _____

   _____

2. My neighbor will trim his bushes.

   _____

   _____

3. John will trim his sideburns.

   _____

   _____

4. Anna will go on a blind date.

   _____

   _____

5. You will recognize me with my wig.

   _____

   _____

6. They will allow you to stay overnight.

   _____

   _____

7. We will celebrate on New Year's Eve.

   _____

   _____

8. The man will confess to the murder.

   _____

   _____

9. I will pawn my guitar.

   _____

   _____

Use your dictionary to find the meaning of the following verbs and vocabulary words needed for this exercise before you begin. Write the words in your language in the space provided.

to delay	_____	to operate	_____
to betray	_____	to issue	_____
to hand	_____	to benefit	_____
to tolerate	_____	to guess	_____
to pierce	_____	to purchase	_____
to cure	_____	to clog	_____
to improve	_____	to attempt	_____
to ruin	_____	to compensate	_____
tool	_____	drain	_____
soap	_____	guilty	_____
job	_____	weight	_____
flight	_____	hell	_____
heaven	_____	spine	_____
breast	_____	custody	_____
suit	_____	rundown	_____
tongue	_____	jet	_____
newsletter	_____	will (n)	_____
product	_____	wisdom teeth	_____
loss	_____	reputation	_____
agreement	_____	insurance policy	_____

Complete the following sentences by using the contraction **won't** and the simple form of the verb in parentheses.

1. You _____ (to ruin) your reputation.

2. It _____ (to clog) the drain.

3. My company _____ (to issue) the newsletter.

4. We _____ (to improve) our products this year.

5. I _____ (to guess) your weight.

6. They _____ (to discuss) heaven and hell.

7. We _____ (to benefit) from this insurance policy.

8. It _____ (to delay) our flight.

9. They _____ (to compensate) us for our loss.

10. She _____ (to allow) me to pierce my tongue.

11. The treatment _____ (to cure) breast cancer.

12. He _____ (to purchase) new tools for his job.

13. The students _____ (to listen) to their teacher.

14. The pilot _____ (to attempt) to fly the jet.

15. He _____ (to wear) his black suit.

16. They _____ (to sign) the agreement.

17. My aunt _____ (to make) a will.

18. The doctors _____ (to operate) on my spine.

19. We _____ (to betray) you.

20. My dentist _____ (to remove) my wisdom teeth.

21. She _____ (to have) custody of the children.

22. They _____ (to live) in a rundown building.

23. It _____ (to mean) that he is guilty.

24. I _____ (to tolerate) this behavior.

25. Louise _____ (to hand) me the soap.

26. You _____ (to fail) your exam.

Will: Future Tense: Question Form

Place **will** before the subject to create questions in the future tense. The simple form of the verb is always used when forming questions with **will**.

I will	→	will I like	→	Will I like it?
you will	→	will you call	→	Will you call me?
he will	→	will he write	→	Will he write a book?
she will	→	will she join	→	Will she join us for dinner?
it will	→	will it annoy	→	Will it annoy you?
we will	→	will we need	→	Will we need a new car?
they will	→	will they worry	→	Will they worry about me?

EXERCISE
39·1

Use your dictionary to find the meaning of the following verbs and vocabulary words needed for this exercise before you begin. Write the words in your language in the space provided.

to travel	_____	to punish	_____
to spray	_____	to disappear	_____
to rescue	_____	to mention	_____
to kick	_____	to partake	_____
to accuse	_____	to show	_____
to poison	_____	to measure	_____
fang	_____	island	_____
wasp	_____	pajamas	_____
bee	_____	writing	_____
muscle	_____	eagle	_____
toaster	_____	ironing board	_____
poison	_____	tape measure	_____
brand-new	_____	foreman	_____
competition	_____	last name	_____

Rewrite the following sentences to create the question form of the future tense by placing **will** *before the subject. Don't forget to include a question mark (?) in your answer.*

1. The snow will disappear in the spring.

   _____

2. Your mother will punish you for that.

   _____

3. The police will accuse Sara.

   _____

4. You will spell your last name for me.

   _____

5. She will throw her old pajamas in the garbage.

   _____

   _____

6. He will measure it with his brand-new tape measure.

   _____

   _____

7. Bobby will show the judges his muscles.

   _____

   _____

8. It will poison you with its fangs.

   _____

9. They will mention it to their foreman.

   _____

10. The gardener will spray the wasps and bees with poison.

    _____

    _____

11. They will rescue the eagles on the island.

    _____

    _____

12. Your boyfriend will partake in the writing competition.

    _____

    _____

13. We will travel a lot next year.

    _____

14. It will kick me.

_____

15. She will buy a new ironing board and toaster for her apartment.

_____

_____

Use your dictionary to find the meaning of the following verbs and vocabulary words needed for this exercise before you begin. Write the words in your language in the space provided.

to grind	_____	to publish	_____
to produce	_____	to require	_____
to sag	_____	to regret	_____
to respond	_____	to pause	_____
to blame	_____	to arrive	_____
to trade	_____	to expand	_____
stitch	_____	magnet	_____
rush hour	_____	painting	_____
mouth	_____	on time	_____
ivory	_____	trailer	_____

Rewrite the following sentences to create questions in the future tense by placing **will** _before the subject. Don't forget to include a question mark (?) in your answer._

1. It will arrive on time.

_____

2. He will publish his report.

_____

3. They will blame me.

_____

4. We will be in rush hour traffic.

_____

5. Our country will ban the sale of ivory.

_____

6. Sheila will stick the magnet on the fridge.

_____

7. You will close your mouth when you eat.

_____

8. We will produce a lot of corn this year.

_____

9. Our company will expand next year.

_____

10. It will rain tomorrow.

_____

11. We will trade our trailer for a boat.

_____

12. He will pause the movie for a few minutes.

_____

13. I will regret it.

_____

14. It will grind the coffee beans.

_____

15. You will require stitches in your knee.

_____

16. The roof will sag with all the snow on it.

_____

17. They will bid on the famous painting.

_____

18. I will gain weight if I eat this.

_____

19. He will respond.

_____

20. I will have enough time.

_____

·40· Be Going To: Future Tense

The future tense can also be expressed by using **be going to**. Use the correct form of the verb **to be** for each person. The simple form of the verb always follows **be going to**.

I am going to	→	I am going to explain	→	I am going to explain it to you again.
you are going to	→	you are going to need	→	You are going to need a hammer.
he is going to	→	he is going to answer	→	He is going to answer the question.
she is going to	→	she is going to have	→	She is going to have a baby.
it is going to	→	it is going to be	→	It is going to be expensive.
we are going to	→	we are going to prove	→	We are going to prove it to you.
they are going to	→	they are going to meet	→	They are going to meet downtown.

EXERCISE 40·1

Use your dictionary to find the meaning of the following verbs and vocabulary words needed for this exercise before you begin. Write the words in your language in the space provided.

to lift	_____	to spread	_____
to dirty	_____	to injure	_____
to shine	_____	to vomit	_____
to check	_____	to create	_____
to hurry	_____	to applaud	_____
to remove	_____	to surprise	_____
sun	_____	lobby	_____
end	_____	schedule	_____
deep	_____	too much	_____
upset	_____	manager	_____

shallow _____   audience _____

muddy _____   waterbed _____

Rewrite the following sentences in the future tense using **be going to**. *Use the correct form of the verb* **to be** *and the simple form of the verb in parentheses.*

1. I (be) going to (to hurry) because I don't want to miss my bus.

   _____

   _____

2. He drank too much, and now he (be) going to (to vomit).

   _____

   _____

3. You (be) going to (to dirty) my floor with your muddy shoes.

   _____

   _____

4. The sun (be) going to (to shine) all day today.

   _____

   _____

5. I (be) going to (to wait) for you in the lobby downstairs.

   _____

   _____

6. We (be) going to (to sell) our waterbed in our garage sale.

   _____

   _____

7. The kids (be) going to (to swim) in the shallow end of the pool.

   _____

   _____

8. The adults (be) going to (to dive) in the deep end of the pool.

   _____

   _____

9. You (be) going to (to injure) your back if you lift that heavy box.

   _____

   _____

10. It (be) going to (to create) problems in the office.

_____

_____

11. I (be) going to (to spread) the jam on my toast.

_____

_____

12. My manager (be) going to (to check) his schedule for next week.

_____

_____

13. You (be) going to (to be) upset if the audience doesn't applaud.

_____

_____

14. He (be) going to (to surprise) her with a diamond ring.

_____

_____

15. She (be) going to (to remove) your name from the list.

_____

_____

Use your dictionary to find the meaning of the following verbs and vocabulary words needed for this exercise before you begin. Write the words in your language in the space provided.

to tighten	_____	to commute	_____
to assume	_____	to admit	_____
to skip	_____	to suggest	_____
to remind	_____	to clip	_____
to tap	_____	to vanish	_____
to seem	_____	to charge	_____
sample	_____	hairspray	_____
dawn	_____	someday	_____
partner	_____	interest	_____
receipt	_____	turnip	_____

shallot	_____	leash	_____
innocent	_____	noon	_____
proud	_____	at first	_____
difficult	_____	painful	_____

*Complete the sentences using the correct form of the verb **to be** and the simple form of the verb in parentheses to create the future tense with **be going to**.*

1. We _____ going to _____ (to assume) that he is innocent.

2. He _____ going to _____ (to suggest) something better at the meeting.

3. She _____ going to _____ (to tighten) the leash on the dog.

4. I _____ going to _____ (to clip) the receipts together.

5. We _____ going to _____ (to observe) the students in the cafeteria at noon.

6. I _____ going to _____ (to give) you a sample.

7. It _____ going to _____ (to seem) difficult at first.

8. We _____ going to _____ (to remind) you in the morning.

9. We _____ going to _____ (to admit) the truth.

10. It _____ going to _____ (to be) very painful.

11. He _____ going to _____ (to ask) his partner.

12. I _____ going to _____ (to tap) him on the shoulder.

13. The students _____ going to _____ (to commute) by train.

14. The boys _____ going to _____ (to skip) school this afternoon.

15. I _____ going to _____ (to put) shallots and turnips in the stew.

16. She _____ going to _____ (to marry) Edward someday.

17. It _____ going to _____ (to occur) at dawn.

18. They _____ going to _____ (to charge) us interest.

19. This car _____ going to _____ (to belong) to me someday.

20. The fog _____ going to _____ (to vanish) soon.

21. I _____ going to _____ (to buy) a can of hairspray.

22. You _____ going to _____ (to be) very proud.

·41· Be Going To: Future Tense: Negative Form

Place **not** after the verb **to be** to create the negative form of the future tense with **be going to**. The simple form of the verb always follows the negative form of **be going to**.

I am going to	→	I am not going to	→	I am not going to lose.
you are going to	→	you are not going to	→	You are not going to win.
he is going to	→	he is not going to	→	He is not going to be there.
she is going to	→	she is not going to	→	She is not going to eat it.
it is going to	→	it is not going to	→	It is not going to run.
we are going to	→	we are not going to	→	We are not going to leave.
they are going to	→	they are not going to	→	They are not going to talk.

The negative form of the future tense with **be going to** can also be expressed with the contraction **isn't** or **aren't**. There is no contraction for **am not**.

I am not going to	→		→	I am not going to drive.
you are not going to	→	you aren't going to	→	You aren't going to forget.
he is not going to	→	he isn't going to	→	He isn't going to play.
she is not going to	→	she isn't going to	→	She isn't going to study.
it is not going to	→	it isn't going to	→	It isn't going to rain.
we are not going to	→	we aren't going to	→	We aren't going to try it.
they are not going to	→	they aren't going to	→	They aren't going to like it.

EXERCISE 41·1

Use your dictionary to find the meaning of the following verbs and vocabulary words needed for this exercise before you begin. Write the words in your language in the space provided.

to haunt	_____	to submit	_____
to chill	_____	to invest	_____
to withdraw	_____	to announce	_____
to reuse	_____	to divorce	_____
funds	_____	report	_____
life	_____	ostrich	_____
rest	_____	cutbacks	_____
experience	_____	stock market	_____

Rewrite the following sentences to create the negative form of the future tense of **be going to**. *Write your answer once with* **am not, is not,** *or* **are not** *and once with the contraction* **isn't** *or* **aren't**.

1. My company is going to announce cutbacks for the new year.

   _____

   _____

2. We are going to submit the report in the morning.

   _____

   _____

3. I am going to withdraw all my money.

   _____

   _____

4. They are going to invest the funds in the stock market.

   _____

   _____

5. This experience is going to haunt me for the rest of my life.

   _____

   _____

6. Annie is going to chill the wine before she serves it.

   _____

   _____

7. The ostrich is going to attack you.

   _____

   _____

8. You are going to reuse the bags.

   _____

   _____

9. He is going to divorce his wife.

   _____

   _____

Use your dictionary to find the meaning of the following verbs and vocabulary words needed for this exercise before you begin. Write the words in your language in the space provided.

to judge	_____	to wrestle	_____
to steer	_____	to quarrel	_____
to pry	_____	to trick	_____
to curse	_____	to care	_____
to lessen	_____	to leap	_____
to empty	_____	to trap	_____
to label	_____	to ensure	_____
to respect	_____	to can	_____
checkers	_____	safety	_____
subpoena	_____	January	_____
February	_____	March	_____
April	_____	May	_____
June	_____	beet	_____
pain	_____	bailiff	_____

*Complete the following sentences using **am not** or the contraction **isn't** or **aren't** to create the negative form of the future tense of **be going to**.*

1. We _____ going to trick you again.

2. She _____ going to circle the right answer.

3. We _____ going to respect his decision.

4. They _____ going to ensure our safety.

5. You _____ going to curse in my class.

6. She _____ going to empty her purse.

7. I _____ going to label all the items in the store.

8. We _____ going to can beets this year.

9. She _____ going to care about that.

10. We _____ going to send the subpoena by bailiff.

11. It _____ going to snow in June.

12. I _____ going to be twenty-five years old in January.

13. She _____ going to visit me in March.

14. You _____ going to have another operation.

15. They _____ going to play checkers all night.

16. I _____ going to bake a cake.

17. Nancy _____ going to place the names in a hat.

18. We _____ going to judge you.

19. It _____ going to lessen the pain.

20. The frog _____ going to leap on you.

21. They _____ going to quarrel again.

22. He _____ going to pry the door open.

23. Sidney _____ going to steer the boat.

24. The boys _____ going to wrestle in the living room.

25. We _____ going to be in Tokyo in April.

26. He _____ going to start his new job in May.

27. It _____ going to open in February.

28. We _____ going to trap beavers.

Be Going To: Future Tense: Question Form

Place the verb **to be** before the subject to create questions in the future tense of **be going to**. The simple form of the verb is always used when forming questions with **be going to**.

I am going to	→	am I going to	→	Am I going to see you?
you are going to	→	are you going to	→	Are you going to visit me?
he is going to	→	is he going to	→	Is he going to believe you?
she is going to	→	is she going to	→	Is she going to be here?
it is going to	→	is it going to	→	Is it going to start soon?
we are going to	→	are we going to	→	Are we going to agree?
they are going to	→	are they going to	→	Are they going to park there?

EXERCISE
42·1

Use your dictionary to find the meaning of the following verbs and vocabulary words needed for this exercise before you begin. Write the words in your language in the space provided.

to dip	_____	to store	_____
to graze	_____	to apply	_____
to turn	_____	to scrub	_____
to drain	_____	to immigrate	_____
to cooperate	_____	to process	_____
to supply	_____	to provide	_____
July	_____	August	_____
September	_____	October	_____
November	_____	December	_____
peace	_____	United States	_____
supplies	_____	explanation	_____
parents	_____	knowledge	_____
war	_____	immigration	_____
bathtub	_____	snowblower	_____

*Rewrite the following sentences to create the question form of the future tense of **be going to** by placing the verb **to be** before the subject. Don't forget to include a question mark (?) in your answer.*

1. He is going to share this knowledge with the world.

   _____

   _____

2. She is going to cooperate with us.

   _____

3. You are going to provide me with a good explanation.

   _____

   _____

4. They are going to immigrate to the United States in August.

   _____

   _____

5. It is going to turn green when I put it in water.

   _____

   _____

6. The immigration office is going to process my file in July.

   _____

   _____

7. My parents are going to supply me with my school supplies in September.

   _____

   _____

8. I am going to drain the vegetables with this.

   _____

   _____

9. They are going to complete the project in November or December.

   _____

   _____

10. She is going to apply for a new job in October.

    _____

    _____

11. You are going to scrub the bathtub now.

    _____

    _____

12. The cows and horses are going to graze in the field.

_____

_____

13. You are going to dip the apple in honey.

_____

14. We are going to store the snowblower in the garage during the summer.

_____

_____

15. The teacher is going to talk about war and peace in history class today.

_____

_____

Use your dictionary to find the meaning of the following verbs and vocabulary words needed for this exercise before you begin. Write the words in your language in the space provided.

to compete	_____	to tidy	_____
to promise	_____	to assess	_____
to rest	_____	to whistle	_____
to wish	_____	to sort	_____
second	_____	sunny	_____
werewolf	_____	customs	_____
icicle	_____	oven mitts	_____
shrimp	_____	interview	_____

Rewrite the following sentences to create questions in the future tense of **be going to** *by placing the verb* **to be** *before the subject. Don't forget to include a question mark (?) in your answer.*

1. He is going to promise to be good.

_____

2. You are going to wish for a car again.

_____

3. I am going to compete with you.

_____

4. She is going to rest on the couch.

_____

5. You are going to fake that you are sick.

_____

6. He is going to break the icicles with the shovel.

_____

7. Sonia is going to buy new oven mitts.

_____

8. The insurance company is going to assess the damage.

_____

_____

9. You are going to cry.

_____

10. It is going to be sunny tomorrow.

_____

11. I am going to have a second interview.

_____

12. We are going to wait a long time at customs.

_____

13. She is going to sort the dirty laundry.

_____

14. Bobby is going to tidy his room.

_____

15. We are going to watch the scary movie about the werewolf.

_____

_____

16. They are going to whistle the song.

_____

17. They are going to bring shrimp to the party tomorrow night.

_____

_____

18. It is going to be good.

_____

The Indefinite Articles: A and An

The indefinite articles **a** and **an** are used with singular nouns. Use **a** before most nouns or adjectives that begin with a consonant. Use **an** before most nouns or adjectives that begin with a vowel.

a cup	a ball	a class	a bug
an empty cup	an orange ball	an English class	an ugly bug
an egg	an idea	an owl	an accident
a brown egg	a good idea	a white owl	a bad accident

Use **a** before nouns or adjectives that begin with a pronounced **h**, but use **an** before nouns or adjectives when the **h** is not pronounced.

a house	a horse	a hammer	a hurricane
an honor	an hour	an heir	an honest mistake

Use **a** before nouns or adjectives if the vowel is pronounced as a consonant. The following words are pronounced with a **y** sound.

a union	a university	a uniform	a utensil

The following words are pronounced with a **w** sound.

a one-hour class	a once-in-a-lifetime opportunity

EXERCISE 43·1

*Rewrite the following sentences correctly by choosing **a** or **an**.*

1. We saw (a, an) horrible accident this morning.

_____

2. This is (a, an) one-way street.

_____

3. My uncle has (a, an) ostrich on his farm.

_____

4. He is (a, an) American citizen.

_____

5. I wear (a, an) uniform to work.

_____

6. There was (a, an) earthquake last night.

_____

7. You are (a, an) excellent student.

_____

8. I need (a, an) hammer to fix the roof.

_____

9. It was (a, an) useful tool.

_____

10. I have (a, an) red apple in my lunch bag.

_____

11. We bought (a, an) oil painting at the market.

_____

_____

12. This is (a, an) busy airport.

_____

13. Give me (a, an) example, please.

_____

14. We played the game for (a, an) hour and (a, an) half.

_____

_____

EXERCISE

43·2

Complete the following sentences with **a** *or* **an**.

1. I ate _____ orange, _____ banana, and _____ peach today.

2. There is _____ wild ostrich in the field.

3. I want to live on _____ island for _____ month.

4. Give her _____ application, please.

5. There is _____ spider, _____ ant, and _____ fly in the kitchen.

6. You made _____ excellent effort.

7. Do you want _____ oatmeal cookie?

8. We have _____ union at work.

9. Do you have _____ horse?

10. I had _____ egg sandwich for lunch.

11. She married _____ wealthy American.

12. We made _____ apple cake, _____ salad, and _____ onion dip for the picnic.

13. Do you have _____ yellow umbrella?

14. I saw _____ owl, _____ tiger, _____ eagle, _____ zebra, and _____ elephant at the zoo.

15. She has _____ blue eye and _____ green eye.

16. Do you have _____ appointment?

17. She is _____ heir to the estate.

18. I have _____ idea.

19. He drew _____ picture of _____ unicorn.

20. We had _____ ice storm and _____ hurricane last year.

21. I prefer to wear _____ one-piece bathing suit to the beach.

22. It is _____ honor to meet you.

23. Is there _____ university in your city?

24. That is _____ honest opinion.

25. I want _____ ice cube and _____ cherry in my drink.

26. We had _____ easy test at school.

27. I need _____ cup of olive oil.

28. There is _____ oil lamp in the living room.

29. We saw _____ dead octopus on the beach.

30. I found _____ old sock under the bed.

31. It was _____ expensive ring.

32. There is _____ pen, _____ pencil, and _____ eraser on the table.

33. You are _____ hero.

34. You need _____ envelope and _____ stamp if you want to send _____ letter.

35. My sister had _____ baby; now I am _____ aunt.

36. Is there _____ elevator in the building?

37. It has _____ long nose.

38. We have _____ uncle in Germany.

39. I want _____ second opinion.

40. Do you want _____ ice-cream cone?

Irregular Verbs Table

Study and learn the past participles of the following irregular verbs.

SIMPLE FORM	SIMPLE PAST	PAST PARTICIPLE
awake	awoke	awoken
be	was/were	been
beat	beat	beaten
become	became	become
begin	began	begun
bend	bent	bent
bet	bet	bet
bite	bit	bitten
bleed	bled	bled
blow	blew	blown
break	broke	broken
bring	brought	brought
broadcast	broadcast	broadcast
build	built	built
burn	burned/burnt	burned/burnt
burst	burst	burst
buy	bought	bought
cast	cast	cast
catch	caught	caught
choose	chose	chosen
come	came	come
cost	cost	cost
creep	crept	crept
cut	cut	cut
deal	dealt	dealt
dig	dug	dug
dive	dived/dove	dived/dove
do	did	done
draw	drew	drawn
dream	dreamed/dreamt	dreamed/dreamt
drink	drank	drunk
drive	drove	driven
eat	ate	eaten
fall	fell	fallen
feed	fed	fed

SIMPLE FORM	SIMPLE PAST	PAST PARTICIPLE
feel	felt	felt
fight	fought	fought
find	found	found
fit	fit	fit
flee	fled	fled
fly	flew	flown
forbid	forbade	forbidden
forget	forgot	forgotten
forgive	forgave	forgiven
freeze	froze	frozen
get	got	got/gotten
give	gave	given
go	went	gone
grind	ground	ground
grow	grew	grown
hang	hung	hung
have	had	had
hear	heard	heard
hide	hid	hidden
hit	hit	hit
hold	held	held
hurt	hurt	hurt
keep	kept	kept
kneel	knelt	knelt
knit	knitted/knit	knitted/knit
know	knew	known
lay (to place, put down)	laid	laid
lead	led	led
leave	left	left
lend	lent	lent
let	let	let
lie (to lie down)	lay	lain
light	lit	lit
lose	lost	lost
make	made	made
mean	meant	meant
meet	met	met
mistake	mistook	mistaken
pay	paid	paid
prove	proved	proved/proven
put	put	put
quit	quit	quit
read	read	read
ride	rode	ridden
ring	rang	rung
rise	rose	risen
run	ran	run
say	said	said

SIMPLE FORM	SIMPLE PAST	PAST PARTICIPLE
see	saw	seen
seek	sought	sought
sell	sold	sold
send	sent	sent
set	set	set
sew	sewed	sewed/sewn
shake	shook	shaken
shave	shaved	shaved/shaven
shear	sheared	sheared/shorn
shed	shed	shed
shine	shined/shone	shined/shone
shoot	shot	shot
show	showed	shown
shrink	shrank	shrunk
shut	shut	shut
sing	sang	sung
sink	sank	sunk
sit	sat	sat
sleep	slept	slept
slide	slid	slid
speak	spoke	spoken
spend	spent	spent
spill	spilled/spilt	spilled/spilt
spin	spun	spun
spit	spit/spat	spit/spat
split	split	split
spread	spread	spread
spring	sprang	sprung
stand	stood	stood
steal	stole	stolen
stick	stuck	stuck
sting	stung	stung
strike	struck	struck
swear	swore	sworn
sweep	swept	swept
swell	swelled	swelled/swollen
swim	swam	swum
swing	swung	swung
take	took	taken
teach	taught	taught
tear	tore	torn
tell	told	told
think	thought	thought
throw	threw	thrown
understand	understood	understood
upset	upset	upset
wake	woke	woken

SIMPLE FORM	SIMPLE PAST	PAST PARTICIPLE
wear	wore	worn
weep	wept	wept
win	won	won
write	wrote	written

The Present Perfect Tense

The present perfect tense is used when the time of a past activity is not important or is not known in the sentence. Use **has** or **have** and the past participle of the verb with both regular and irregular verbs to form the present perfect tense.

Contractions can also be used with the pronouns to create the present perfect tense.

Regular

SIMPLE PRESENT	SIMPLE PAST	PRESENT PERFECT	CONTRACTION
I work	I worked	I have worked	I've worked
you work	you worked	you have worked	you've worked
he works	he worked	he has worked	he's worked
she works	she worked	she has worked	she's worked
it works	it worked	it has worked	it's worked
we work	we worked	we have worked	we've worked
they work	they worked	they have worked	they've worked

Irregular

SIMPLE PRESENT	SIMPLE PAST	PRESENT PERFECT	CONTRACTION
I take	I took	I have taken	I've taken
you take	you took	you have taken	you've taken
he takes	he took	he has taken	he's taken
she takes	she took	she has taken	she's taken
it takes	it took	it has taken	it's taken
we take	we took	we have taken	we've taken
they take	they took	they have taken	they've taken

The past participle of all regular verbs is the same as the simple past tense form (add -**ed**).

INFINITIVE	SIMPLE PAST	PAST PARTICIPLE
to borrow	borrowed	borrowed
to cheat	cheated	cheated
to try	tried	tried
to offend	offended	offended
to work	worked	worked

The past participle of all irregular verbs has a different form and must be studied and learned. Refer to Lesson 44.

INFINITIVE	SIMPLE PAST	PAST PARTICIPLE
to grow	grew	grown
to teach	taught	taught
to be	was/were	been
to hear	heard	heard
to take	took	taken

It takes a lot of practice to be able to correctly use the present perfect tense. Learn the past participles of all the irregular verbs by heart, and you will quickly be able to use this tense proficiently.

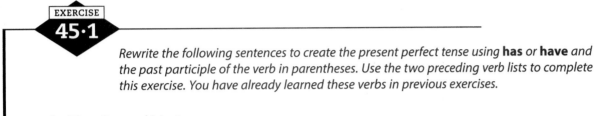

EXERCISE
45·1

*Rewrite the following sentences to create the present perfect tense using **has** or **have** and the past participle of the verb in parentheses. Use the two preceding verb lists to complete this exercise. You have already learned these verbs in previous exercises.*

1. They (to work) in Japan.

   _____

2. William (to grow) a lot since the last time I saw him.

   _____

   _____

3. My parents (to be) together for twenty years.

   _____

   _____

4. They (to borrow) a lot of money from their friends.

   _____

   _____

5. She (to teach) English in many different schools.

   _____

   _____

6. You (to offend) everybody in the office.

   _____

7. I (to hear) that noise in my car several times.

   _____

8. He (to cheat) on every one of his tests.

   _____

9. We (to try) to help them.

_____

10. It (to take) a long time.

_____

Complete the sentences that follow to create the present perfect tense. Use the contracted pronoun and the past participle of the verb in parentheses. You have already learned these verbs in previous exercises.

Regular

INFINITIVE	SIMPLE PAST	PAST PARTICIPLE
to offer	offered	offered
to climb	climbed	climbed
to use	used	used
to discuss	discussed	discussed
to warn	warned	warned
to accuse	accused	accused
to suffer	suffered	suffered
to help	helped	helped
to start	started	started
to thank	thanked	thanked

Irregular

INFINITIVE	SIMPLE PAST	PAST PARTICIPLE
to forgive	forgave	forgiven
to bite	bit	bitten
to make	made	made
to sing	sang	sung
to see	saw	seen
to tear	tore	torn
to choose	chose	chosen
to know	knew	known
to break	broke	broken
to fly	flew	flown

1. He _____ (to break) the law many times.

2. I _____ (to use) this product before.

3. We _____ (to see) that movie several times.

4. He _____ (to make) many mistakes in his life.

5. It _____ (to bite) a few people.

6. You _____ (to offer) to help.

7. I _____ (to fly) many times.

8. They _____ (to suffer) enough.

9. You _____ (to tear) all the clothes I lent you.

10. She _____ (to forgive) you many times.

11. I _____ (to know) Mary since high school.

12. He _____ (to accuse) me of that before.

13. It _____ (to start).

14. We _____ (to discuss) this many times.

15. I _____ (to warn) you about that.

16. It _____ (to help) me to be a better person.

17. We _____ (to choose) to live in the city.

18. She _____ (to sing) that song before.

19. They _____ (to thank) us ten times.

20. He _____ (to climb) many mountains.

·46· The Present Perfect Tense: Negative Form

Place **not** after **has** or **have** to create the negative form of the present perfect tense. Use the past participle of the verb in the negative form.

I have been	→	I have not been	→	I have not been to Paris.
you have been	→	you have not been	→	You have not been there.
he has been	→	he has not been	→	He has not been nice.
she has been	→	she has not been	→	She has not been happy.
it has been	→	it has not been	→	It has not been cold.
we have been	→	we have not been	→	We have not been busy.
they have been	→	they have not been	→	They have not been on a boat.

The negative form of the present perfect tense can also be expressed with the contraction **hasn't** or **haven't**.

I have not seen	→	I haven't seen	→	I haven't seen it.
you have not seen	→	you haven't seen	→	You haven't seen the play.
he has not seen	→	he hasn't seen	→	He hasn't seen his sister.
she has not seen	→	she hasn't seen	→	She hasn't seen her brother.
it has not seen	→	it hasn't seen	→	It hasn't seen me.
we have not seen	→	we haven't seen	→	We haven't seen the movie.
they have not seen	→	they haven't seen	→	They haven't seen Sara.

The past participle of all regular verbs is the same as the simple past tense form (add **-ed**).

INFINITIVE	SIMPLE PAST	PAST PARTICIPLE
to attract	attracted	attracted
to wait	waited	waited
to accept	accepted	accepted
to invent	invented	invented

The past participle of all irregular verbs has a different form and must be studied and learned. Refer to Lesson 44.

INFINITIVE	SIMPLE PAST	PAST PARTICIPLE
to find	found	found
to become	became	become
to write	wrote	written

*Rewrite the following sentences to create the negative form of the present perfect tense. Write your answer once with **has not** or **have not** and once with the contraction **hasn't** or **haven't**. Use the past participle of the verb in parentheses. You have already learned these verbs in previous exercises.*

1. My teacher (to write) two books.

   _____

   _____

2. I (to accept) the offer.

   _____

   _____

3. They (to invent) many fun games.

   _____

   _____

4. The light (to attract) all the bugs.

   _____

   _____

5. Joe and Lynn (to become) rich and famous.

   _____

   _____

6. We (to find) that he works very hard.

   _____

   _____

7. Cassandra (to wait) a long time for the news.

   _____

   _____

Use your dictionary to find the meaning of the new vocabulary words needed for this exercise before you begin. Write the words in your language in the space provided.

chore _____   chance _____

prisoner _____   feelings _____

tattoo _____   Italy _____

team _____   secret _____

Complete the sentences that follow by using the contraction **hasn't** *or* **haven't** *and the past participle of the verb in parentheses. You have already learned these verbs in previous exercises.*

Regular

INFINITIVE	SIMPLE PAST	PAST PARTICIPLE
to solve	solved	solved
to waste	wasted	wasted
to express	expressed	expressed
to convince	convinced	convinced
to notice	noticed	noticed
to escape	escaped	escaped
to ask	asked	asked

Irregular

INFINITIVE	SIMPLE PAST	PAST PARTICIPLE
to give	gave	given
to have	had	had
to keep	kept	kept
to build	built	built
to go	went	gone
to fall	fell	fallen
to beat	beat	beaten
to do	did	done
to forget	forgot	forgotten

1. We _____ _____ (to keep) it a secret.

2. She _____ _____ (to notice) your new tattoo.

3. They _____ _____ (to go) to Italy.

4. Laura _____ _____ (to convince) me.

5. Mr. Lawrence _____ _____ (to build) three houses.

6. I _____ _____ (to do) all my chores.

7. Cindy _____ _____ (to express) her feelings.

8. You _____ _____ (to waste) my time.

9. You _____ _____ (to give) it a chance.

10. I _____ _____ (to solve) the mystery.

11. Jarrod _____ _____ (to have) his vacation.

12. I _____ _____ (to ask) for a raise twice.

13. My team _____ _____ (to beat) their team.

14. The prisoners _____ _____ (to escape) from jail.

15. It _____ _____ (to fall) asleep.

16. She _____ _____ (to forget) that it's your birthday.

·47· ◆ The Present Perfect Tense: Question Form

Place **has** or **have** before the subject to create questions with the present perfect tense. The past participle of the verb is used when forming questions with the present perfect tense.

I have begun	→	have I begun	→	Have I begun to sing better?
you have begun	→	have you begun	→	Have you begun your course?
he has begun	→	has he begun	→	Has he begun to realize it?
she has begun	→	has she begun	→	Has she begun to understand?
it has begun	→	has it begun	→	Has it begun to melt?
we have begun	→	have we begun	→	Have we begun to eat right?
they have begun	→	have they begun	→	Have they begun to worry?

The past participle of all regular verbs is the same as the simple past tense form (add **-ed**).

INFINITIVE	SIMPLE PAST	PAST PARTICIPLE
to apologize	apologized	apologized
to benefit	benefited	benefited
to chew	chewed	chewed
to follow	followed	followed
to correct	corrected	corrected
to wrap	wrapped	wrapped

The past participle of all irregular verbs has a different form and must be studied and learned. Refer to Lesson 44.

INFINITIVE	SIMPLE PAST	PAST PARTICIPLE
to rise	rose	risen
to hide	hid	hidden
to show	showed	shown
to bring	brought	brought
to awake	awoke	awoken
to pay	paid	paid
to draw	drew	drawn
to blow	blew	blown

*Rewrite the following sentences to create the question form of the present perfect tense by placing **has** or **have** before the subject. Use the past participle of the verb in parentheses. You have already learned these verbs in previous exercises. Don't forget to include a question mark (?) in your answer.*

1. You (to show) your report card to your parents.

   _____

2. The teacher (to correct) all the exams.

   _____

3. I (to bring) enough for everybody.

   _____

4. My dog (to chew) all the furniture.

   _____

5. It (to follow) me to school often.

   _____

6. We (to wrap) all the gifts.

   _____

7. She (to blow) out all the candles on the cake.

   _____

8. They (to apologize) many times.

   _____

9. He (to draw) many beautiful pictures for her.

   _____

10. We (to benefit) from that.

    _____

11. It (to hide) the peanuts.

    _____

12. I (to pay) all the bills.

    _____

13. The sun (to rise).

    _____

14. I (to awake) the baby again.

    _____

Rewrite the sentences that follow to create questions in the present perfect tense. Place **has** *or* **have** *before the subject, and use the past participle of the verb in parentheses. You have already learned these verbs in previous exercises. Don't forget to include a question mark (?) in your answer.*

Regular

INFINITIVE	SIMPLE PAST	PAST PARTICIPLE
to invest	invested	invested
to occur	occurred	occurred
to iron	ironed	ironed
to answer	answered	answered
to park	parked	parked
to disappear	disappeared	disappeared
to manage	managed	managed

Irregular

INFINITIVE	SIMPLE PAST	PAST PARTICIPLE
to leave	left	left
to read	read	read
to drive	drove	driven
to meet	met	met
to sleep	slept	slept
to lose	lost	lost
to feed	fed	fed

1. You (to iron) the clothes.

   _____

2. He (to drive) many miles.

   _____

3. Leora (to answer) all the questions.

   _____

4. They (to feed) the animals.

   _____

5. It (to occur) a few times.

   _____

6. I (to read) that book before.

   _____

7. We (to invest) all our money.

   _____

8. I (to park) here before.

   _____

9. You (to lose) a lot of weight.

_____

10. He (to manage) the company alone.

_____

11. Elvis (to leave) the building.

_____

12. It (to disappear).

_____

13. Robin (to meet) many famous people.

_____

14. George (to sleep) late many times.

_____

·48· The Past Perfect Tense

The past perfect tense is used to describe a past action that occurred before another past action. For example, one past action occurred at 8:00 P.M., and the previous past action occurred at 7:00 P.M. Use **had** for all persons and the past participle of the verb to create the past perfect tense.

I have heard	→	I had heard	→ I had heard the news.
you have heard	→	you had heard	→ You had heard the guitar.
he has heard	→	he had heard	→ He had heard you scream.
she has heard	→	she had heard	→ She had heard the song.
it has heard	→	it had heard	→ It had heard the noise.
we have heard	→	we had heard	→ We had heard everything.
they have heard	→	they had heard	→ They had heard nothing.

The contraction **'d** is often used with the pronouns when using the past perfect tense.

I had learned	→	I'd learned	→ I'd learned my lesson.
you had learned	→	you'd learned	→ You'd learned how to do it.
he had learned	→	he'd learned	→ He'd learned the rules.
she had learned	→	she'd learned	→ She'd learned our names.
it had learned	→	it'd learned	→ It'd learned how to speak.
we had learned	→	we'd learned	→ We'd learned to add.
they had learned	→	they'd learned	→ They'd learned to spell.

The past participle of all regular verbs is the same as the simple past tense form (add -**ed**).

INFINITIVE	SIMPLE PAST	PAST PARTICIPLE
to stop	stopped	stopped
to expect	expected	expected
to pass	passed	passed
to explain	explained	explained
to die	died	died
to decide	decided	decided

The past participle of all irregular verbs has a different form and must be studied and learned. Refer to Lesson 44.

INFINITIVE	SIMPLE PAST	PAST PARTICIPLE
to sell	sold	sold
to see	saw	seen
to have	had	had
to do	did	done

*Rewrite the following sentences to create the past perfect tense. Use **had** and the past participle of the verb in parentheses. You have already learned these verbs in previous exercises.*

1. We (to decide) to stay home when they asked us to go out for dinner.

   _____

   _____

2. They (to sell) their boat when they bought the motorcycle.

   _____

   _____

3. He (to expect) to see you before you left.

   _____

4. I (to have) supper, so I only ate the dessert.

   _____

5. My grandmother (to die) when I was born.

   _____

6. The rain (to stop), so we went for a walk.

   _____

7. I (to do) the laundry when he brought me his dirty clothes.

   _____

   _____

8. She (to see) the movie before, so she went to bed.

   _____

   _____

9. The teacher (to explain) the lesson twice, but we didn't understand.

   _____

   _____

10. We (to pass) all our exams, so we celebrated all night.

    _____

    _____

*Complete the sentences that follow using **had** and the past participle of the verb in parentheses. You have already learned these verbs in previous exercises.*

Regular

INFINITIVE	SIMPLE PAST	PAST PARTICIPLE
to finish	finished	finished
to order	ordered	ordered
to divorce	divorced	divorced
to rescue	rescued	rescued
to open	opened	opened
to complete	completed	completed
to worry	worried	worried

Irregular

INFINITIVE	SIMPLE PAST	PAST PARTICIPLE
to sweep	swept	swept
to throw	threw	thrown
to ring	rang	rung
to run	ran	run
to ride	rode	ridden
to sing	sang	sung
to cut	cut	cut

1. She _____ (to throw) it in the garbage when you asked for it.

2. We _____ (to sing) the song several times, but we forgot the words.

3. I _____ (to open) the gift when I realized it was for you.

4. They _____ (to order) the pizza when we arrived.

5. I _____ (to sweep) the floor when he dropped the plate of cookies.

6. We _____ (to worry) all night; then he finally called.

7. She _____ (to ride) the horse many times before she fell and broke her leg.

8. I _____ (to run) five miles when they cancelled the race.

9. He _____ (to complete) his homework, so he went to bed.

10. The class _____ (to finish) when we arrived.

11. The bell _____ (to ring) for twenty minutes before the janitor came to fix it.

12. We _____ (to rescue) the little girl in the water when the police came.

13. I _____ (to cut) my hair when he told me that he liked it long.

14. They _____ (to divorce) but remained good friends.

The Past Perfect Tense: Negative Form

Place **not** after **had** to create the negative form of the past perfect tense. The past participle of the verb is always used in the negative form.

I had run	→	I had not run	→	I had not run after school.
you had run	→	you had not run	→	You had not run very far.
he had run	→	he had not run	→	He had not run the race.
she had run	→	she had not run	→	She had not run with shoes.
it had run	→	it had not run	→	It had not run across the road.
we had run	→	we had not run	→	We had not run together.
they had run	→	they had not run	→	They had not run outside.

The negative form of the past perfect tense can also be expressed with the contraction **hadn't**.

I had not opened	→	I hadn't opened	→	I hadn't opened the mail.
you had not opened	→	you hadn't opened	→	You hadn't opened the book.
he had not opened	→	he hadn't opened	→	He hadn't opened the letter.
she had not opened	→	she hadn't opened	→	She hadn't opened her gifts.
it had not opened	→	it hadn't opened	→	It hadn't opened its mouth.
we had not opened	→	we hadn't opened	→	We hadn't opened the store.
they had not opened	→	they hadn't opened	→	They hadn't opened it.

The past participle of all regular verbs is the same as the simple past tense form (add **-ed**).

INFINITIVE	SIMPLE PAST	PAST PARTICIPLE
to notice	noticed	noticed
to follow	followed	followed
to arrive	arrived	arrived

The past participle of all irregular verbs has a different form and must be studied and learned. Refer to Lesson 44.

INFINITIVE	SIMPLE PAST	PAST PARTICIPLE
to fly	flew	flown
to pay	paid	paid
to see	saw	seen
to hold	held	held

*Rewrite the following sentences to create the negative form of the past perfect tense. Write your answer once with **had not** and once with the contraction **hadn't**. Use the past participle of the verb in parentheses. You have already learned these verbs in previous exercises.*

1. He (to hold) a baby before today.

   _____

   _____

2. It (to arrive), so I called the store.

   _____

   _____

3. I (to notice) that you were standing there.

   _____

   _____

4. She (to pay) the phone bill, so I paid it.

   _____

   _____

5. They (to see) that movie before, and they really enjoyed it.

   _____

   _____

6. We (to fly) before, so we were very nervous on the airplane.

   _____

   _____

7. You (to follow) the instructions, and you made a mistake.

   _____

   _____

*Complete the sentences that follow by using the contraction **hadn't** and the past participle of the verb in parentheses. You have already learned these verbs in previous exercises.*

Regular

INFINITIVE	SIMPLE PAST	PAST PARTICIPLE
to rain	rained	rained
to smoke	smoked	smoked
to talk	talked	talked
to start	started	started
to clean	cleaned	cleaned
to borrow	borrowed	borrowed
to wait	waited	waited

Irregular

INFINITIVE	SIMPLE PAST	PAST PARTICIPLE
to have	had	had
to drive	drove	driven
to drink	drank	drunk
to hang	hung	hung
to make	made	made
to send	sent	sent
to eat	ate	eaten
to buy	bought	bought
to give	gave	given

1. We _____ (to eat) our breakfast, so we were hungry.

2. She _____ (to clean) the fridge, so I cleaned it for her.

3. It _____ (to rain), so the streets were dry.

4. She _____ (to drive) on icy roads before, so she had a bad

   accident.

5. My husband _____ (to hang) the clothes on the clothesline,

   so I did it when I got home.

6. You _____ (to talk) about that before today.

7. I _____ (to buy) butter, so I went to the store again.

8. We _____ (to send) the check, so we sent it this morning.

9. She _____ (to have) her shower, so I left without her.

10. They _____ (to borrow) enough money, so we lent them

    $1,000.

11. He _____ (to give) me his address.

12. I _____ (to wait) a long time before it arrived in the mail.

13. My uncle _____ (to smoke) in three years, and he started again.

14. He _____ (to drink) his juice, so I drank it.

15. The movie _____ (to start), so we went to buy some chocolates and candies.

16. My wife _____ (to make) supper, so we went to a restaurant.

The Past Perfect Tense: Question Form

Place **had** before the subject to create the question form of the past perfect tense. The past participle of the verb is used when forming questions in the past perfect tense.

I had worked	→	had I worked	→	Had I worked with you?
you had worked	→	had you worked	→	Had you worked in Mexico?
he had worked	→	had he worked	→	Had he worked for his father?
she had worked	→	had she worked	→	Had she worked in the city?
it had worked	→	had it worked	→	Had it worked well?
we had worked	→	had we worked	→	Had we worked together?
they had worked	→	had they worked	→	Had they worked late?

The past participle of all regular verbs is the same as the simple past tense form (add -**ed**).

INFINITIVE	SIMPLE PAST	PAST PARTICIPLE
to plan	planned	planned
to live	lived	lived
to end	ended	ended
to happen	happened	happened
to taste	tasted	tasted
to try	tried	tried

The past participle of all irregular verbs has a different form and must be studied and learned. Refer to Lesson 44.

INFINITIVE	SIMPLE PAST	PAST PARTICIPLE
to withdraw	withdrew	withdrawn
to know	knew	known
to speak	spoke	spoken
to see	saw	seen
to make	made	made
to have	had	had
to wear	wore	worn
to give	gave	given

*Rewrite the following sentences to create the question form of the past perfect tense by placing **had** before the subject. Use the past participle of the verb in parentheses. You have already learned these verbs in previous exercises. Don't forget to include a question mark (?) in your answer.*

1. He (to know) that you were my brother.

   _____

2. They (to withdraw) all the money from their savings account.

   _____

   _____

3. You (to try) to ski before you bought the skis.

   _____

   _____

4. The play (to end) when she arrived.

   _____

5. You (to give) him your phone number.

   _____

6. Your aunt (to wear) this dress before.

   _____

7. They (to taste) seafood before today.

   _____

8. Richard and Jennifer (to plan) their vacation together.

   _____

   _____

9. Wade (to make) coffee for everybody.

   _____

10. You (to have) your breakfast before you went to school.

   _____

   _____

11. The teacher (to speak) to you before she called your parents.

   _____

   _____

12. It (to happen) before.

   _____

13. You (to see) that woman before she came to your house.

_____

_____

14. They (to live) in Ontario before they moved to British Columbia.

_____

_____

Rewrite the sentences that follow to create the question form of the past perfect tense. Place **had** *before the subject, and use the past participle of the verb in parentheses. You have already learned these verbs in previous exercises. Don't forget to include a question mark (?) in your answer.*

Regular

INFINITIVE	SIMPLE PAST	PAST PARTICIPLE
to realize	realized	realized
to play	played	played
to work	worked	worked
to notice	noticed	noticed
to belong	belonged	belonged
to seem	seemed	seemed

Irregular

INFINITIVE	SIMPLE PAST	PAST PARTICIPLE
to take	took	taken
to find	found	found
to leave	left	left
to take	took	taken
to read	read	read
to pay	paid	paid
to be	was/were	been
to bring	brought	brought

1. She (to realize) what she did.

_____

2. You (to take) the wrong bus.

_____

3. It (to seem) fair to everyone.

_____

4. Your boss (to bring) his dog to work before today.

_____

_____

5. Tony (to be) in the hospital before he had his operation.

_____

_____

6. They (to leave) the building before the fire started.

_____

_____

7. Jessica (to work) as a flight attendant before she became a nurse.

_____

_____

8. He (to take) the time to do it right.

_____

9. They (to notice) where you put it.

_____

10. You (to pay) cash for it.

_____

11. Maria (to find) a new job before she quit her old job.

_____

_____

12. He (to play) hockey before he joined our team.

_____

_____

13. You (to read) the contract before you signed it.

_____

_____

14. It (to belong) to your grandmother before your mother gave it to you.

_____

_____

·51· The Future Perfect Tense

The future perfect tense is used to describe an action that will happen in the future before another action happens. Place **will** after the subject and use **have** for all persons. The past participle of the verb is used for both regular and irregular verbs.

I have built	→	I will have built	→	I will have built a sandcastle.
you have built	→	you will have built	→	You will have built another house.
he has built	→	he will have built	→	He will have built a birdhouse.
she has built	→	she will have built	→	She will have built a big company.
it has built	→	it will have built	→	It will have built a nest in the tree.
we have built	→	we will have built	→	We will have built a snowman.
they have built	→	they will have built	→	They will have built a garage.

Contractions can also be used with the pronouns to create the future perfect tense.

I will have done	→	I'll have done	→	I'll have done the housework.
you will have done	→	you'll have done	→	You'll have done the chores.
he will have done	→	he'll have done	→	He'll have done his work.
she will have done	→	she'll have done	→	She'll have done everything.
it will have done	→	it'll have done	→	It'll have done something.
we will have done	→	we'll have done	→	We'll have done enough.
they will have done	→	they'll have done	→	They'll have done it.

The past participle of all regular verbs is the same as the simple past tense form (add **-ed**).

INFINITIVE	SIMPLE PAST	PAST PARTICIPLE
to start	started	started
to die	died	died
to complete	completed	completed
to finish	finished	finished

The past participle of all irregular verbs has a different form and must be studied and learned. Refer to Lesson 44.

INFINITIVE	SIMPLE PAST	PAST PARTICIPLE
to leave	left	left
to find	found	found
to spend	spent	spent
to read	read	read
to teach	taught	taught
to eat	ate	eaten
to take	took	taken

EXERCISE 51·1

*Rewrite the following sentences to create the future perfect tense using **will** and **have** and the past participle of the verb in parentheses. You have already learned these verbs in previous exercises.*

1. She (to finish) all the housework by lunch time.

   _____

   _____

2. I (to take) my shower by the time you arrive.

   _____

   _____

3. The flowers in my garden (to die) by the end of October.

   _____

   _____

4. Mrs. Stacey (to teach) for 30 years when she finally retires.

   _____

   _____

5. They (to eat) supper by the time we arrive.

   _____

   _____

6. The plane (to leave) by the time we arrive at the airport.

   _____

   _____

7. The girls (to complete) their project by Saturday.

   _____

   _____

8. Chris (to find) a new job by the end of the summer.

_____

_____

9. I (to start) school by September.

_____

10. Benjamin (to read) the complete series by the time he finishes this book.

_____

_____

11. We (to spend) all our money by the time we finish our vacation.

_____

_____

Complete the following sentences to create the future perfect tense. Use the contraction **'ll** with the pronouns and **will** with the nouns. Use **have** and the past participle of the verb in parentheses. You have already learned these verbs in previous exercises.

INFINITIVE	SIMPLE PAST	PAST PARTICIPLE
to learn	learned	learned
to elect	elected	elected
to complete	completed	completed
to receive	received	received
to work	worked	worked
to melt	melted	melted
to speak	spoke	spoken
to see	saw	seen
to lose	lost	lost
to leave	left	left
to freeze	froze	frozen
to drive	drove	driven
to be	was/were	been
to forget	forgot	forgotten
to fly	flew	flown
to have	had	had

1. She _____ (to lose) 40 pounds by the end of the year.

2. He _____ (to have) my car for a month by the time he returns it to me.

3. We _____ (to receive) our order by the end of the week.

4. Jesse _____ (to leave) if you arrive at 9 o'clock.

5. They _____ (to elect) a new president by the spring.

6. The birds _____ (to fly) south for the winter by November.

7. I _____ (to speak) to every student by Friday.

8. My mother-in-law _____ (to be) at my house for 23 days and 9 hours by Saturday.

9. You _____ (to learn) many things by the time you finish this book.

10. She _____ (to work) in many countries by the time she retires.

11. They _____ (to complete) the work on the bridge before the winter comes.

12. The lake _____ (to freeze) by December.

13. We _____ (to drive) for four days by the time we arrive in Chicago.

14. I _____ (to forget) everything by the time the teacher gives us the test.

15. The snow _____ (to melt) by May.

16. They _____ (to see) many plays by the time they leave New York City.

 **·52·** # The Future Perfect Tense: Negative Form

The future perfect negative form is used to describe an action that will not happen in the future before another action happens. Place **not** after **will** and use **have** for all persons. The past participle of the verb is used for both regular and irregular verbs.

I will have left	→ I will not have left	→ I will not have left the house.
you will have left	→ you will not have left	→ You will not have left the office.
he will have left	→ he will not have left	→ He will not have left the museum.
she will have left	→ she will not have left	→ She will not have left the restaurant.
it will have left	→ it will not have left	→ It will not have left without its baby.
we will have left	→ we will not have left	→ We will not have left the parking lot.
they will have left	→ they will not have left	→ They will not have left the arena.

The contraction **won't** can be used in place of **will not** when using the future perfect negative form.

I will not have heard	→ I won't have heard	→ I won't have heard you.
you will not have heard	→ you won't have heard	→ You won't have heard me.
he will not have heard	→ he won't have heard	→ He won't have heard her.
she will not have heard	→ she won't have heard	→ She won't have heard it.
it will not have heard	→ it won't have heard	→ It won't have heard him.
we will not have heard	→ we won't have heard	→ We won't have heard them.
they will not have heard	→ they won't have heard	→ They won't have heard us.

The past participle of all regular verbs is the same as the simple past tense form (add -*ed*).

INFINITIVE	SIMPLE PAST	PAST PARTICIPLE
to convince	convinced	convinced
to discuss	discussed	discussed
to open	opened	opened

The past participle of all irregular verbs has a different form and must be studied and learned. Refer to Lesson 44.

INFINITIVE	SIMPLE PAST	PAST PARTICIPLE
to meet	met	met
to eat	ate	eaten
to become	became	become
to be	was/were	been

EXERCISE

52·1

*Rewrite the following sentences to create the negative form of the future perfect tense. Write your answer once with **will not** and once with the contraction **won't**. Use **have** and the past participle of the verb in parentheses. You have already learned these verbs in previous exercises.*

1. We (to be) here for two hours by the time the bus arrives.

   _____

   _____

2. They (open) all the gifts by noon.

   _____

   _____

3. You (to convince) the judges by the time you finish your song.

   _____

   _____

4. We (to meet) the neighbors by the time we move.

   _____

   _____

5. My parents (to discuss) it by the weekend.

   _____

   _____

6. The kids (to eat) by 5 o'clock.

   _____

   _____

7. He (to become) famous by the time he is 30 years old.

_____

_____

*Complete the sentences that follow to create the negative form of the future perfect tense. Use the contraction **won't** and **have** and the past participle of the verb in parentheses. You have already learned these verbs in previous exercises.*

INFINITIVE	SIMPLE PAST	PAST PARTICIPLE
to help	helped	helped
to show	showed	shown
to prevent	prevented	prevented
to talk	talked	talked
to slice	sliced	sliced
to purchase	purchased	purchased
to postpone	postponed	postponed
to sort	sorted	sorted
to complete	completed	completed
to sweep	swept	swept
to make	made	made
to go	went	gone
to bring	brought	brought
to speak	spoke	spoken
to choose	chose	chosen
to leave	left	left

1. Tim _____ (to choose) his courses by the end of the week.

2. She _____ (to speak) to her sister by Monday.

3. The new law _____ (to prevent) many road accidents.

4. Sandra _____ (to talk) to her doctor by the weekend.

5. They _____ (to purchase) their new car by the end of the month.

6. It _____ (to help) us very much by the time we finish.

7. Elizabeth _____ (to show) us the new puppy by the time we leave.

8. My uncle _____ (to bring) the kids for ice cream before supper time.

9. You _____ (to sort) the dirty clothes by the time I am ready to do the laundry.

10. She _____ (to sweep) all the rooms in the house before noon.

11. They _____ (to make) enough food for everyone.

12. He _____ (to go) to the bank by the time you come to get your money.

13. Daniel _____ (to complete) the program by February.

14. I _____ (to slice) the bread by the time you put the spaghetti on the table.

15. We _____ (to leave) the country by March.

16. They _____ (to postpone) the trip three times.

·53· The Future Perfect Tense: Question Form

Place *will* before the subject to create questions with the future perfect tense. The past participle of the verb is used when forming questions with the future perfect tense.

I will have had	→	will I have had	→	Will I have had the tests?
you will have had	→	will you have had	→	Will you have had time?
he will have had	→	will he have had	→	Will he have had his supper?
she will have had	→	will she have had	→	Will she have had a vacation?
it will have had	→	will it have had	→	Will it have had enough food?
we will have had	→	will we have had	→	Will we have had lunch?
they will have had	→	will they have had	→	Will they have had the meeting?

The past participle of all regular verbs is the same as the simple past tense form (add *-ed*).

INFINITIVE	SIMPLE PAST	PAST PARTICIPLE
to clean	cleaned	cleaned
to stop	stopped	stopped
to move	moved	moved
to work	worked	worked
to finish	finished	finished
to save	saved	saved
to sign	signed	signed

The past participle of all irregular verbs has a different form and must be studied and learned. Refer to Lesson 44.

INFINITIVE	SIMPLE PAST	PAST PARTICIPLE
to write	wrote	written
to fly	flew	flown
to see	saw	seen
to be	was/were	been
to eat	ate	eaten
to go	went	gone
to speak	spoke	spoken

Rewrite the following sentences to create the question form of the future perfect tense by placing **will** *before the subject. Use the past participle of the verb in parentheses. You have already learned these verbs in previous exercises. Don't forget to include a question mark (?) in your answer.*

1. We (to sign) all the necessary documents.

   _____

2. You (to speak) to Bob before Friday.

   _____

3. Joanie (to clean) the basement before everybody arrives for the party.

   _____

   _____

4. They (to save) enough money to visit their cousins in California.

   _____

   _____

5. It (to be) in the oven for four hours by 6 o'clock.

   _____

   _____

6. He (to work) there long enough to get a bonus at the end of the year.

   _____

   _____

7. The kids (to go) to bed by the time I arrive tonight.

   _____

   _____

8. You (to eat) your dessert by the time I finish my meal.

   _____

   _____

9. She (to finish) her exams by May.

   _____

10. Dennis (to write) the report by Tuesday.

    _____

11. We (to see) everything before we leave.

    _____

12. They (to move) by July.

_____

13. The rain (to stop) by the morning.

_____

14. The birds (to fly) south by November.

_____

Rewrite the sentences that follow to create questions in the future perfect tense. Place **will** before the subject and use the past participle of the verb in parentheses. You have already learned these verbs in previous exercises. Don't forget to include a question mark (?) in your answer.

INFINITIVE	SIMPLE PAST	PAST PARTICIPLE
to repair	repaired	repaired
to remove	removed	removed
to start	started	started
to feed	fed	fed
to read	read	read
to catch	caught	caught
to forget	forgot	forgotten
to meet	met	met
to pay	paid	paid
to begin	began	begun
to sweep	swept	swept
to send	sent	sent

1. You (to pay) all the bills by the end of the month.

_____

_____

2. The game (to start) if we arrive at 7 o'clock.

_____

_____

3. The secretary (to send) all the letters by next Thursday.

_____

_____

4. She (to sweep) the bedrooms by the time I finish the dishes.

_____

_____

5. You (to feed) the baby before the movie starts.

_____

_____

6. We (to catch) many trout by sunset.

_____

7. Wendy (to begin) her painting class by September.

_____

_____

8. I (to meet) all the new students by the end of the day.

_____

_____

9. He (to read) the newspaper by the time I finish my book.

_____

_____

10. You (to remove) all the furniture by the time the painters come.

_____

_____

11. The mechanic (to repair) the car by 6 o'clock.

_____

_____

12. You (to forget) about us by then.

_____

REVIEW EXERCISES

Verb Tenses Review: 1  ·54·

Study the following verb tenses for the verb **to play**.

Simple present tense

AFFIRMATIVE FORM	NEGATIVE FORM	QUESTION FORM
I play	I do not (don't) play	do I play
you play	you do not (don't) play	do you play
he plays	he does not (doesn't) play	does he play
she plays	she does not (doesn't) play	does she play
it plays	it does not (doesn't) play	does it play
we play	we do not (don't) play	do we play
they play	they do not (don't) play	do they play

Simple past tense

AFFIRMATIVE FORM	NEGATIVE FORM	QUESTION FORM
I played	I did not (didn't) play	did I play
you played	you did not (didn't) play	did you play
he played	he did not (didn't) play	did he play
she played	she did not (didn't) play	did she play
it played	it did not (didn't) play	did it play
we played	we did not (didn't) play	did we play
they played	they did not (didn't) play	did they play

Present progressive tense

AFFIRMATIVE FORM	NEGATIVE FORM	QUESTION FORM
I am playing	I am not playing	am I playing
you are playing	you are not (aren't) playing	are you playing
he is playing	he is not (isn't) playing	is he playing
she is playing	she is not (isn't) playing	is she playing
it is playing	it is not (isn't) playing	is it playing
we are playing	we are not (aren't) playing	are we playing
they are playing	they are not (aren't) playing	are they playing

Past progressive tense

AFFIRMATIVE FORM	NEGATIVE FORM	QUESTION FORM
I was playing	I was not (wasn't) playing	was I playing
you were playing	you were not (weren't) playing	were you playing
he was playing	he was not (wasn't) playing	was he playing
she was playing	she was not (wasn't) playing	was she playing
it was playing	it was not (wasn't) playing	was it playing
we were playing	we were not (weren't) playing	were we playing
they were playing	they were not (weren't) playing	were they playing

Future tense (will)

AFFIRMATIVE FORM	NEGATIVE FORM	QUESTION FORM
I will play	I will not (won't) play	will I play
you will play	you will not (won't) play	will you play
he will play	he will not (won't) play	will he play
she will play	she will not (won't) play	will she play
it will play	it will not (won't) play	will it play
we will play	we will not (won't) play	will we play
they will play	they will not (won't) play	will they play

Future tense (be going to)

AFFIRMATIVE FORM	NEGATIVE FORM	QUESTION FORM
I am going to play	I am not going to play	am I going to play
you are going to play	you are not (aren't) going to play	are you going to play
he is going to play	he is not (isn't) going to play	is he going to play
she is going to play	she is not (isn't) going to play	is she going to play
it is going to play	it is not (isn't) going to play	is it going to play
we are going to play	we are not (aren't) going to play	are we going to play
they are going to play	they are not (aren't) going to play	are they going to play

Present perfect tense

AFFIRMATIVE FORM	NEGATIVE FORM	QUESTION FORM
I have played	I have not (haven't) played	have I played
you have played	you have not (haven't) played	have you played
he has played	he has not (hasn't) played	has he played
she has played	she has not (hasn't) played	has she played
it has played	it has not (hasn't) played	has it played
we have played	we have not (haven't) played	have we played
they have played	they have not (haven't) played	have they played

Past perfect tense

AFFIRMATIVE FORM	NEGATIVE FORM	QUESTION FORM
I had played	I had not (hadn't) played	had I played
you had played	you had not (hadn't) played	had you played
he had played	he had not (hadn't) played	had he played
she had played	she had not (hadn't) played	had she played
it had played	it had not (hadn't) played	had it played
we had played	we had not (hadn't) played	had we played
they had played	they had not (hadn't) played	had they played

Future perfect tense

AFFIRMATIVE FORM	NEGATIVE FORM	QUESTION FORM
I will have played	I will not (won't) have played	will I have played
you will have played	you will not (won't) have played	will you have played
he will have played	he will not (won't) have played	will he have played
she will have played	she will not (won't) have played	will she have played
it will have played	it will not (won't) have played	will it have played
we will have played	we will not (won't) have played	will we have played
they will have played	they will not (won't) have played	will they have played

Using the verb **to play** *and the information in parentheses, rewrite the following sentences in the correct verb tense.*

1. The kids (to play) outside in the leaves. (past progressive, affirmative)

_____

2. Tommy (to play) baseball until he started school. (past perfect, negative)

_____

_____

3. Your brother (to play) football at the university. (simple present, question)

_____

_____

4. She (to play) the piano at church many times. (present perfect, affirmative)

_____

_____

5. You (to play) with Bobby at school today. (simple past, question)

_____

6. They (to play) with their friends at the park. (future, question, *be going to*)

_____

_____

7. We (to play) hockey on the street in the summer. (simple present, affirmative)

_____

_____

8. I (to play) games on my phone in the waiting room. (future, affirmative, *will*)

_____

_____

9. My cat (to play) with the puppy. (present progressive, negative, contraction)

_____

10. They (to play) hide and seek in the dark. (simple present, negative, contraction)

_____

11. Kristy (to play) with her dolls all week. (present perfect, negative, contraction)

_____

12. Your sisters (to play) in the sandbox. (past progressive, question)

_____

13. We (to play) with water guns in the house, Mom. (future, negative, *will*, contraction)

_____

_____

14. My parents (to play) cards with the neighbors. (present progressive, affirmative)

_____

_____

15. You (to play) with a yo-yo before. (present perfect, question)

_____

16. Derek (to play) the drums all night, I hope. (future, negative, *be going to*)

_____

_____

17. She (to play) that song 50 times by tonight. (future perfect, affirmative)

_____

_____

18. You (to play) with fire and you got burned. (simple past, affirmative)

_____

_____

19. Jordan and Julien (to play) with their trucks. (present progressive, question)

_____

_____

20. He (to play) the guitar for us. (future, question, *will*)

_____

21. They (to play) on the swings during recess. (future, affirmative, *be going to*)

_____

_____

22. We (to play) checkers or chess in a long time. (present perfect, negative)

_____

_____

23. You (to play) dice with me later. (future, question, *will*)

_____

_____

Verb Tenses Review: 2

Study the following verb tenses for the verb **to buy**.

Simple present tense

AFFIRMATIVE FORM	NEGATIVE FORM	QUESTION FORM
I buy	I do not (don't) buy	do I buy
you buy	you do not (don't) buy	do you buy
he buys	he does not (doesn't) buy	does he buy
she buys	she does not (doesn't) buy	does she buy
it buys	it does not (doesn't) buy	does it buy
we buy	we do not (don't) buy	do we buy
they buy	they do not (don't) buy	do they buy

Simple past tense

AFFIRMATIVE FORM	NEGATIVE FORM	QUESTION FORM
I bought	I did not (didn't) buy	did I buy
you bought	you did not (didn't) buy	did you buy
he bought	he did not (didn't) buy	did he buy
she bought	she did not (didn't) buy	did she buy
it bought	it did not (didn't) buy	did it buy
we bought	we did not (didn't) buy	did we buy
they bought	they did not (didn't) buy	did they buy

Present progressive tense

AFFIRMATIVE FORM	NEGATIVE FORM	QUESTION FORM
I am buying	I am not buying	am I buying
you are buying	you are not (aren't) buying	are you buying
he is buying	he is not (isn't) buying	is he buying
she is buying	she is not (isn't) buying	is she buying
it is buying	it is not (isn't) buying	is it buying
we are buying	we are not (aren't) buying	are we buying
they are buying	they are not (aren't) buying	are they buying

Past progressive tense

AFFIRMATIVE FORM	NEGATIVE FORM	QUESTION FORM
I was buying	I was not (wasn't) buying	was I buying
you were buying	you were not (weren't) buying	were you buying
he was buying	he was not (wasn't) buying	was he buying
she was buying	she was not (wasn't) buying	was she buying
it was buying	it was not (wasn't) buying	was it buying
we were buying	we were not (weren't) buying	were we buying
they were buying	they were not (weren't) buying	were they buying

Future tense (will)

AFFIRMATIVE FORM	NEGATIVE FORM	QUESTION FORM
I will buy	I will not (won't) buy	will I buy
you will buy	you will not (won't) buy	will you buy
he will buy	he will not (won't) buy	will he buy
she will buy	she will not (won't) buy	will she buy
it will buy	it will not (won't) buy	will it buy
we will buy	we will not (won't) buy	will we buy
they will buy	they will not (won't) buy	will they buy

Future tense (be going to)

AFFIRMATIVE FORM	NEGATIVE FORM	QUESTION FORM
I am going to buy	I am not going to buy	am I going to buy
you are going to buy	you are not (aren't) going to buy	are you going to buy
he is going to buy	he is not (isn't) going to buy	is he going to buy
she is going to buy	she is not (isn't) going to buy	is she going to buy
it is going to buy	it is not (isn't) going to buy	is it going to buy
we are going to buy	we are not (aren't) going to buy	are we going to buy
they are going to buy	they are not (aren't) going to buy	are they going to buy

Present perfect tense

AFFIRMATIVE FORM	NEGATIVE FORM	QUESTION FORM
I have bought	I have not (haven't) bought	have I bought
you have bought	you have not (haven't) bought	have you bought
he has bought	he has not (hasn't) bought	has he bought
she has bought	she has not (hasn't) bought	has she bought
it has bought	it has not (hasn't) bought	has it bought
we have bought	we have not (haven't) bought	have we bought
they have bought	they have not (haven't) bought	have they bought

Past perfect tense

AFFIRMATIVE FORM	NEGATIVE FORM	QUESTION FORM
I had bought	I had not (hadn't) bought	had I bought
you had bought	you had not (hadn't) bought	had you bought
he had bought	he had not (hadn't) bought	had he bought
she had bought	she had not (hadn't) bought	had she bought
it had bought	it had not (hadn't) bought	had it bought
we had bought	we had not (hadn't) bought	had we bought
they had bought	they had not (hadn't) bought	had they bought

Future perfect tense

AFFIRMATIVE FORM	NEGATIVE FORM	QUESTION FORM
I will have bought	I will not (won't) have bought	will I have bought
you will have bought	you will not (won't) have bought	will you have bought
he will have bought	he will not (won't) have bought	will he have bought
she will have bought	she will not (won't) have bought	will she have bought
it will have bought	it will not (won't) have bought	will it have bought
we will have bought	we will not (won't) have bought	will we have bought
they will have bought	they will not (won't) have bought	will they have bought

*Using the verb **to buy** and the information in parentheses, rewrite the following sentences in the correct verb tense.*

1. You (to buy) enough plates for all the guests. (past perfect, question)

_____

_____

2. I (to buy) it at the garage sale down the street. (simple past, affirmative)

_____

_____

3. She (to buy) new clothes for the trip. (future, negative, *be going to*, contraction)

_____

4. They (to buy) butter before. (past perfect, negative)

_____

5. You (to buy) that for me. (present progressive, question)

_____

6. Jessica (to buy) balloons for the party. (past tense, negative, contraction)

_____

_____

7. I (to buy) my lunch in the cafeteria tomorrow. (future, affirmative, *will*)

_____

_____

8. You (to buy) this kind of toothpaste. (present perfect, question)

_____

9. My husband (to buy) a lot of tools. (simple present, affirmative)

_____

10. Rachel (to buy) all her school books by next week. (future perfect, affirmative)

_____

_____

11. They (to buy) a new truck when you saw them. (past progressive, question)

_____

_____

12. We (to buy) fur products. (simple present, negative, contraction)

_____

13. Tony (to buy) furniture before he moves into his house. (future perfect, question)

_____

_____

14. My mother (to buy) a lot of vegetables at the market. (simple past, negative)

_____

_____

15. Joseph (to buy) flowers for his girlfriend. (present progressive, affirmative)

_____

_____

16. You (to buy) the tickets. (simple past, question)

_____

17. They (to buy) bagels and cheese. (future, question, _will_)

_____

18. We (to buy) from that store again. (future, negative, _will_, contraction)

_____

19. The boys (to buy) everything for their camping trip. (past perfect, affirmative)

_____

_____

20. Sonia (to buy) her wedding dress. (present perfect, negative)

_____

21. I (to buy) new tires. (future, negative, _be going to_)

_____

22. She (to buy) the newspaper this morning. (simple past, question)

_____

_____

23. Your brother (to buy) a new calculator. (future, question, _be going to_)

_____

_____

Verb Tenses Review: 3

Study the following verb tenses for the verb *to call*.

Simple present tense

AFFIRMATIVE FORM	NEGATIVE FORM	QUESTION FORM
I call	I do not (don't) call	do I call
you call	you do not (don't) call	do you call
he calls	he does not (doesn't) call	does he call
she calls	she does not (doesn't) call	does she call
it calls	it does not (doesn't) call	does it call
we call	we do not (don't) call	do we call
they call	they do not (don't) call	do they call

Simple past tense

AFFIRMATIVE FORM	NEGATIVE FORM	QUESTION FORM
I called	I did not (didn't) call	did I call
you called	you did not (didn't) call	did you call
he called	he did not (didn't) call	did he call
she called	she did not (didn't) call	did she call
it called	it did not (didn't) call	did it call
we called	we did not (didn't) call	did we call
they called	they did not (didn't) call	did they call

Present progressive tense

AFFIRMATIVE FORM	NEGATIVE FORM	QUESTION FORM
I am calling	I am not calling	am I calling
you are calling	you are not (aren't) calling	are you calling
he is calling	he is not (isn't) calling	is he calling
she is calling	she is not (isn't) calling	is she calling
it is calling	it is not (isn't) calling	is it calling
we are calling	we are not (aren't) calling	are we calling
they are calling	they are not (aren't) calling	are they calling

Past progressive tense

AFFIRMATIVE FORM	NEGATIVE FORM	QUESTION FORM
I was calling	I was not (wasn't) calling	was I calling
you were calling	you were not (weren't) calling	were you calling
he was calling	he was not (wasn't) calling	was he calling
she was calling	she was not (wasn't) calling	was she calling
it was calling	it was not (wasn't) calling	was it calling
we were calling	we were not (weren't) calling	were we calling
they were calling	they were not (weren't) calling	were they calling

Future tense (will)

AFFIRMATIVE FORM	NEGATIVE FORM	QUESTION FORM
I will call	I will not (won't) call	will I call
you will call	you will not (won't) call	will you call
he will call	he will not (won't) call	will he call
she will call	she will not (won't) call	will she call
it will call	it will not (won't) call	will it call
we will call	we will not (won't) call	will we call
they will call	they will not (won't) call	will they call

Future tense (be going to)

AFFIRMATIVE FORM	NEGATIVE FORM	QUESTION FORM
I am going to call	I am not going to call	am I going to call
you are going to call	you are not (aren't) going to call	are you going to call
he is going to call	he is not (isn't) going to call	is he going to call
she is going to call	she is not (isn't) going to call	is she going to call
it is going to call	it is not (isn't) going to call	is it going to call
we are going to call	we are not (aren't) going to call	are we going to call
they are going to call	they are not (aren't) going to call	are they going to call

Present perfect tense

AFFIRMATIVE FORM	NEGATIVE FORM	QUESTION FORM
I have called	I have not (haven't) called	have I called
you have called	you have not (haven't) called	have you called
he has called	he has not (hasn't) called	has he called
she has called	she has not (hasn't) called	has she called
it has called	it has not (hasn't) called	has it called
we have called	we have not (haven't) called	have we called
they have called	they have not (haven't) called	have they called

Past perfect tense

AFFIRMATIVE FORM	NEGATIVE FORM	QUESTION FORM
I had called	I had not (hadn't) called	had I called
you had called	you had not (hadn't) called	had you called
he had called	he had not (hadn't) called	had he called
she had called	she had not (hadn't) called	had she called
it had called	it had not (hadn't) called	had it called
we had called	we had not (hadn't) called	had we called
they had called	they had not (hadn't) called	had they called

Future perfect tense

AFFIRMATIVE FORM	NEGATIVE FORM	QUESTION FORM
I will have called	I will not (won't) have called	will I have called
you will have called	you will not (won't) have called	will you have called
he will have called	he will not (won't) have called	will he have called
she will have called	she will not (won't) have called	will she have called
it will have called	it will not (won't) have called	will it have called
we will have called	we will not (won't) have called	will we have called
they will have called	they will not (won't) have called	will they have called

*Using the verb **to call** and the information in parentheses, rewrite the following sentences in the correct verb tense.*

1. I (to call) my friend. (past progressive, affirmative)

   _____

2. They (to call) you. (present perfect, question)

   _____

3. Sandy (to call) to make a complaint. (future, affirmative, *will*)

   _____

4. You (to call) your mother every week. (simple present, question)

   _____

5. He (to call) me in over a month. (present perfect, negative, contraction)

   _____

6. They (to call) to confirm my appointment. (simple past, question)

   _____

   _____

7. She (to call) by Friday, I hope. (future perfect, affirmative)

   _____

8. You (to call) me a chicken. (present progressive, question)

   _____

9. We (to call) Monique to see if you were there. (simple past, affirmative)

   _____

   _____

10. Stacy (to call) her brother overseas tonight. (future, question, *be going to*)

    _____

    _____

11. I (to call) you several times since your wedding. (present perfect, affirmative)

    _____

    _____

12. They (to call) the fire department. (past perfect, negative, contraction)

    _____

13. You (to call) the plumber, please. (future, question, *will*)

    _____

14. She (to call) the police. (past progressive, negative)

_____

15. I (to call) you again. (future, negative, *be going to*)

_____

16. Jack (to call) every day just to say hello. (simple present, affirmative)

_____

_____

17. I (to call) the doctor, but he was on vacation that week. (past perfect, affirmative)

_____

_____

18. We (to call) to congratulate you. (present progressive, affirmative)

_____

19. They (to call) before we leave next week. (future perfect, question)

_____

_____

20. Janice (to call) him anymore. (simple present, negative)

_____

21. He (to call) too late. (future, negative, *will*, contraction)

_____

22. I (to call) to invite you to our annual barbecue. (present progressive, affirmative)

_____

_____

23. It (to call) to its baby. (present progressive, negative, contraction)

_____

Verb Tenses Review: 4

Study the following verb tenses for the verb *to sleep*.

Simple present tense

AFFIRMATIVE FORM	NEGATIVE FORM	QUESTION FORM
I sleep	I do not (don't) sleep	do I sleep
you sleep	you do not (don't) sleep	do you sleep
he sleeps	he does not (doesn't) sleep	does he sleep
she sleeps	she does not (doesn't) sleep	does she sleep
it sleeps	it does not (doesn't) sleep	does it sleep
we sleep	we do not (don't) sleep	do we sleep
they sleep	they do not (don't) sleep	do they sleep

Simple past tense

AFFIRMATIVE FORM	NEGATIVE FORM	QUESTION FORM
I slept	I did not (didn't) sleep	did I sleep
you slept	you did not (didn't) sleep	did you sleep
he slept	he did not (didn't) sleep	did he sleep
she slept	she did not (didn't) sleep	did she sleep
it slept	it did not (didn't) sleep	did it sleep
we slept	we did not (didn't) sleep	did we sleep
they slept	they did not (didn't) sleep	did they sleep

Present progressive tense

AFFIRMATIVE FORM	NEGATIVE FORM	QUESTION FORM
I am sleeping	I am not sleeping	am I sleeping
you are sleeping	you are not (aren't) sleeping	are you sleeping
he is sleeping	he is not (isn't) sleeping	is he sleeping
she is sleeping	she is not (isn't) sleeping	is she sleeping
it is sleeping	it is not (isn't) sleeping	is it sleeping
we are sleeping	we are not (aren't) sleeping	are we sleeping
they are sleeping	they are not (aren't) sleeping	are they sleeping

Past progressive tense

AFFIRMATIVE FORM	NEGATIVE FORM	QUESTION FORM
I was sleeping	I was not (wasn't) sleeping	was I sleeping
you were sleeping	you were not (weren't) sleeping	were you sleeping
he was sleeping	he was not (wasn't) sleeping	was he sleeping
she was sleeping	she was not (wasn't) sleeping	was she sleeping
it was sleeping	it was not (wasn't) sleeping	was it sleeping
we were sleeping	we were not (weren't) sleeping	were we sleeping
they were sleeping	they were not (weren't) sleeping	were they sleeping

Future tense (will)

AFFIRMATIVE FORM	NEGATIVE FORM	QUESTION FORM
I will sleep	I will not (won't) sleep	will I sleep
you will sleep	you will not (won't) sleep	will you sleep
he will sleep	he will not (won't) sleep	will he sleep
she will sleep	she will not (won't) sleep	will she sleep
it will sleep	it will not (won't) sleep	will it sleep
we will sleep	we will not (won't) sleep	will we sleep
they will sleep	they will not (won't) sleep	will they sleep

Future tense (be going to)

AFFIRMATIVE FORM	NEGATIVE FORM	QUESTION FORM
I am going to sleep	I am not going to sleep	am I going to sleep
you are going to sleep	you are not (aren't) going to sleep	are you going to sleep
he is going to sleep	he is not (isn't) going to sleep	is he going to sleep
she is going to sleep	she is not (isn't) going to sleep	is she going to sleep
it is going to sleep	it is not (isn't) going to sleep	is it going to sleep
we are going to sleep	we are not (aren't) going to sleep	are we going to sleep
they are going to sleep	they are not (aren't) going to sleep	are they going to sleep

Present perfect tense

AFFIRMATIVE FORM	NEGATIVE FORM	QUESTION FORM
I have slept	I have not (haven't) slept	have I slept
you have slept	you have not (haven't) slept	have you slept
he has slept	he has not (hasn't) slept	has he slept
she has slept	she has not (hasn't) slept	has she slept
it has slept	it has not (hasn't) slept	has it slept
we have slept	we have not (haven't) slept	have we slept
they have slept	they have not (haven't) slept	have they slept

Past perfect tense

AFFIRMATIVE FORM	NEGATIVE FORM	QUESTION FORM
I had slept	I had not (hadn't) slept	had I slept
you had slept	you had not (hadn't) slept	had you slept
he had slept	he had not (hadn't) slept	had he slept
she had slept	she had not (hadn't) slept	had she slept
it had slept	it had not (hadn't) slept	had it slept
we had slept	we had not (hadn't) slept	had we slept
they had slept	they had not (hadn't) slept	had they slept

Future perfect tense

AFFIRMATIVE FORM	NEGATIVE FORM	QUESTION FORM
I will have slept	I will not (won't) have slept	will I have slept
you will have slept	you will not (won't) have slept	will you have slept
he will have slept	he will not (won't) have slept	will he have slept
she will have slept	she will not (won't) have slept	will she have slept
it will have slept	it will not (won't) have slept	will it have slept
we will have slept	we will not (won't) have slept	will we have slept
they will have slept	they will not (won't) have slept	will they have slept

Using the verb **to sleep** *and the information in parentheses, rewrite the following sentences in the correct verb tense.*

1. You (to sleep) in my bed. (past progressive, question)

   _____

2. We (to sleep) until dawn. (simple past, affirmative)

   _____

3. Mary (to sleep) at that hotel before. (past perfect, negative, contraction)

   _____

4. They (to sleep) enough by the time the plane lands. (future perfect, question)

   _____

   _____

5. I (to sleep) in the car on the way to Nova Scotia. (future, negative, *will*, contraction)

   _____

   _____

6. Joe (to sleep) all afternoon. (simple past, negative)

   _____

7. The girls (to sleep) in a tent before they went camping with Sandra. (past perfect, negative, contraction)

   _____

   _____

8. It (to sleep) on my pillow. (past progressive, question)

   _____

9. We (to sleep) if you are not home. (future, negative, *be going to*)

   _____

10. I (to sleep) all night. (simple past, negative, contraction)

    _____

11. She (to sleep) in days. (present perfect, negative, contraction)

    _____

12. Mike (to sleep) in my sleeping bag. (present progressive, question)

    _____

13. He (to sleep) with the light on. (simple present, affirmative)

    _____

14. You (to sleep) well last night. (simple past, question)

_____

15. The dog (to sleep) in the dog house. (future, question, *will*)

_____

_____

16. I (to sleep) when you called. (past progressive, affirmative)

_____

17. He (to sleep) on the couch often. (present perfect, question)

_____

18. A bear (to sleep) all winter. (simple present, question)

_____

19. We (to sleep) under the stars many times. (present perfect, affirmative)

_____

_____

20. Crystal (to sleep) with her favorite doll. (present progressive, affirmative)

_____

_____

21. My cat (to sleep) outside. (simple present, negative, contraction)

_____

22. I (to sleep) until noon tomorrow. (future, affirmative, *will*)

_____

23. Gerry (to sleep) 12 hours by 8 o'clock. (future perfect, affirmative)

_____

_____

Verb Tenses Practice: 1

EXERCISE
58·1

To ask *Create complete sentences using the model sentence and the verb tenses indicated at left. Use* **I** *for all your answers.*

I (to ask) the right questions.

PRESENT TENSE, AFFIRMATIVE	1. _____
PRESENT TENSE, NEGATIVE	2. _____
PRESENT TENSE, QUESTION	3. _____
PAST TENSE, AFFIRMATIVE	4. _____
PAST TENSE, NEGATIVE	5. _____
PAST TENSE, QUESTION	6. _____
PRESENT PROGRESSIVE TENSE, AFFIRMATIVE	7. _____
PRESENT PROGRESSIVE TENSE, NEGATIVE	8. _____
PRESENT PROGRESSIVE TENSE, QUESTION	9. _____
PAST PROGRESSIVE TENSE, AFFIRMATIVE	10. _____
PAST PROGRESSIVE TENSE, NEGATIVE	11. _____
PAST PROGRESSIVE TENSE, QUESTION	12. _____
FUTURE TENSE, AFFIRMATIVE (*will*)	13. _____
FUTURE TENSE, NEGATIVE (*will*)	14. _____
FUTURE TENSE, QUESTION (*will*)	15. _____

FUTURE TENSE, AFFIRMATIVE (*be going to*)	16. _____
FUTURE TENSE, NEGATIVE (*be going to*)	17. _____
FUTURE TENSE, QUESTION (*be going to*)	18. _____
PRESENT PERFECT TENSE, AFFIRMATIVE	19. _____
PRESENT PERFECT TENSE, NEGATIVE	20. _____
PRESENT PERFECT TENSE, QUESTION	21. _____
PAST PERFECT TENSE, AFFIRMATIVE	22. _____
PAST PERFECT TENSE, NEGATIVE	23. _____
PAST PERFECT TENSE, QUESTION	24. _____
FUTURE PERFECT TENSE, AFFIRMATIVE	25. _____
FUTURE PERFECT TENSE, NEGATIVE	26. _____
FUTURE PERFECT TENSE, QUESTION	27. _____

EXERCISE
58·2

To take *Create complete sentences using the model sentence and the verb tenses indicated at left. Use* **you** *for all your answers.*

You (to take) the bus.

PRESENT TENSE, AFFIRMATIVE	1. _____
PRESENT TENSE, NEGATIVE	2. _____
PRESENT TENSE, QUESTION	3. _____
PAST TENSE, AFFIRMATIVE	4. _____
PAST TENSE, NEGATIVE	5. _____
PAST TENSE, QUESTION	6. _____
PRESENT PROGRESSIVE TENSE, AFFIRMATIVE	7. _____
PRESENT PROGRESSIVE TENSE, NEGATIVE	8. _____
PRESENT PROGRESSIVE TENSE, QUESTION	9. _____
PAST PROGRESSIVE TENSE, AFFIRMATIVE	10. _____
PAST PROGRESSIVE TENSE, NEGATIVE	11. _____
PAST PROGRESSIVE TENSE, QUESTION	12. _____
FUTURE TENSE, AFFIRMATIVE (*will*)	13. _____
FUTURE TENSE, NEGATIVE (*will*)	14. _____
FUTURE TENSE, QUESTION (*will*)	15. _____

FUTURE TENSE, AFFIRMATIVE (*be going to*)	16. _____
FUTURE TENSE, NEGATIVE (*be going to*)	17. _____
FUTURE TENSE, QUESTION (*be going to*)	18. _____
PRESENT PERFECT TENSE, AFFIRMATIVE	19. _____
PRESENT PERFECT TENSE, NEGATIVE	20. _____
PRESENT PERFECT TENSE, QUESTION	21. _____
PAST PERFECT TENSE, AFFIRMATIVE	22. _____
PAST PERFECT TENSE, NEGATIVE	23. _____
PAST PERFECT TENSE, QUESTION	24. _____
FUTURE PERFECT TENSE, AFFIRMATIVE	25. _____
FUTURE PERFECT TENSE, NEGATIVE	26. _____
FUTURE PERFECT TENSE, QUESTION	27. _____

EXERCISE
58·3

To clean *Create complete sentences using the model sentence and the verb tenses indicated at left. Use* **he** *for all your answers.*

He (to clean) his car.

PRESENT TENSE, AFFIRMATIVE	1. _____
PRESENT TENSE, NEGATIVE	2. _____
PRESENT TENSE, QUESTION	3. _____
PAST TENSE, AFFIRMATIVE	4. _____
PAST TENSE, NEGATIVE	5. _____
PAST TENSE, QUESTION	6. _____
PRESENT PROGRESSIVE TENSE, AFFIRMATIVE	7. _____
PRESENT PROGRESSIVE TENSE, NEGATIVE	8. _____
PRESENT PROGRESSIVE TENSE, QUESTION	9. _____
PAST PROGRESSIVE TENSE, AFFIRMATIVE	10. _____
PAST PROGRESSIVE TENSE, NEGATIVE	11. _____
PAST PROGRESSIVE TENSE, QUESTION	12. _____
FUTURE TENSE, AFFIRMATIVE (*will*)	13. _____
FUTURE TENSE, NEGATIVE (*will*)	14. _____
FUTURE TENSE, QUESTION (*will*)	15. _____

FUTURE TENSE, AFFIRMATIVE (*be going to*)	16. _____
FUTURE TENSE, NEGATIVE (*be going to*)	17. _____
FUTURE TENSE, QUESTION (*be going to*)	18. _____
PRESENT PERFECT TENSE, AFFIRMATIVE	19. _____
PRESENT PERFECT TENSE, NEGATIVE	20. _____
PRESENT PERFECT TENSE, QUESTION	21. _____
PAST PERFECT TENSE, AFFIRMATIVE	22. _____
PAST PERFECT TENSE, NEGATIVE	23. _____
PAST PERFECT TENSE, QUESTION	24. _____
FUTURE PERFECT TENSE, AFFIRMATIVE	25. _____
FUTURE PERFECT TENSE, NEGATIVE	26. _____
FUTURE PERFECT TENSE, QUESTION	27. _____

EXERCISE
58·4

To speak *Create complete sentences using the model sentence and the verb tenses indicated at left. Use* **she** *for all your answers.*

She (to speak) on the phone.

PRESENT TENSE, AFFIRMATIVE	1. _____
PRESENT TENSE, NEGATIVE	2. _____
PRESENT TENSE, QUESTION	3. _____
PAST TENSE, AFFIRMATIVE	4. _____
PAST TENSE, NEGATIVE	5. _____
PAST TENSE, QUESTION	6. _____
PRESENT PROGRESSIVE TENSE, AFFIRMATIVE	7. _____
PRESENT PROGRESSIVE TENSE, NEGATIVE	8. _____
PRESENT PROGRESSIVE TENSE, QUESTION	9. _____
PAST PROGRESSIVE TENSE, AFFIRMATIVE	10. _____
PAST PROGRESSIVE TENSE, NEGATIVE	11. _____
PAST PROGRESSIVE TENSE, QUESTION	12. _____
FUTURE TENSE, AFFIRMATIVE (*will*)	13. _____
FUTURE TENSE, NEGATIVE (*will*)	14. _____
FUTURE TENSE, QUESTION (*will*)	15. _____

FUTURE TENSE, AFFIRMATIVE (*be going to*)   16. _____

FUTURE TENSE, NEGATIVE (*be going to*)   17. _____

FUTURE TENSE, QUESTION (*be going to*)   18. _____

PRESENT PERFECT TENSE, AFFIRMATIVE   19. _____

PRESENT PERFECT TENSE, NEGATIVE   20. _____

PRESENT PERFECT TENSE, QUESTION   21. _____

PAST PERFECT TENSE, AFFIRMATIVE   22. _____

PAST PERFECT TENSE, NEGATIVE   23. _____

PAST PERFECT TENSE, QUESTION   24. _____

FUTURE PERFECT TENSE, AFFIRMATIVE   25. _____

FUTURE PERFECT TENSE, NEGATIVE   26. _____

FUTURE PERFECT TENSE, QUESTION   27. _____

Verb Tenses Practice: 2

To eat *Create complete sentences using the model sentence and the verb tenses indicated at left. Use* **it** *for all your answers.*

It (to eat) bugs.

PRESENT TENSE, AFFIRMATIVE   1. _____

PRESENT TENSE, NEGATIVE   2. _____

PRESENT TENSE, QUESTION   3. _____

PAST TENSE, AFFIRMATIVE   4. _____

PAST TENSE, NEGATIVE   5. _____

PAST TENSE, QUESTION   6. _____

PRESENT PROGRESSIVE TENSE,   7. _____
AFFIRMATIVE

PRESENT PROGRESSIVE TENSE,   8. _____
NEGATIVE

PRESENT PROGRESSIVE TENSE,   9. _____
QUESTION

PAST PROGRESSIVE TENSE,   10. _____
AFFIRMATIVE

PAST PROGRESSIVE TENSE,   11. _____
NEGATIVE

PAST PROGRESSIVE TENSE,   12. _____
QUESTION

FUTURE TENSE,   13. _____
AFFIRMATIVE (*will*)

FUTURE TENSE,   14. _____
NEGATIVE (*will*)

FUTURE TENSE,   15. _____
QUESTION (*will*)

FUTURE TENSE, AFFIRMATIVE (*be going to*)   16. _____

FUTURE TENSE, NEGATIVE (*be going to*)   17. _____

FUTURE TENSE, QUESTION (*be going to*)   18. _____

PRESENT PERFECT TENSE, AFFIRMATIVE   19. _____

PRESENT PERFECT TENSE, NEGATIVE   20. _____

PRESENT PERFECT TENSE, QUESTION   21. _____

PAST PERFECT TENSE, AFFIRMATIVE   22. _____

PAST PERFECT TENSE, NEGATIVE   23. _____

PAST PERFECT TENSE, QUESTION   24. _____

FUTURE PERFECT TENSE, AFFIRMATIVE   25. _____

FUTURE PERFECT TENSE, NEGATIVE   26. _____

FUTURE PERFECT TENSE, QUESTION   27. _____

EXERCISE
59·2

To live *Create complete sentences using the model sentence and the verb tenses indicated at left. Use* **we** *for all your answers.*

We (to live) in an apartment.

PRESENT TENSE, AFFIRMATIVE   1. _____

PRESENT TENSE, NEGATIVE   2. _____

PRESENT TENSE, QUESTION   3. _____

PAST TENSE, AFFIRMATIVE   4. _____

PAST TENSE, NEGATIVE   5. _____

PAST TENSE, QUESTION   6. _____

PRESENT PROGRESSIVE TENSE, AFFIRMATIVE   7. _____

PRESENT PROGRESSIVE TENSE, NEGATIVE   8. _____

PRESENT PROGRESSIVE TENSE, QUESTION   9. _____

PAST PROGRESSIVE TENSE, AFFIRMATIVE   10. _____

PAST PROGRESSIVE TENSE, NEGATIVE   11. _____

PAST PROGRESSIVE TENSE, QUESTION   12. _____

FUTURE TENSE, AFFIRMATIVE (*will*)   13. _____

FUTURE TENSE, NEGATIVE (*will*)   14. _____

FUTURE TENSE, QUESTION (*will*)   15. _____

FUTURE TENSE, AFFIRMATIVE (*be going to*)	16.	_____
FUTURE TENSE, NEGATIVE (*be going to*)	17.	_____
FUTURE TENSE, QUESTION (*be going to*)	18.	_____
PRESENT PERFECT TENSE, AFFIRMATIVE	19.	_____
PRESENT PERFECT TENSE, NEGATIVE	20.	_____
PRESENT PERFECT TENSE, QUESTION	21.	_____
PAST PERFECT TENSE, AFFIRMATIVE	22.	_____
PAST PERFECT TENSE, NEGATIVE	23.	_____
PAST PERFECT TENSE, QUESTION	24.	_____
FUTURE PERFECT TENSE, AFFIRMATIVE	25.	_____
FUTURE PERFECT TENSE, NEGATIVE	26.	_____
FUTURE PERFECT TENSE, QUESTION	27.	_____

EXERCISE
59·3

To go *Create complete sentences using the model sentence and the verb tenses indicated at left. Use* **they** *for all your answers.*

They (to go) to college.

PRESENT TENSE, AFFIRMATIVE	1.	_____
PRESENT TENSE, NEGATIVE	2.	_____
PRESENT TENSE, QUESTION	3.	_____
PAST TENSE, AFFIRMATIVE	4.	_____
PAST TENSE, NEGATIVE	5.	_____
PAST TENSE, QUESTION	6.	_____
PRESENT PROGRESSIVE TENSE, AFFIRMATIVE	7.	_____
PRESENT PROGRESSIVE TENSE, NEGATIVE	8.	_____
PRESENT PROGRESSIVE TENSE, QUESTION	9.	_____
PAST PROGRESSIVE TENSE, AFFIRMATIVE	10.	_____
PAST PROGRESSIVE TENSE, NEGATIVE	11.	_____
PAST PROGRESSIVE TENSE, QUESTION	12.	_____
FUTURE TENSE, AFFIRMATIVE (*will*)	13.	_____
FUTURE TENSE, NEGATIVE (*will*)	14.	_____
FUTURE TENSE, QUESTION (*will*)	15.	_____

FUTURE TENSE, AFFIRMATIVE (*be going to*)   16. _____

FUTURE TENSE, NEGATIVE (*be going to*)   17. _____

FUTURE TENSE, QUESTION (*be going to*)   18. _____

PRESENT PERFECT TENSE, AFFIRMATIVE   19. _____

PRESENT PERFECT TENSE, NEGATIVE   20. _____

PRESENT PERFECT TENSE, QUESTION   21. _____

PAST PERFECT TENSE, AFFIRMATIVE   22. _____

PAST PERFECT TENSE, NEGATIVE   23. _____

PAST PERFECT TENSE, QUESTION   24. _____

FUTURE PERFECT TENSE, AFFIRMATIVE   25. _____

FUTURE PERFECT TENSE, NEGATIVE   26. _____

FUTURE PERFECT TENSE, QUESTION   27. _____

Regular and Irregular Verbs Review

EXERCISE

60·1

Complete the following sentences with the correct past tense form of the verb in parentheses.

1. I _____ (to do) all my homework at school.

2. The girls _____ (to scream) when they

   _____ (to see) the spider.

3. Adam _____ (to fill) the glass to the top.

4. It _____ (to fall) on my head.

5. Amy _____ (to feel) very sad when she

   _____ (to fail) her test.

6. They _____ (to walk) and _____

   (to talk) in the park for over an hour.

7. I _____ (to burn) my toast this morning.

8. We _____ (to put) the cake and the presents on the

   table.

9. My friend _____ (to break) his leg and he

   _____ (to need) crutches to walk.

10. The painter _____ (to paint) a beautiful painting of

    his wife.

11. I _____ (to read) that book twice.

12. Samantha _____ (to wear) her new dress to school.

13. We _____ (to forget) to tell you that Lenny

    _____ (to bring) his cousin Lana.

14. Samuel _____ (to borrow) my baseball bat and he

    _____ (to lend) me his basketball.

15. The little girl _____ (to run) toward her mother.

16. He _____ (to climb) the ladder and _____ (to dive) into the pool.

17. Jonathan _____ (to lose) his glasses at school.

18. My class _____ (to go) to New York City last month.

19. My dog _____ (to bark) and _____ (to growl) when he saw the mailman.

20. You _____ (to leave) the block of ice on the picnic table and it _____ (to melt).

21. Oliver _____ (to blow) out the candles and _____ (to make) a wish.

22. The old man _____ (to snore) during the movie and _____ (to annoy) everyone.

23. She _____ (to thank) her friends and family for their support.

24. Sarah _____ (to dream) about monsters last night.

25. It _____ (to cost) too much, so we didn't buy it.

26. My grandfather _____ (to own) the restaurant, but he _____ (to sell) it to my father in 2005.

27. The puppy _____ (to follow) us home, and we _____ (to keep) it.

28. Tommy _____ (to mail) the letter to Santa Claus.

29. We _____ (to order) most of our supplies online.

30. Your dog _____ (to chew) the leg on my couch.

31. You really _____ (to hurt) my feelings when you _____ (to say) that.

32. The party and the noise _____ (to last) all night.

33. Grandma _____ (to knit) slippers for everyone.

34. I _____ (to think) it was Saturday today.

35. He _____ (to hide) it in the bottom drawer.

36. We _____ (to wake) up when we _____ (to hear) the alarm.

37. John _____ (to sell) his truck and _____ (to buy) a small car.

38. I _____ (to forget) to wear my socks this morning, and my feet
_____ (to freeze).

39. You _____ (to shine) the light in my eyes.

40. My grandmother _____ (to sew) the squares together to make the
quilt.

41. The kids _____ (to play) soccer all afternoon.

42. They _____ (to move) to San Diego.

43. I _____ (to spend) too much money at the mall.

44. We _____ (to convince) them to come with us.

45. Jennifer _____ (to find) the answer in the book.

46. We _____ (to give) it to Sonny.

47. She _____ (to type) the report on my computer.

48. Jeremy _____ (to spill) his glass of milk all over the table.

49. I _____ (to ask) for a raise, and my boss _____
(to say), "No."

50. The fly _____ (to fly) into my house.

Grammar Review

EXERCISE
61·1

*Review the following sentences. If a sentence is incorrect, rewrite it correctly. If the sentence is correct, write **OK**.*

1. Is this his eraser?

   _____

2. She goes at the corner to wait for the bus.

   _____

   _____

3. Will she have talks to her mother by tonight?

   _____

   _____

4. He has already taken his medication.

   _____

5. They decide to leave before midnight last Wednesday night.

   _____

   _____

6. We lend them our sleeping bags and tent last weekend.

   _____

   _____

7. Has you been to the museum?

   _____

8. We drived to Toronto for the weekend.

   _____

9. I already red that book.

   _____

10. She isn't my cousin, she's my friend.

_____

11. We are going to see a play to the theater tonight.

_____

_____

12. Why are you shouting at me?

_____

13. There are three eggs in the nest.

_____

14. Put it on the garbage can.

_____

15. They won't have notice the changes we made to the document.

_____

_____

16. Will they publishing your story?

_____

17. We only stayed for a hour.

_____

18. She was eating carrots while we were talking on the phone.

_____

_____

19. He go to the store for milk and bread last night.

_____

20. She had broke my favorite glass yesterday morning.

_____

_____

21. Don't walk on the puddle.

_____

22. Is there enough toys for the kids to play with?

_____

23. He is going to goes to the circus with his niece.

_____

*Review the following sentences. If a sentence is incorrect, rewrite it correctly. If the sentence is correct, write **OK**.*

1. We like to look at the stars in the night.

_____

2. She goes at the library to study.

_____

3. Are they watching the kids in the pool?

_____

4. I talked to the owner from the building.

_____

5. Don't worry. They willn't forget about it.

_____

6. I have broughten cookies for everyone many times.

_____

_____

7. Our girls like strawberries ice cream.

_____

8. Why did you did that?

_____

9. Tracy have many new friends at school.

_____

10. We send the package last week.

_____

11. She really misses her parents.

_____

12. I have five golds rings on my fingers.

_____

13. It weren't raining yesterday.

_____

14. The twins have 10 years old.

_____

15. Janet trys to exercise every morning.

_____

16. I will call you tonight before I go to bed.

_____

17. I have really cold. I will put on my slippers.

_____

18. Do they your brothers?

_____

19. Susan hasn't very tall for her age.

_____

20. We flied to Boston for their wedding.

_____

21. The princess wept alone in her room.

_____

22. He will have written the whole book by Tuesday.

_____

_____

23. They met their friends at Quebec City.

_____

EXERCISE
61·3

*Review the following sentences. If a sentence is incorrect, rewrite it correctly. If the sentence is correct, write **OK**.*

1. Mrs. Fletcher teaches eighth grade last year.

_____

2. He washes her car in our driveway.

_____

3. There wasn't enough chairs in the classroom for all the students.

_____

_____

4. Did you answered the phone?

_____

5. It is a birthday card very special.

_____

6. I hope he like his gift.

_____

7. She wants to buy a horse next summer.

_____

8. You need an uniform to enter the building.

_____

9. I hasn't seen the results of the tests.

_____

10. Arnold likes blacks cats.

_____

11. We have offered to help several times.

_____

12. We want to go at Alaska next summer.

_____

13. She will holds the baby while I go in the bank.

_____

14. There is a few foxes in the woods.

_____

15. It hasn't helped much.

_____

16. They aren't going to need the big blue plastic bucket.

_____

_____

17. I sat next to Philip in the plane.

_____

18. The baby cries all night last night.

_____

19. Give the screwdriver at Justin, please.

_____

20. Katie took a lot of candies from the bowl.

_____

21. Do they watch the baseball game last night?

_____

22. We eat to the restaurant every Friday night.

_____

23. There weren't enough time.

_____

Vocabulary Review

·62·

EXERCISE

62·1

Choose the word in parentheses that best completes each sentence.

1. You need a _____ (locksmith, corkscrew) to open the bottle of wine.

2. I use the _____ (lawn mower, vacuum) to cut the grass.

3. My mother hangs the wet clothes on the _____ (dryer, clothesline).

4. I fry my eggs in a _____ (pan, pen).

5. You have to wear a clean _____ (sheet, shirt) for your interview.

6. He washes his body with _____ (soap, soup).

7. You need a _____ (kitten, kettle) to boil the water.

8. She forgot her _____ (watch, witch) this morning.

9. There are a lot of minnows in the _____ (pond, pound).

10. I will give you an _____ (accountant, appointment) for tomorrow morning.

11. Please put a lot of _____ (needles, noodles) in the soup.

12. Did she give you her _____ (receipt, recipe) for this delicious _____ (dessert, desert)?

13. Don't put too much _____ (butter, bitter) on my toast.

14. Every time I see Danny, I _____ (flush, blush).

15. Isabelle had a very difficult _____ (pregnant, pregnancy).

16. My neighbors make a lot of _____ (nose, noise).

17. Is it the _____ (true, truth)?

18. The housekeeper does my _____ (housework, homework).

19. He is going to meet us at the _____ (mall, mail) this afternoon.

20. We need a better _____ (plan, plain).

21. Can you _____ (sign, sing) the national anthem?

22. Look at the huge _____ (sheep, ship) on the ocean.

23. There are a lot of _____ (hangers, hunters) in the closet.

24. Don't put that in your _____ (month, mouth).

25. My grandmother likes to work in the _____ (gardener, garden).

26. You are very _____ (niece, nice).

27. The _____ (icing, icicle) on the cake is delicious.

28. Peggy forgot to put the _____ (bib, lid) on the jar.

29. There is a _____ (scar, scarf) on his left hand.

30. I am not hungry because I ate my _____ (snack, snake).

31. My socks are wet because of the _____ (dough, dew) on the grass.

32. You need a better _____ (raisin, reason).

33. An elephant has two _____ (brains, tusks).

34. The little girl kissed her mother on the _____ (cheek, chick).

35. We will have several _____ (ghosts, guests) for dinner tonight.

36. You wear a watch on your _____ (wrist, waist).

37. The students will paint the _____ (blisters, bleachers) at school.

38. Can you _____ (borrow, lend) me a few dollars?

39. Uncle Joe grew a _____ (bear, beard) for the winter.

40. My grandmother has _____ (wrinkles, antlers) on her forehead.

41. We will have _____ (peacocks, pancakes) for breakfast.

42. Please close the _____ (window, widow).

43. Her skirt is made of _____ (yolk, silk).

44. The king lost his _____ (crowd, crown) in the

    _____ (crowd, crown).

45. He thinks he knows _____ (everywhere, everything).

46. Do you want a piece of my _____ (pie, pea)?

47. My _____ (landlord, mortgage) is due on Friday.

48. I feel _____ (dizzy, fuzzy) when I close my eyes and spin around.

49. We will paint our _____ (chicken, kitchen) next week.

50. She is wearing a pink _____ (lip, wig).

51. I hurt my _____ (elbow, eyelash) when I fell.

52. The _____ (fairy, ferry) will take you across the lake.

53. There is a _____ (wasp, shark) in the house.

54. He dropped the _____ (oar, row) in the middle of the lake.

55. David is a very handsome _____ (bride, groom).

56. There is an _____ (ant, aunt) on the floor.

57. Do you need _____ (flower, flour) to make cookies?

58. I have a _____ (pebble, pickle) in my shoe.

59. There are a lot of _____ (dentures, leftovers) in the fridge.

60. We love to watch the beautiful _____ (sunset, sunrise) on the lake in the morning.

Word Search Puzzles

Clothesline *Find the words listed below in the following word search puzzle. Words may be horizontal, vertical, or diagonal; they may be left to right or right to left, top to bottom or bottom to top.*

pajamas	socks	underwear	shirt
blouse	jacket	ties	scarf
jeans	pants	rags	sheets
tablecloth	towels	shorts	clothespin
dress	skirt	curtains	quilts
pantyhose	blankets	facecloths	coat

```
Z   S   C   A   R   F   S   A   T   C   Z   D   S   H   U
J   J   N   C   O   A   I   O   T   S   R   S   Y   N   X
M   E   W   I   M   K   W   B   S   E   S   P   D   S   F
V   D   A   A   A   E   F   G   S   V   U   E   A   T   O
Z   C   J   N   L   T   A   S   W   I   R   F   I   E   Z
G   A   L   S   S   R   R   G   L   W   H   A   N   K   P
P   B   L   O   U   S   E   U   E   J   T   C   Z   N   A
C   O   A   T   T   S   T   A   C   R   A   E   V   A   N
T   R   I   K   S   H   R   L   I   P   V   C   W   L   T
F   S   P   I   Q   E   E   H   I   F   I   L   K   B   S
V   N   W   Q   F   E   S   S   Q   U   S   O   S   E   P
E   S   O   H   Y   T   N   A   P   B   Q   T   K   S   T
S   T   R   O   H   S   B   A   K   I   S   H   C   E   D
T   A   B   L   E   C   L   O   T   H   N   S   O   I   V
B   Y   G   L   N   P   G   O   B   T   Q   B   S   T   U
```

254

Animals *Find the words listed below in the following word search puzzle. Words may be horizontal, vertical, or diagonal; they may be left to right or right to left, top to bottom or bottom to top.*

pigs	horse	cow	bull
goats	duck	ducklings	cats
foxes	monkey	donkey	wolves
piglet	bunny	swan	goose
peacock	rooster	chicken	bears
raccoon	skunk	porcupine	dogs
kitten	puppy	elephant	groundhog

```
E  N  S  S  S  G  S  R  Y  P  S  Y  Y  P  S
P  L  K  E  E  K  O  F  E  U  G  S  N  E  T
Y  C  E  S  X  O  N  N  K  P  N  J  N  A  A
S  V  O  P  S  O  I  O  N  P  I  X  U  C  C
K  O  R  T  H  P  F  A  O  Y  L  Q  B  O  M
G  C  E  B  U  A  C  P  M  C  K  D  W  C  R
S  R  U  C  U  W  N  O  Z  A  C  M  F  K  H
Y  H  R  D  L  P  N  T  W  U  U  A  Y  O  K
T  O  N  E  K  C  I  H  C  P  D  E  R  N  I
P  W  O  L  V  E  S  G  I  L  K  S  A  T  T
B  E  A  R  S  R  S  G  L  N  E  W  Q  H  T
L  L  U  B  V  X  S  K  O  E  S  A  M  O  E
D  O  G  S  R  Q  E  D  U  S  T  A  O  G  N
G  R  O  U  N  D  H  O  G  N  S  X  K  L  O
V  R  Q  G  G  F  D  Z  S  A  K  G  Z  P  V
```

Aquarium *Find the words listed below in the following word search puzzle. Words may be horizontal, vertical, or diagonal; they may be left to right or right to left, top to bottom or bottom to top.*

rocks	seaweed	shark	whale
bubbles	ship	colorful	treasure
goldfish	water	shells	filter
heater	trout	catfish	eel
sunfish	frogs	waves	dolphins
sand	divers	snorkel	goggles
frogmen	octopus	clams	minnows

```
T  S  H  E  L  L  S  D  J  G  W  H  A  L  E
C  R  Z  F  T  U  O  R  T  O  W  A  V  E  S
L  S  E  S  L  L  R  B  C  G  D  N  A  S  W
A  W  H  A  P  S  Z  G  T  G  K  I  C  W  M
M  O  S  H  S  S  Y  C  O  L  O  R  F  U  L
S  N  I  S  G  U  E  D  E  E  W  A  E  S  S
X  N  F  K  O  X  R  L  J  S  G  T  H  H  W
S  I  T  C  L  Q  M  E  B  E  J  S  I  H  A
G  M  A  O  D  Z  Q  S  T  B  I  P  M  E  T
O  L  C  R  F  S  S  L  U  F  U  P  M  A  E
R  O  E  U  I  I  E  N  P  Q  B  K  T  R
F  O  X  E  S  B  L  U  S  N  O  R  K  E  L
D  U  B  W  H  H  S  T  L  M  A  T  W  R  L
N  E  M  G  O  R  F  S  E  H  R  S  C  H  H
S  R  E  V  I  D  G  O  S  R  K  G  P  O  A
```

Garage sale *Find the words listed below in the following word search puzzle. Words may be horizontal, vertical, or diagonal; they may be left to right or right to left, top to bottom or bottom to top.*

pots	hammer	tools	blankets
jars	cups	shoes	toys
puzzle	skis	kettle	furniture
lamp	books	bike	radio
pans	dishes	chair	stroller
crib	bowls	dolls	hairdryer
clothes	skates	teapot	rake

```
V  B  H  S  E  O  H  S  Q  R  X  E  E  Q  A
M  L  N  A  B  I  K  E  A  M  T  L  O  J  Q
D  A  I  Q  I  R  S  K  I  S  Q  Z  I  R  N
M  N  S  R  V  R  E  K  D  I  E  Z  D  K  J
P  K  O  K  D  A  D  M  O  M  P  U  A  A  P
O  E  D  J  A  O  S  R  M  O  U  P  R  M  T
T  T  A  Z  Q  T  L  Y  Y  A  B  S  A  S  E
S  S  P  U  C  R  E  L  O  E  H  L  T  L  A
S  E  H  T  O  L  C  S  S  T  R  R  T  C  P
D  I  S  H  E  S  J  E  O  R  O  T  S  R  O
F  U  R  N  I  T  U  R  E  L  E  T  I  I  T
B  O  W  L  S  P  G  Z  L  K  O  A  K  B  C
K  S  A  P  R  H  A  E  L  O  H  X  S  N  R
I  R  L  O  Y  A  R  N  L  C  V  F  U  M  S
Y  W  U  O  P  R  G  S  S  T  F  E  T  L  X
```

Scrambled Sentences

EXERCISE

64·1

Put the scrambled words into the correct order to form a complete sentence.

1. you / time / me / week / if / please / next / call / have.

   _____

   _____

2. her / for / gave / daughter / she / her / to / it / birthday.

   _____

   _____

3. late / am / so / I / I / today / night / very / last / tired / worked.

   _____

   _____

4. of / many / there / at / ocean / the / the / ships / are / bottom.

   _____

   _____

5. there / my / walk / I / from / crutches / need / to / to / here.

   _____

   _____

6. clothesline / nice / I / on / dry / to / my / so / the / sheets / was / day / it / hung / a.

   _____

   _____

7. fireplace / I / the / night / when / in / light / finger / match / fire / I / to / the / my / lit / burned / the / last.

_____

_____

_____

8. birthday / mother / a / with / cake / Mary / that / party / hopes / for / chocolate / week / vanilla / her / next / her / makes / icing.

_____

_____

_____

9. bill / I / three / me / dollar / quarters / give / so / two / gave / coins / four / dollar / a / you / one / dimes / a / and / five / nickel.

_____

_____

_____

10. supper / in / started / the / when / were / basement / in / making / fire / the / we / kitchen / the.

_____

_____

Put the scrambled words into the correct order to form a complete sentence.

1. landlord / year / the / to / lease / again / raised / my / me / this / sign / and / a / wants / new / rent / he.

_____

_____

2. class / wrote / in / parents / I / teacher / about / my / trouble / note / my / to / a / behavior / in / bad / am / my / because.

_____

_____

_____

3. that / wearing / out / at / arrived / I / I / I / my / inside / was / realized / this / when / morning / shirt / work.

_____

_____

_____

4. because / bird / down / with / wrong / flying / it / there / that / is / upside / something / is.

_____

_____

5. back / nephew / dent / the / car / my / it / new / he / and / my / was / lent / in / when / to / I / door / there / brought / a.

_____

_____

_____

6. had / suit / very / and / because / work / to / brother / important / a / wore / a / my / new / today / black / meeting / a / he / tie.

_____

_____

_____

7. a / minimum / for / because / is / only / new / Martin / he / job / looking / is / making / wage / the.

_____

_____

8. in / quiet / live / friendly / close / I / and / Montreal / neighborhood / a / to / very.

_____

_____

Appendix
Pronunciation Exercises

The following exercises focus on sounds and individual words in English that learners find particularly challenging. After an explanation, thirty model sentences are provided that include examples of the sound or word. Consult the McGraw Hill Language Lab app for streaming audio recordings of all the example sentences; pauses are provided in the recording for you to repeat, following the model pronunciation.

Pronunciation Exercises

Pronunciation of Contractions

Contractions are often used with the verb **to be** *in the present tense, in both written and spoken form. The ending of the contraction must be firmly pronounced.*

I am	→	I'**m**
you are	→	you'**re**
he is	→	he'**s**
she is	→	she'**s**
it is	→	it'**s**
we are	→	we'**re**
they are	→	they'**re**

Listen carefully and repeat the following sentences.

1. She'**s** a hairdresser and I'**m** a real estate agent.
2. He'**s** in love with her.
3. It'**s** not true.
4. We'**re** so proud of you.
5. They'**re** best friends.
6. You'**re** a funny guy.
7. She'**s** a nurse at the clinic.
8. We'**re** happy to be here tonight.
9. He'**s** the owner of the company.
10. We'**re** late for work again.
11. They'**re** outside.
12. She'**s** my sister.
13. You'**re** welcome.
14. I'**m** from Montreal.
15. She'**s** a big star in Hollywood.
16. We'**re** staying home tonight.
17. They'**re** getting married in June.
18. He'**s** a very tall man.
19. I'**m** listening to the news on the radio.
20. She'**s** always busy on the weekends.
21. It'**s** time for lunch and I'**m** hungry.
22. You'**re** a very interesting person.
23. I'**m** sorry for saying that about you.
24. He'**s** mad that you did that.
25. They'**re** waiting for us downstairs.
26. I'**m** making a cake for your birthday.
27. It'**s** better like that.
28. She'**s** afraid of you.
29. We'**re** leaving now.
30. You'**re** so nice.

Pronunciation of Contractions: To Be – Present Tense – Negative Form

Contractions are often used with the verb **to be** *in the present tense negative form, in both written and spoken form. The* **-n't** *ending of the contraction must be firmly pronounced.*

I am not	→	no contraction
you are not	→	you are**n't**
he is not	→	he is**n't**
she is not	→	she is**n't**
it is not	→	it is**n't**
we are not	→	we are**n't**
they are not	→	they are**n't**

Listen carefully and repeat the following sentences.

1. They are**n't** cousins.
2. She is**n't** a secretary.
3. We are**n't** twins.
4. It is**n't** clean.
5. You are**n't** the boss.
6. He is**n't** a policeman.
7. We are**n't** proud of it.
8. Sara is**n't** mad at you.
9. David is**n't** here.
10. Max and Melanie are**n't** in the house.
11. It is**n't** fair.
12. You are**n't** on my list.
13. He is**n't** a doctor.
14. They are**n't** in a meeting.
15. My brother is**n't** a student.
16. We are**n't** ready for the test.
17. The milk is**n't** in the fridge.
18. He is**n't** on vacation this week.
19. We are**n't** busy today.
20. The cat is**n't** under the bed.
21. My shoes are**n't** dirty.
22. She is**n't** a nurse.
23. The car is**n't** in the garage.
24. The eggs are**n't** broken.
25. It is**n't** necessary.
26. The boys are**n't** at the park.
27. Melanie is**n't** serious.
28. Jenny and I are**n't** hungry right now.
29. He is**n't** joking.
30. It is**n't** my birthday today.

Pronunciation of Contractions: To Be – Past Tense – Negative Form

Contractions are often used with the verb **to be** *in the past tense negative form, in both written and spoken form. The* **-n't** *ending of the contraction must be firmly pronounced.*

I was not	→	I was**n't**
you were not	→	you were**n't**
he was not	→	he was**n't**
she was not	→	she was**n't**
it was not	→	it was**n't**
we were not	→	we were**n't**
they were not	→	they were**n't**

Listen carefully and repeat the following sentences.

1. She was**n't** ready.
2. They were**n't** in class today
3. It was**n't** in my purse.
4. He was**n't** there.
5. We were**n't** at the mall.
6. I was**n't** late.
7. You were**n't** very nice to her.
8. The house was**n't** for sale
9. Mark and John were**n't** hungry.
10. Jennifer was**n't** with us.
11. The cows were**n't** in the barn.
12. It was**n't** a good plan.
13. Tanya and Lynn were**n't** on the bus.
14. The letter was**n't** on my desk.
15. You were**n't** on time for class.
16. He was**n't** happy about it.
17. The children were**n't** at the playground.
18. It was**n't** important.
19. We were**n't** at the Mexican restaurant.
20. My grandparents were**n't** in the waiting room.
21. The girls were**n't** at the dance last night.
22. I was**n't** the first to finish the exam.
23. The lights were**n't** on.
24. They were**n't** at the concert.
25. Michelle was**n't** in class today.
26. He was**n't** sick yesterday.
27. The pie was**n't** very good.
28. The apples were**n't** ripe.
29. It was**n't** a very good idea.
30. The restaurant was**n't** open.

Pronunciation of -S on Plural Nouns

The -s on plural nouns must be firmly pronounced.

| dog<u>s</u> | cat<u>s</u> | monkey<u>s</u> | hand<u>s</u> | trip<u>s</u> |
| song<u>s</u> | pen<u>s</u> | towel<u>s</u> | lamp<u>s</u> | fork<u>s</u> |

Listen carefully and repeat the following sentences.

1. Her rings, chains, and earrings are gold.
2. I bought apples, pears, bananas, and grapes to make my famous fruit salad.
3. Mary has two brothers and four sisters.
4. The cups, forks, and spoons are already on the table.
5. Put on your socks and shoes.
6. My uncle has cows, pigs, and chickens on his farm.
7. We saw raccoons, skunks, birds, and bears in the woods.
8. I need pencils, pens, erasers, books, and binders to start school.
9. The kids left the toys, marbles, games, and puzzles all over the floor.
10. She washed the plates, bowls, and utensils but left the pots and pans for me.
11. Most pet stores sell puppies, kittens, birds, hamsters, and pet supplies.
12. Johnny has jellybeans, lollipops, and gumballs in his pockets.
13. We bought blueberries, strawberries, and raspberries at the market.
14. We will serve hamburgers and hot dogs to our friends.
15. I need stamps and envelopes to send the letters to our customers.
16. What are the reasons for her decisions?
17. Put the lifejackets, paddles, fishing rods, and worms in the boat.
18. He is afraid of storms, clowns, dogs, and bugs.
19. We went to shows, museums, and plays in New York City.
20. Mike gave his girlfriend flowers and chocolates for her birthday.
21. There are no periods, commas, question marks, or exclamation marks in your documents.
22. The students and teachers sold muffins, cookies, and doughnuts at the bake sale.
23. My mother will wash the sheets and blankets today.
24. I put onions, carrots, green beans, and potatoes in the beef stew.
25. They need more nails and screws to finish the renovations.
26. The days, weeks, months, and years pass by so quickly.
27. There are many great high schools and universities in the United States.
28. The bathrooms, bedrooms, and closets are not very big in my house.
29. We forgot the batteries for the flashlights when we went camping.
30. The frogs are sitting on the lily pads.

Pronunciation of -*ES* on Plural Nouns

When **-es** *is added to nouns that end in* **ch, sh, x, z,** *or* **s** *to create the plural form, the* **-es** *is firmly pronounced as a separate syllable.*

brush**es**   dress**es**   box**es**   peach**es**   quizz**es**

Listen carefully and repeat the following sentences.

1. How many class**es** do you have this semester?
2. How did you get the scratch**es** on your leg?
3. We want to test your reflex**es**.
4. Please send all the fax**es** today.
5. You need to trim the branch**es** on your trees.
6. All the waitress**es** in this restaurant are nice.
7. What would you wish for if you had three wish**es**?
8. She had several illness**es** last year.
9. Put the dirty dish**es** in the sink please.
10. There is a pack of match**es** in my coat pocket.
11. She has two e-mail address**es**.
12. The box**es** are full of books and magazines.
13. He had many success**es** in his life.
14. I have a couple of watch**es**.
15. Where are my glass**es**?
16. I need crutch**es** to walk because I broke my ankle.
17. Are the bus**es** on strike today?
18. Thank you for all the kiss**es**.
19. Why are there four brush**es** in your purse?
20. The insurance company will compensate you for your loss**es**.
21. My teacher always gives us quizz**es**.
22. There are many old church**es** in Montreal.
23. Do you like peach**es** or pears?
24. The beach**es** are beautiful in Hawaii.
25. Look at the wild fox**es** near the tree.
26. All the boss**es** are in a meeting.
27. There are ash**es** on the carpet.
28. What are the municipal tax**es** on this property?
29. Leave the toothbrush**es** in the bathroom.
30. There were many cockroach**es** in the hotel.

Pronunciation of -*S* on Verbs

When -s is added to the verb for third person singular in the simple present tense, it must be firmly pronounced.

he runs	the boy jumps
she sings	my mother cooks
it walks	the dog barks

Listen carefully and repeat the following sentences.

1. She eats meat and poultry.
2. It barks all day.
3. Roy writes music.
4. The phone rings all day.
5. My boss wears a tie every day.
6. She drinks black coffee.
7. It needs some work.
8. The machine gives change.
9. She buys nice perfume.
10. Not everybody snores.
11. He hates winter but he loves summer.
12. Marco rents a small apartment.
13. It reminds me of you.
14. The movie ends in 20 minutes.
15. It bothers me when you do that.
16. She swims like a fish.
17. That man says hello to everybody.
18. He owes me money.
19. Caroline believes you.
20. Bobby acts like a child.
21. Sandra gossips about everyone.
22. It jumps really high.
23. Linda feels better today.
24. It disturbs everyone around you.
25. Jeremy earns a good salary.
26. My husband makes breakfast for me every morning.
27. He parks his car in the parking lot.
28. The show starts at 8 o'clock.
29. She owns a busy restaurant downtown.
30. Your son draws really well for his age.

Pronunciation of -S on Nouns and Verbs

When -s is added to the verb for third person singular in the simple present tense and the nouns that follow are plural, the -s must be firmly pronounced on the verb and all nouns.

He likes apples, pears, and bananas.
She plays with kittens, puppies, and dolls.
It buries balls, bones, and sticks.

Listen carefully and repeat the following sentences.

1. My dog likes bones and other treats.
2. He blames the girls for that.
3. She dislikes spiders and snakes.
4. He works with his hands.
5. Marco lives with his friends.
6. He sells cars, trucks, and motorcycles.
7. Grace thinks that cookies are better than muffins.
8. Ruby writes short stories and poems.
9. It weighs 40 pounds.
10. My aunt moves every two years.
11. She wears blue jeans and white socks almost every day.
12. Anne likes braids and bows in her hair.
13. My teacher uses pictures and lots of examples when she explains the lessons.
14. Mr. King paints bedrooms and bathrooms but not kitchens.
15. My neighbor grows carrots, peppers, tomatoes, yellow beans, and cucumbers in her garden.
16. The maid cleans bathtubs, sinks, and showers but not toilets.
17. She knows the names of all the students.
18. He collects stamps and old coins.
19. Uncle George repairs bikes, clocks, and broken toys.
20. It costs thousands of dollars.
21. Elizabeth wears rings on her fingers and toes.
22. My grandmother knits slippers, scarves, mittens, and hats for the kids.
23. Chris scribbles on the lockers and desks at school.
24. He works days, nights, and weekends.
25. That store sells balloons, candles, games, and other things for birthday parties.
26. Judy sees birds and butterflies when she walks in the woods.
27. She plants tulips, daffodils, lilies, and daisies in the summer.
28. Virginia spends her money on shoes, belts, hats, and coats.
29. He brings snacks and drinks when he travels with his kids.
30. My son orders books, lamps, blankets, and other household items online.

Pronunciation of -*ES* on Verbs

*When -**es** is added to verbs that end in **ch**, **ss**, **se**, **ge**, **ce**, **sh**, **x**, and **z** for third person singular in the simple present tense, the -**es** ending is firmly pronounced as a separate syllable.*

he fix**es**	he pass**es**	he chang**es**
she wash**es**	she los**es**	she quizz**es**
it catch**es**	it bounc**es**	it sneez**es**

Listen carefully and repeat the following sentences.

1. She teach**es** French at the adult education center.
2. David seiz**es** every opportunity.
3. He crush**es** grapes to make wine
4. Ronald pass**es** by my house every day.
5. He push**es** the employees too hard.
6. Jean watch**es** every game on TV.
7. He fix**es** all the broken furniture.
8. My brother kiss**es** all the girls in school.
9. She mix**es** all the ingredients in a bowl.
10. She match**es** her pants with her sweaters.
11. It bounc**es** when you drop it.
12. Claude manag**es** four apartment buildings.
13. The bee buzz**es** in my garden.
14. Ben choos**es** to join the army.
15. He guess**es** all the answers in class.
16. Paul recogniz**es** a lot of people at the conference.
17. She excus**es** herself every time she sneez**es**.
18. Lynn discuss**es** everything with her husband.
19. Our boss notic**es** our hard work and dedication.
20. Robert chang**es** his car every two years.
21. Katrina blush**es** when the teacher asks her a question.
22. My aunt wash**es** her pantyhose in the sink.
23. The baby reach**es** for everything.
24. It reduc**es** the risk of heart disease.
25. The lake freez**es** in November.
26. Tina wax**es** her legs for the summer.
27. Sara wish**es** that she never quit her job.
28. He rais**es** the pric**es** every year.
29. Roxanne miss**es** her boyfriend.
30. My dog damag**es** everything in the house.

Pronunciation of *-ED* on Verbs Ending in *T* or *D*

*When **-ed** is added to verbs that end in **t** or **d**, the ending **-ted** or **-ded** must be firmly pronounced as a separate syllable.*

to want	→	wan**ted**
to accept	→	accep**ted**
to paint	→	pain**ted**
to attend	→	atten**ded**
to decide	→	deci**ded**
to guide	→	gui**ded**

Listen carefully and repeat the following sentences.

1. His father foun**ded** this company in 1953.
2. We expec**ted** a better return from our investment.
3. We loa**ded** everything into the truck.
4. The snowman mel**ted** in the spring.
5. Our relationship en**ded** last summer.
6. The two colors blen**ded** well together.
7. We chat**ted** for a long time on the computer.
8. Not everyone atten**ded** the annual company picnic.
9. Laura ha**ted** vegetables when she was young.
10. I pos**ted** the job openings on the bulletin board.
11. Randy presen**ted** the prize to the winner.
12. It soun**ded** like my boss on the phone.
13. We deci**ded** to move to the country.
14. It tas**ted** like chicken.
15. Sue star**ted** her new job yesterday.
16. He nod**ded** to show his approval.
17. I negotia**ted** the terms of the contract.
18. He inclu**ded** pictures in his presentation.
19. Suzanne consul**ted** a specialist for her skin condition.
20. I wai**ted** outside in the car.
21. Everybody benefi**ted** from the profits we made.
22. She ad**ded** more garlic to the sauce.
23. They visi**ted** Niagara Falls last summer.
24. I pain**ted** my room blue but I don't think I like it.
25. He adjus**ted** the mirrors on the car.
26. He dona**ted** it to charity.
27. The teacher divi**ded** the kids into groups of four.
28. We elec**ted** Steven.
29. She depen**ded** on the support of her family.
30. I submit**ted** the report last Thursday.

Pronunciation of -*ED* on Verbs Not Ending in *T* or *D*

When -**ed** *is added to verbs that do not end in* **t** *or* **d**, *the* -**ed** *is not pronounced as a separate syllable but as a one syllable ending. The final sound for verbs ending in* **f, k, p, s, ch,** *and* **sh** *is* **t**. *The final sound for verbs ending in* **b, g, j, l, m, n, r, v,** *and* **z** *is* **d**. *Note that sometimes other sounds are produced by certain letters. The letter* **c** *may sound like* **s**, *the* **gh** *may sound like* **f** *and the* **s** *may sound like* **z**.

to share	→	shar**ed** (d)
to walk	→	walk**ed** (t)
to raise	→	rais**ed** (d)
to chase	→	chas**ed** (t)

Listen carefully and repeat the following sentences.

1. I dream**ed** that I danc**ed** with a prince.
   (d)   (t)

2. She complain**ed** about everything the whole time we talk**ed**.
   (d)   (t)

3. It surpris**ed** me when she sign**ed** the check.
   (d)   (d)

4. The children touch**ed** and smell**ed** the flowers in the garden.
   (t)   (d)

5. She blush**ed** when he whisper**ed** in her ear.
   (t)   (d)

6. We walk**ed** along the river and talk**ed** all afternoon.
   (t)   (t)

7. I brush**ed** the cat and watch**ed** the news at the same time.
   (t)   (t)

8. She punish**ed** her son because he scratch**ed** her car with his bike.
   (t)   (t)

9. He hurri**ed** into the house and answer**ed** the phone but he miss**ed** the call.
   (d)   (d)   (t)

10. She notic**ed** that she earn**ed** more than her husband last year.
    (t)   (d)

11. As soon as he arriv**ed**, I told him that he still ow**ed** me money.
    (d)   (d)

12. Mario deni**ed** that he fail**ed** the exam because he was embarrass**ed** and asham**ed**.
    (d)   (d)   (d)   (d)

13. It bother**ed** and annoy**ed** me when you pick**ed** my roses.
    (d)   (d)   (t)

14. I scrap**ed** my elbow and injur**ed** my arm when I tumbl**ed** down the stairs.
      t   d   d

15. He smil**ed** and kiss**ed** me then vanish**ed** into the night.
    d   t   t

16. The man reach**ed** into his pocket, pull**ed** out a tissue, and wip**ed** her tears.
        t   d   t

17. I clos**ed** my eyes and listen**ed** to the soft music.
   d   d

18. We believ**ed** her because she prov**ed** it.
    d   d

19. He destroy**ed** my grass when he park**ed** his tractor on it.
     d   t

20. We all agre**ed** that Simon manag**ed** the company very well.
     d   d

21. She spell**ed** my name wrong, so I eras**ed** it.
    d   t

22. We order**ed** a lot of wood for the winter and we chopp**ed** it all weekend.
    d   t

23. It rain**ed** after we wash**ed** our car.
   d   t

24. She cook**ed** the meat and boil**ed** the vegetables.
    t   d

25. Cory pass**ed** his final exam and obtain**ed** his certificate.
     t   d

26. The boat sail**ed** peacefully on the lake while we observ**ed** the stars in the sky.
      d   d

27. She dress**ed** the baby before the babysitter arriv**ed**.
     t   d

28. My students laugh**ed** and jok**ed** all day in class.
       t   t

29. She mix**ed** and stirr**ed** my drink, then pour**ed** it into a tall glass.
    t   d   d

30. We thank**ed** her for her hospitality, then we wav**ed** goodbye.
    t   d

Pronunciation of Verbs Ending in -*ED* – Mixed Exercise
*Pronounce the following past tense verbs ending in -ed with the **ted**, **ded**, **t**, or **d** sound as indicated.*

Listen carefully and repeat the following sentences.

1. We ren**ted** a car for the weekend.
2. I clean**ed** and tid**ied** the house, then I relax**ed** all evening.

      d   d   t
3. Sara inheri**ted** the property from her grandparents.
4. She dedica**ted** the book to her children.
5. They lower**ed** the price, so we purchas**ed** two.

       d   t
6. Frank repea**ted** the same mistake twice.
7. The teacher exten**ded** the due date to Friday.
8. My plane lan**ded** at eleven o'clock.
9. That's why I sugges**ted** that you stay overnight.
10. The mechanic repair**ed** my car and I sav**ed** a lot of money.

                        d   d
11. They nee**ded** help with the fundraiser, so we help**ed** them.

                                                t
12. They argu**ed** and yell**ed** all night and it disturb**ed** the neighbors.

      d   d   d
13. We repor**ted** it to the police.
14. The storm only las**ted** a couple of hours.
15. Amanda wish**ed**, hop**ed**, and pray**ed** for a baby sister.

             t   t   d
16. We toas**ted** the marshmallows over the fire.
17. No one accep**ted** the new working conditions.
18. I ask**ed** the waiter for the bill, then realiz**ed** that I had forgotten my wallet.

     t   d
19. It help**ed** when we employ**ed** extra workers for the season.

    t   d
20. I wan**ted** to call you but I fell asleep.
21. Our employer provi**ded** all the training.
22. He connec**ted** the two wires together.
23. Your dog chas**ed** me and I jump**ed** over the fence and I ripp**ed** my pants.

          t   t   t
24. I look**ed** both ways, then procee**ded** to cross the street.

   t

25. Who crea**ted** this work of art?

26. All the money was there when I coun**ted** it.

27. The kids play**ed** in the pool and jump**ed** on the trampoline all afternoon.
             d   t

28. I indica**ted** my overtime hours on my timesheet.

29. She reques**ted** a slow song.

30. We lik**ed** it when you liv**ed** next door.
      t   d

Pronunciation of S like Z

The **s** *in most words is pronounced like* **s** *as in:*

cla**ss**	**s**ee	tap**s**	fir**s**t	hope**s**
s	s	s	s	s

The **s** *in some words is pronounced like* **z** *as in:*

mu**s**ic	ha**s**	arrive**s**	bean**s**	choo**s**e
z	z	z	z	z

Listen carefully and repeat the following sentences.

1. How many day**s** are in a week?

z

2. Did you **s**ee the big moo**s**e in the fore**s**t?

s   s   s

3. It wa**s** our anniver**s**ary ye**s**terday.

z   s   s

4. Doe**s** the train **s**top at all the **s**tation**s**?

z   s   s   z

5. She **s**tudie**s** Chine**s**e and find**s** that it i**s s**o ea**s**y to learn.

s   z   z   z   z s   z

6. I am a**s** wi**s**e a**s** you.

z   z   z

7. Who i**s** making all the noi**s**e down**s**tair**s**?

z   z   s   z

8. The bu**s** i**s** alway**s** late.

s z   z

9. Blow your no**s**e, plea**s**e.

z   z

10. I like country mu**s**ic al**s**o.

z   s

11. Her eye**s** are blue.

z

12. Which pur**s**e did you choo**s**e?

s   z

13. Don't **s**tand **s**o clo**s**e to the flame**s**.

s   s   s   z

14. Please clo**s**e all the blind**s** and the door**s**.

z   z   z   z

15. I will adverti**s**e my new bu**s**ine**ss** in the new**s**paper**s**.

z   z   s   z   z

16. He advi**s**ed u**s** that he wa**s** working at the ca**s**ino.

z   s   z   s

17. She **says** that she**'s** busy, **so** please be **s**ilent for a few **seconds**.
        s z   z   z s   z   s   s   z

18. I cut the ro**s**e**s** with the **scissors**.
              z z   s z z

19. I gue**ss** that my cou**s**in know**s** the an**s**wer becau**s**e he **is smart**.
          s   z   z   s   z z s

20. He get**s** ga**s** near hi**s** hou**s**e when he goe**s** to work.
             s   s   z   s   z

21. Our bo**ss is** very wi**s**e to give u**s** a rai**s**e thi**s** year.
            s z   z   s   z   s

22. **S**usan crie**s** when she **s**ee**s** **s**pider**s** and **s**nake**s**.
        s z   z   s z s   z   s   s

23. She pretend**s** that she know**s** what it mean**s**.
               z   z   z

24. My hu**s**band **s**nore**s** when he **s**nooze**s** on the **s**ofa.
          z   s   z   s   z   s

25. It **s**eem**s** that he approve**s** of my grade**s** thi**s** **s**eme**s**ter.
        s   z   z   z s s   s

26. He live**s** in a big old hou**s**e that belong**s** to hi**s** relative**s**.
          z   s   z   z   z

27. Thi**s** mean**s** that if he decide**s** to quit, I get the promotion and rai**s**e that I de**s**erve.
        s   z   z   z   z

28. She **says** that she hear**s** **s**trange noi**s**e**s** in the ba**s**ement.
        s z   z s   z z   s

29. Bear**s**, wolve**s**, raccoon**s**, and **s**kunk**s** live in the wood**s**.
       z   z   z   s   s   z

30. He love**s** to eat bean**s**, egg**s**, and toa**s**t with hi**s** **s**ister every **S**unday.
         z   z   z   s   z s s   s

EXERCISE
P·13

Pronunciation of Words with *TH* (1)
One of the most difficult sounds to pronounce in English is **th**. *It takes a lot of practice to be able to correctly pronounce this letter combination.*

Sometimes **th** *has a very pronounced and distinct sound.*
ba**th**   **th**ree   **th**esaurus   **th**umb   **Th**ursday

Other times **th** *is more subtle and has a softer pronunciation.*
that   **th**e   wea**th**er   fa**th**er   **th**ey

Listen carefully and repeat the following sentences.

1. I **th**ought of **th**inking of **th**anking you—so **th**anks.
2. He has a **th**orn in his **th**umb.
3. I am very **th**irsty.
4. I **th**ink **th**at **Th**elma has **th**irteen **th**ousand dollars in **th**e bank.
5. **Th**is is **th**e **th**ousand**th** **th**oughtful **th**ank-you card **th**at I received **th**is week.
6. My mo**th**er, bro**th**er, and fa**th**er **th**ought **th**at **Th**eodore **th**e **Th**ird was **th**irteen on **Th**ursday.
7. **Th**ere's a **th**ick **th**esaurus over **th**ere.
8. We are en**th**usiastic about **th**e grow**th** in our company **th**is year.
9. The pan**th**er is a ru**th**less hunter.
10. **Th**is faceclo**th** is fil**th**y.
11. He can't talk because he has a mou**th**ful of mou**th**wash.
12. I won **th**ree hundred and **th**irty-**th**ree **th**ousand **th**ree hundred and **th**irty-**th**ree dollars on the lottery.
13. Bo**th** birds are ba**th**ing in the birdba**th**.
14. It is an au**th**entic ame**th**yst and it is my bir**th**stone.
15. Never**th**eless, your **th**eory is bo**th**ersome.
16. What are **th**e leng**th**, wid**th**, and dep**th** of **th**is ba**th**tub?
17. **Th**ere are o**th**er soo**th**ing me**th**ods for childbir**th**.
18. **Th**ey will ga**th**er berries fur**th**er down the pa**th**.
19. One of my bro**th**ers is a blacksmi**th** and **th**e o**th**er is a locksmi**th**.
20. Nei**th**er **th**e au**th**or nor **th**e coau**th**or told **th**e tru**th** about every**th**ing.
21. You have to swear, o**th**erwise **th**e oa**th** means no**th**ing.
22. Did **th**e a**th**lete finish nin**th** or ten**th** in **th**e mara**th**on?
23. You don't have **th**e au**th**ority to au**th**orize any**th**ing.
24. What is **th**e afterma**th** of **th**e ear**th**quake?
25. Al**th**ough he has ar**th**ritis, he is heal**th**y and a**th**letic.
26. An**th**ony wants to celebrate his **th**irtie**th** birthday wi**th** **th**em in A**th**ens.
27. Your ba**th**robe is on **th**e ba**th**mat in **th**e ba**th**room.
28. **Th**ere is a **th**umbtack undernea**th** the desk.
29. I don't know whe**th**er **th**ey went nor**th** or sou**th**.
30. **Th**ey **th**ink **th**at **th**eir **th**in **th**ighs are **th**ick.

Pronunciation of Words with *TH* (2)

One of the most difficult sounds to pronounce in English is **th**. *It takes a lot of practice to be able to correctly pronounce this letter combination.*

Sometimes **th** *has a very pronounced and distinct sound.*

my**th**   **th**read   weal**th**y   **th**ird   fai**th**

Other times **th** *is more subtle and has a softer pronunciation.*

bro**th**er   **th**ough   ano**th**er   fea**th**er   lea**th**er

Listen carefully and repeat the following sentences.

1. An**th**ropology is **th**e study of human beings.
2. Mo**th**s don't bo**th**er **th**em ei**th**er.
3. **Th**ank you for **th**e lea**th**er shoes. You are so **th**oughtful.
4. I have to buy some **th**read and a **th**imble.
5. E**th**ics is a **th**eory of moral values.
6. I would ra**th**er have a fea**th**er pillow.
7. You don't need a **th**esaurus for your ma**th** class.
8. Don't **th**row **th**ose **th**ings at your bro**th**er.
9. I **th**ink **th**at he **th**ought I was **th**rough **th**ough.
10. Looking at **th**e Ear**th** from a satellite is **th**rilling and brea**th**taking.
11. Can you **th**aw some**th**ing for supper?
12. **Th**is **th**ermometer is broken; **th**erefore I need ano**th**er one.
13. It is a my**th** **th**at **th**e king sat on his **th**rone on his bir**th**day and **th**anked **th**e goldsmi**th** **th**ree times.
14. I have fai**th** in **th**e you**th** of today.
15. **Th**ey don't know **th**e rhy**th**m ei**th**er.
16. My **th**roat hurt **th**roughout **th**e day on **Th**ursday.
17. He committed **th**e crime wi**th** malice afore**th**ought.
18. **Th**ey sang **th**e national an**th**em in class today.
19. Was **th**at a **th**reat?
20. The baby likes to ba**th**e in **th**e ba**th** wi**th** fro**th**y bubbles.
21. My fa**th**er took **th**e **th**ermos to work **th**is morning.
22. I can't brea**th**e wi**th** all **th**e **th**ick smoke in **th**e air.
23. I am **th**ankful **th**at **th**e **th**ief didn't steal my **th**oroughbred or my **th**esis.
24. I **th**ink Ar**th**ur is very weal**th**y because he just bought his **th**irteen**th** ba**th**ing suit.
25. My grandmo**th**er has trouble brea**th**ing in hot and humid wea**th**er.
26. **Th**ey did a **th**orough search benea**th** **th**e bridge.
27. I **th**ink **th**at **th**ere were **th**irty **th**ousand mo**th**s in **th**e **th**eatre.
28. Don't bo**th**er me please. I have a too**th**ache.
29. On **th**e **th**ird **Th**ursday of every mon**th**, we buy **th**irty-**th**ree spools of **th**read.
30. I **th**ink **th**at **th**e **th**under bo**th**ers my grandfa**th**er.

When *TH* is not Pronounced *TH*
Sometimes the letter combination **th** *is not pronounced as such.*
It can be pronounced as a **t** *sound as in:*

an**th**ill   **Th**omas   cour**th**ouse

Or it can be silent, as in:

as**th**ma   clo**th**es   clo**th**esline

Listen carefully and repeat the following sentences.

1. The transition to adul**th**ood has many challenges.
2. She lives in a beautiful pen**th**ouse in New York City.
3. I am happy that I don't have an ou**th**ouse in my back yard.
4. We are going to move to Cha**th**am.
5. There are enormous po**th**oles on the roads in Montreal.
6. Did you ever go to **Th**ailand?
7. I felt a little ligh**th**eaded on the plane.
8. Use the po**th**older to take the pot out of the oven.
9. There are many an**th**ills on the patio in my back yard.
10. Have you ever climbed to the top of a ligh**th**ouse?
11. They were rewarded with knigh**th**ood for their bravery.
12. The rat ran down the ra**th**ole.
13. Many years ago, secretaries were required to know shor**th**and.
14. She had seen firs**th**and the effects of the experiment.
15. He wants to go into the pries**th**ood.
16. We rent a boa**th**ouse to park our boat for the summer months.
17. The television reporters were at the cour**th**ouse today.
18. **Th**omas and Terry are twins.
19. I need new clo**th**es to start school.
20. As**th**ma is a chronic lung disease.
21. Nelson Mandela helped to end Apar**th**eid in South Africa.
22. Did you hang the sheets on the clo**th**esline?
23. You forgot to put the clo**th**espins back in the bag.
24. They are very young and not ready for paren**th**ood.
25. A foo**th**ill is a small hill at the foot of a higher hill.
26. I looked out the por**th**ole and finally saw land.
27. **Th**yme leaves are used for seasoning.
28. An is**th**mus is a narrow strip of land with sea on either side.
29. They say that one child in ten is as**th**matic.
30. Fla**th**ead Lake is a large natural lake in northwest Montana.

Pronunciation of Ordinal Numbers and Fractions

*The sound of **th** is used after each ordinal number except for all numbers ending in 1, 2, and 3. The three exceptions to this rule are 11, 12, and 13, which take the **-th** ending. All letter endings for each ordinal number must be firmly pronounced.*

1st	fir**st**	4th	four**th**	11th	eleven**th**
2nd	seco**nd**	5th	fif**th**	12th	twel**fth**
3rd	thi**rd**	6th	six**th**	13th	thirteen**th**
21st	twenty-fir**st**	43rd	forty-thi**rd**	87th	eighty-seven**th**
38th	thirty-eigh**th**	71st	seventy-fir**st**	64th	sixty-four**th**
92nd	ninety-seco**nd**	55th	fifty-fif**th**	22nd	twenty-seco**nd**

To pronounce ordinal numbers that are multiples of 10 starting with 20, add **-eth** as the pronunciation ending. In the written form, the **y** is changed to **i**.

20th	twent**ieth**	50th	fift**ieth**	80th	eight**ieth**
30th	thirt**ieth**	60th	sixt**ieth**	90th	ninet**ieth**
40th	fort**ieth**	70th	sevent**ieth**		

When pronouncing fractions, if the numerator is 1, then the denominator is firmly pronounced with a singular ending.

1/6	one six**th**	1/9	one nin**th**	1/17	one seventeen**th**
1/3	one thi**rd**	1/8	one eigh**th**	1/11	one eleven**th**
1/5	one fif**th**	1/14	one fourteen**th**	1/10	one ten**th**

When the numerator is 2 or more, then the denominator is firmly pronounced with a plural ending.

2/6	two six**ths**	7/10	seven ten**ths**	3/5	three fif**ths**
4/9	four nin**ths**	6/8	six eigh**ths**	9/17	nine seventeen**ths**
2/3	two thi**rds**	8/11	eight eleven**ths**	4/21	four twenty-fir**sts**

Notes:

The fraction ½ is always read as *one half*.

The fraction ¼ can be read as *one quarter* or *one fourth*.

The fraction ¾ can be read as *three quarters* or *three fourths*.

Fractions with a denominator of 12 are pronounced with an **f** sound and not a **v** sound.

12	twel**ve**	1/12	one twel**fth**	5/12	five twel**fths***

(*possibly the most difficult letter combination to pronounce in the English language!)

Listen carefully and repeat the following sentences.

1. We are now living in the **twenty-first** century.
   (21st)

2. I need **three-quarters** of a cup of butter for this recipe.
   (3/4)

3. My birthday is on January **nineteenth**.
   (19th)

4. I also need **one-eighth** teaspoon of cinnamon for this recipe.
   (1/8)

5. Christmas is on December **twenty-fifth**.
   (25th)

6. **Seventeen thirtieths** of the kids in my class are boys.
   (17/30)

7. Christmas Eve is on December **twenty-fourth**.
   (24th)

8. He wants only **one-quarter** teaspoon of sugar in his tea.
   (1/4)

9. The mortgage is due on the **twelfth** of every month.
   (12th)

10. Valentine's Day is on February **fourteenth**.
    (14th)

11. Can you cut off **three-sixteenths** of an inch from this piece of wood?
    (3/16)

12. New Year's Eve is on December **thirty-first**.
    (31st)

13. Can you lend me **two-thirds** of a cup of vegetable oil?
    (2/3)

14. **Five-twelfths** of the girls in my class have blond hair.
    (5/12)

15. My parents are celebrating their **thirtieth** wedding anniversary this weekend.
    (30th)

16. What is on the **ninety-ninth** page of that book?
    (99th)

17. My grandmother just had her **ninety-second** birthday.
    (92nd)

18. They live on **Forty-Seventh** Avenue.
    (47th)

19. **Eighty eightieths**, **twelve twelfths,** and **six sixths** all equal one.
    (80/80)   (12/12)   (6/6)

20. My accountant works on the **thirty-third** floor in that building.
    (33rd)

21. Bill Clinton was the **forty-second** president of the United States.
    (42nd)

22. John A. Macdonald was the **first** prime minister of Canada.
    (1st)

23. **Eighteen twenty-ninths** of the people voted for Peter.
    (18/29)

24. Friday the **thirteenth** is an unlucky day.
    (13th)

25. The **Second** World War lasted from 1939 to1945.
    (2nd)

26. The rate of interest increased **seven-tenths** of a percent.
    (7/10)

27. I can't believe you ate **one half** of the extra large pizza.
    (1/2)

28. It's even harder to believe that you also ate **eleven-twelfths** of the cookies.
    (11/12)

29. We had a big party for his **fortieth** birthday.
    (40th)

30. Spring is **three-twelfths** or **one-fourth** of the calendar year.
    (3/12)   (1/4)

Pronunciation of Words Containing the Hard *G* Sound
*Sometimes the **g** in words is pronounced as a hard **g** sound.*

goat   bu**g**   **g**lass   **g**reat   pro**g**ress

Listen carefully and repeat the following sentences.

1. Are you married or sin**g**le?
2. Don't ar**g**ue with your sister.
3. You have **g**um on your shoe.
4. I saw a **g**orilla at the zoo.
5. Do you want to play **g**olf this afternoon?
6. We made a lot of pro**g**ress on our report this week.
7. She has two **g**old rin**g**s.
8. I have a **g**ift for you.
9. Look at the **g**oose near the lake.
10. I need to stop for **g**as.
11. That is a bi**g** pi**g**.
12. The **g**irls are **g**i**gg**ling a**g**ain.
13. I for**g**et my **g**lasses re**g**ularly.
14. It's a **g**ood idea to use **g**loves to **g**ather **g**rapes.
15. **G**ive your **g**randmother a bi**g** hu**g**.
16. I **g**uess this **g**uy is **g**uilty.
17. She has **g**one to the **g**rocery store to **g**et some **g**arlic.
18. A **g**roup of **g**eese is called a **g**a**gg**le.
19. **G**o **g**et e**gg**s please.
20. **G**reen **g**rass **g**rows on the **g**round.
21. We have a **g**reat **g**roup of **g**raduates this year.
22. It was a **g**loomy and fo**gg**y day.
23. The apple tree will **g**row **g**radually.
24. I can **g**uarantee you that my do**g** is not a**gg**ressive.
25. The tall **g**uy in the **g**rey suit is the **g**room.
26. I already said **g**oodbye to **G**re**gg**.
27. The **g**re**g**arious **g**irl be**g**an to wi**gg**le her nose for the **g**uests.
28. My **g**irlfriend and I made whole **g**rain ba**g**els to**g**ether.
29. Don't **g**ar**g**le with your milk.
30. I am **g**lad that they are **g**one.

Pronunciation of Words Containing the Soft *G* Sound

Sometimes the **g** *in words is pronounced as a soft* **g** *which is pronounced like* **j**.

ca**g**e   dan**g**er   **g**entle   a**g**ent   **g**enius

Listen carefully and repeat the following sentences.

1. You will have more ener**g**y if you exercise.
2. It is ur**g**ent that we do emer**g**ency sur**g**ery on the **g**iraffe.
3. He is a **g**entleman from **G**ermany.
4. Don't run too close to the ed**g**e.
5. I am aller**g**ic to your cat.
6. Do you have the ori**g**inal copy of this document?
7. The left mar**g**in is one inch.
8. We have a hu**g**e bud**g**et for that.
9. He is a secret a**g**ent.
10. Can you enlar**g**e this picture?
11. A banana is not a ve**g**etable.
12. I apolo**g**ize for eating your oran**g**e.
13. He has a lot of knowled**g**e about en**g**ines.
14. Can you change the ink cartrid**g**e for me?
15. Don't exa**gg**erate when you tell a story.
16. **G**erry wants to be an en**g**ineer.
17. It is a challen**g**e for some people to go to colle**g**e.
18. **G**erms are dan**g**erous.
19. Do you like the smell of **g**in**g**er?
20. The story had a tra**g**ic and stran**g**e conclusion.
21. I ur**g**e you to call the police if you see the fu**g**itive in your re**g**ion.
22. Be **g**entle with it because it is very fra**g**ile.
23. Don't talk to stran**g**ers.
24. I saw a **g**iant panda at the zoo.
25. Use your lo**g**ic to solve the puzzle.
26. You are a **g**enius.
27. At what a**g**e will you retire?
28. He knows a lot of ma**g**ic tricks.
29. I don't like to see a bird in a ca**g**e.
30. In **g**eneral, it can **g**enerate a lot of ener**g**y.

Pronunciation of Words Containing the Soft and Hard *G* Sound

*Some words contain both the soft and hard **g** sound. The soft **g** is pronounced like **j**.*

su**gg**est	**g**or**g**eous	**g**eo**g**raphy	**g**arba**g**e	lan**g**ua**g**e
g j	g j	j g	g j	g j

Listen carefully and repeat the following sentences.

1. What a **g**or**g**eous summer day.
   g j

2. He is a pleasant and en**g**a**g**ing person to talk to.
   g j

3. Who is your **g**eo**g**raphy teacher this year?
   j g

4. What is your first lan**g**ua**g**e?
   g j

5. Put the **g**arba**g**e in the **g**arba**g**e can.
   g j g j

6. I finished packing my lu**gg**age last night.
   g j

7. They live in the **g**i**g**antic house on the hill.
   j g

8. Mary is en**g**a**g**ed to Paul.
   g j

9. We want to buy a house with a double **g**ara**g**e.
   g j

10. He buys all kinds of junk and **g**ad**g**ets at **g**ara**g**e sales.
    g j g j

11. Can you su**gg**est a good restaurant in the area?
    g j

12. I left my ba**gg**age on the plane.
    g j

13. You have to pay the mort**g**a**g**e every month.
    g j

14. That was a very good su**gg**estion.
    g j

15. She has **g**or**g**eous long hair.
    g j

16. Please close the **g**ara**g**e door.
    g j

17. There is a lot of **g**run**g**e in the bathtub.
    g j

18. Is your sister en**ga**ged to Julien?
                  g j

19. I will discuss your e**g**re**g**ious behavior in my class with your parents.
                  g   j

20. We can take a survey to **g**au**g**e the opinions of the residents.
                  g   j

21. Did you forgive him or do you still hold a **g**rud**g**e?
                             g   j

22. Do you know how deep the **g**or**g**e is?
                     g   j

23. She is studying **g**ynecolo**g**y at university.
                g   j

24. She will become a **g**ynecolo**g**ist.
               g   j

25. Is it **g**arba**g**e day tomorrow?
       g   j

26. **G**run**g**e music was very popular in the 1990s.
     g   j

27. He won't go in the dark and **g**run**g**y basement alone.
                     g   j

28. She can truly en**ga**ge an audience.
               g j

29. Does anyone have a better su**gg**estion?
                  g j

30. Stella has such an en**ga**ging personality.
               g j

EXERCISE
P·20

Pronunciation of Words Containing the Hard C Sound
*The hard **c** sound is pronounced like **k**.*

cu̱cumber   c̱abin   ele̱ctri̱c   mira̱cle   c̱orre̱ct

Listen carefully and repeat the following sentences.

1. Don't push the panic button.
2. It is music to my ears to hear the cardinals in the morning.
3. What is the forecast for economic development in your country?
4. Did you sign the contract?
5. I will bring my digital camera and camcorder.
6. You need a calculator for that calculus calculation.
7. She has a wonderful collection of cactus plants.
8. All the cabins at the camp were full.
9. The hands on the clock don't move counter clockwise.
10. Do you prefer to have candy or carrots and a cucumber for your snack?
11. He has a good career as an actor.
12. I will contact you in a couple of days.
13. In conclusion, they are trying to control the infection.
14. We will continue this conversation in the cafeteria.
15. Cory wants to communicate with the pilot of the helicopter.
16. I will call you when I get to California.
17. We saw a cocoon on the coconut tree.
18. It's a miracle that my black cat came back from Canada.
19. You will find the correct definition in the dictionary.
20. It's hard to play soccer when you have the hiccups.
21. Can you count the coins in the can?
22. The facts of this case are confusing and complicated.
23. Can you connect the cable to the computer without complaining?
24. Be careful when you cross the intersection at the corner.
25. Do caterpillars eat cauliflower?
26. They are trying to rescue that crazy cow and her calf from the cliff.
27. Your comments are not accurate.
28. The detectives are looking for clues about the crime.
29. Claudia put the candles on the carrot cake.
30. Can a duck catch a cold if it doesn't wear a scarf?

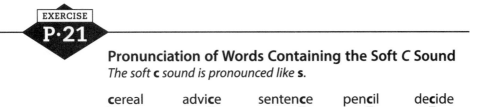

Pronunciation of Words Containing the Soft C Sound

*The soft **c** sound is pronounced like **s**.*

<u>c</u>ereal   advi<u>c</u>e   senten<u>c</u>e   pen<u>c</u>il   de<u>c</u>ide

Listen carefully and repeat the following sentences.

1. We will <u>c</u>ertainly <u>c</u>elebrate your birthday.
2. It is a ni<u>c</u>e <u>c</u>ity.
3. There is a <u>c</u>entipede on the <u>c</u>eiling.
4. I will have a <u>C</u>aesar salad.
5. Do you want a pie<u>c</u>e of <u>c</u>elery?
6. You have spaghetti sau<u>c</u>e on your fa<u>c</u>e.
7. My father de<u>c</u>ided to quit smoking <u>c</u>igars and <u>c</u>igarettes.
8. I hope that Vin<u>c</u>e will ask me to the dan<u>c</u>e.
9. Take a chan<u>c</u>e and throw the di<u>c</u>e.
10. I took my nie<u>c</u>e to the <u>c</u>inema twi<u>c</u>e.
11. There was an in<u>c</u>ident at the <u>c</u>emetery last night.
12. Can I give you some advi<u>c</u>e?
13. Lu<u>c</u>y bought a pen<u>c</u>il for 20 <u>c</u>ents.
14. The prin<u>c</u>e and prin<u>c</u>ess introdu<u>c</u>ed a new poli<u>c</u>y.
15. We are <u>c</u>ertain that there are mi<u>c</u>e in the <u>c</u>ellar.
16. The la<u>c</u>e on your fan<u>c</u>y dress is beautiful.
17. Who has the a<u>c</u>e of diamonds?
18. I noti<u>c</u>ed that there is a footprint in the <u>c</u>ement.
19. <u>I</u>cebergs are amazing to look at.
20. You will re<u>c</u>eive the noti<u>c</u>e in the mail.
21. Are you an American <u>c</u>itizen?
22. It was a pea<u>c</u>eful <u>c</u>eremony.
23. My offi<u>c</u>e is a great pla<u>c</u>e to work.
24. Do you have room servi<u>c</u>e?
25. Is that your best pri<u>c</u>e?
26. Nan<u>c</u>y and Tra<u>c</u>y haven't seen each other sin<u>c</u>e kindergarten.
27. Put the flowers in the <u>c</u>enter of the table.
28. Who won the ra<u>c</u>e during re<u>c</u>ess?
29. I never saw a purple fen<u>c</u>e.
30. Do you like spi<u>c</u>y ri<u>c</u>e?

Pronunciation of Words Containing the Hard and Soft C Sound

*Some words contain both the hard and soft **c** sound. The hard **c** is pronounced like a **k** and the soft **c** like **s**.*

cancel   accident   practice   accept   bicycle
k   s   k s   k   s   k s   s   k

Listen carefully and repeat the following sentences.

1. It is very hard to **conc**entrate when you play your drums.
     k   s

2. We have a lot of **c**onfiden**c**e in you.
      k   s

3. This is a very interesting **conc**ept.
      k   s

4. She is trying to **conc**eal the truth.
      k   s

5. That was a wonderful **conc**ert.
      k   s

6. He hung his **c**ertifi**c**ate on the wall for everyone to see.
      s   k

7. I would like to **canc**el my order.
      k   s

8. We were very **conc**erned about you.
      k   s

9. What is the **c**ir**c**umferen**c**e of this **c**ir**c**le?
      s   k   s   s   k

10. The ele**c**tri**c**ity went out during the storm.
      k   s

11. You should not **c**riti**c**ize other people.
      k   s

12. Don't a**cc**elerate in a residential zone.
      k s

13. I do not have a**cc**ess to your file.
      k s

14. Please be more spe**c**ifi**c** about the details.
      s   k

15. My kids love to go to the **c**ir**c**us.
      s   k

16. He has a French a**cc**ent.
      k s

17. I almost had an a**cc**ident on my way to work.
      k s

18. They say that pra**ctic**e makes perfect.
        k s

19. He is a su**cc**essful businessman in Hong Kong.
        k s

20. We didn't a**cc**ept the offer.
        k s

21. You need more **c**al**c**ium in your diet.
        k   s

22. What is the weight **c**apa**c**ity of this elevator?
        k   s

23. The good news will **c**ir**c**ulate rapidly.
        s   k

24. The i**c**i**c**le fell off the house and hit me on the head.
        s k

25. They are trying to find a va**cc**ine for this disease.
        k s

26. It's a **c**oin**c**iden**c**e that we have the same name and birth date.
        k   s   s

27. Do you re**cyc**le?
        s k

28. I was not aware of the **c**ir**c**umstan**c**es.
        s   k   s

29. He studied **c**ommer**c**e and international relations.
        k   s

30. There was no va**c**an**c**y in the motel, so we slept in the van.
        k   s

Pronunciation of Words with *CH* and *SH*

The letter combination ch *has a strong and firm pronunciation:*

child   **ch**erry   **ch**oose   **ch**ocolate   **ch**eese

The letter combination sh *has a softer and lighter pronunciation:*

she   **sh**ow   fi**sh**   **sh**ower   cra**sh**

Listen carefully and repeat the following sentences.

1. **Sh**e **sh**ould **ch**ange the **ch**annel.
2. I like **sh**redded or **ch**opped **ch**eddar **ch**eese **ch**unks in my **ch**icken soup.
3. I wi**sh** to add **ch**opped **sh**allots on the fre**sh** fi**sh** on my di**sh**.
4. **Sh**e **sh**ould **sh**are the **ch**erries with the **ch**ildren.
5. **Sh**elley **ch**ose to sell **sh**ells and **Sh**ane **ch**ose to sell **sh**oes.
6. The **Ch**inese **ch**ildren **sh**owed their tea**ch**er the **ch**opsticks.
7. Don't **ch**ew the **sh**ellfi**sh** because you will **ch**oke.
8. Ea**ch** egg **sh**ould hat**ch** a **ch**ubby **ch**ick.
9. **Ch**arles put on **ch**eap after**sh**ave after his **sh**ower.
10. The **sh**ip left the **sh**ore.
11. It's a **ch**allenge to **sh**eer a **sh**eep wearing **sh**orts.
12. I sat in the **sh**ade on my **ch**air at the bea**ch**.
13. The tea**ch**er used white **ch**alk to write the new Engli**sh** words on the blackboard.
14. Please put the **sh**ovel in the **sh**ed and the **ch**icken in the kit**ch**en.
15. It's my **ch**oice to work the day**sh**ift.
16. I **ch**eri**sh** our friend**sh**ip.
17. We put fresh mu**sh**rooms, ca**sh**ews, and **ch**ives in the salad.
18. The **sh**ampoo is on the **sh**elf.
19. I had a **ch**eeseburger and **ch**ips for lun**ch**.
20. My publi**sh**er will publi**sh** this **ch**apter.
21. **Sh**irley wants to play **ch**eckers but **Sh**ane wants to play **ch**ess.
22. I have to buy a lea**sh** for my **ch**ihuahua.
23. Pull the **ch**ain to flu**sh** the toilet.
24. Put the cu**sh**ion on the cou**ch**.
25. I took a **ch**ance and ca**sh**ed the **ch**eck.
26. He tried to cat**ch** the **ch**ipmunk with a net.
27. Your **ch**eckered **sh**irt is on the ben**ch** at the park.
28. **Sh**awn greets everyone with a firm hand**sh**ake.
29. The **ch**ildren put the **ch**eese on the di**sh** and the **ch**ocolate **ch**ip cookies on the plate.
30. **Ch**arlie has two scars on his **ch**in and one on his **ch**eek.

Pronunciation of *QU*

The letter combination **qu** *is pronounced like* **kw**.

quick   **qu**iet   a**qu**a   e**qu**al   e**qu**ipment

Listen carefully and repeat the following sentences.

1. Please be **qu**iet in my class.
2. My trip was free with my fre**qu**ent flyer points.
3. Can I **qu**ote you, Mr. Morris?
4. They will have a li**qu**idation sale.
5. Shane is the **qu**arterback on our football team.
6. Did you ever see a black s**qu**irrel?
7. Please indicate the **qu**ality and **qu**antity of the items you need.
8. She is over**qu**alified for this job.
9. Is it a solid or li**qu**id?
10. We re**qu**ire more information from you.
11. Please don't s**qu**eeze the lemons.
12. A s**qu**are has four e**qu**al sides.
13. My a**qu**arium is leaking.
14. He is not a friend, he is just an ac**qu**aintance.
15. We are not e**qu**ipped to go camping in the woods.
16. This will **qu**ench your thirst.
17. Are there any **qu**estions before we continue?
18. Two plus two e**qu**als four.
19. Why do you want to **qu**it the team?
20. I made a beautiful **qu**ilt for my bed.
21. The cows will be in **qu**arantine for six weeks.
22. I'm sorry but you don't have the **qu**alifications for this job.
23. The sea was a**qu**a blue.
24. Did you feel the small earth**qu**ake last night?
25. Can you identify e**qu**ivalent fractions?
26. Why do you always **qu**arrel with her?
27. The **qu**ick duck said, "**Qu**ack, **qu**ack."
28. The **qu**een **qu**ickly **qu**oted her cousin.
29. The s**qu**irrel re**qu**ired **qu**ality care.
30. A **qu**arter is not s**qu**are; it's round.

Pronunciation of *V*

The letter **v** *is often confused with* **w**, *but the pronunciation of* **v** *is very distinct.*

Victor	**v**iolin	lo**v**ely	**v**olcano	ri**v**er

Listen carefully and repeat the following sentences.

1. The results of this new **v**ersion may **v**ary.
2. I have to clean the sto**v**e and o**v**en today.
3. This old **v**ehicle has no **v**alue.
4. We grow **v**egetables in the **v**alley near our **v**illage.
5. **V**eronica is the new **v**ice principal for grade se**v**en.
6. Do you belie**v**e in hea**v**en?
7. That was a mar**v**ellous **v**olleyball game.
8. **V**egetarians ne**v**er eat **v**eal or li**v**er.
9. I take **v**itamins e**v**ery day.
10. E**v**en the **v**olunteers **v**oted for E**v**elyn.
11. We bought **v**arious sou**v**enirs in Las **V**egas.
12. Her **v**oice is **v**ery lo**v**ely.
13. We **v**isited a **v**olcano while we were on **v**acation.
14. **V**alerie lo**v**es to walk along the ri**v**er in the e**v**ening.
15. Ha**v**e you e**v**er been a **v**ictim of **v**iolence?
16. I lo**v**e your black **v**el**v**et glo**v**es.
17. They ha**v**e a **v**ariety of fla**v**ors. They e**v**en ha**v**e **v**anilla.
18. Your **v**ocabulary needs impro**v**ement.
19. The **v**acuum is **v**ery hea**v**y.
20. The **v**iolent wa**v**es made the boat roll o**v**er.
21. Ste**v**en dri**v**es a Cor**v**ette.
22. **V**i**v**iane didn't gi**v**e me a **v**alid reason.
23. Thank you for that **v**aluable ad**v**ice.
24. **V**ampires are more acti**v**e in the e**v**ening.
25. That is an in**v**asion of pri**v**acy.
26. He always tra**v**els with his **v**iolin.
27. She is **v**ery bra**v**e because she remo**v**ed the beehi**v**e.
28. All **v**erbs contain **v**owels.
29. He sol**v**ed the mystery and pro**v**ed it to e**v**erybody.
30. You can buy the **v**ase for **V**icky if you sa**v**e ele**v**en more dollars.

Pronunciation of Words with Silent Letters
Many words contain letters that are not pronounced.

a<u>i</u>s<u>l</u><u>e</u>	**k**now	Feb**r**uary	**k**ni<u>f</u>e	forei**g**n
x x x	x x	x	x x	x x

Listen carefully and repeat the following sentences.

1. Put the ras**p**ber**r**ies in the fri**d**ge not in the cu**p**board.
2. I met a han**d**som**e** man with big mus**c**les and a ya**ch**t.
3. My mor**t**gag**e** is the only de**b**t I hav**e**.
4. Ther**e** wil**l** be **ch**aos if y**o**u resi**g**n from the family busines**s**.
5. **W**hos**e** ve**h**icl**e** sh**ou**ld we tak**e** on We**d**nesda**y**?
6. **W**ho **w**rot**e** the an**sw**er on the board with **w**hit**e** **ch**alk?
7. **Wh**at is **w**rong with yo**u**r s**c**is**s**ors?
8. Do y**o**u **k**now **w**ho wil**l** desi**g**n the new bri**d**ge?
9. Us**e** the **wh**isk to **wh**ip the fu**d**ge.
10. I at**e** the **wh**ol**e** eg**g** even the yo**l**k but not the sa**l**mon san**d**wich.
11. The plum**b**er can't com**e** today bec**au**se he has **p**neumonia.
12. W**ou**ld he lik**e** to ta**l**k to a **p**sy**ch**iatrist?
13. My fol**k**s wil**l** be hom**e** in hal**f** an **h**our.
14. I lov**e** the s**c**ent of yo**u**r new colo**gn**e.
15. It's an **h**onor for me to present the **s**word to the **k**ni**gh**t.
16. He pla**y**ed **g**uitar **wh**ile I drank champa**gn**e under the cres**c**ent moon.
17. I hurt my **k**nee, thum**b**, and **w**rist **wh**ile I was **w**rest**l**ing with the **s**wordfish.

18. Do y**ou** **kno**w wh**e**re that wi**t**ch put my wh**istle**?
    x x   x x   x   x x

19. I g**ue**ss I am g**u**ilty of **kno**cking over that colum**n**.
    x x   x   x   x   x

20. How c**ou**ld I hav**e** **k**nown that the campa**ig**n was in Feb**r**uary?
      x x   x x   x x   x

21. I dou**b**t that the lam**b** and the ca**l**f wil**l** be fri**e**nds.
      x   x   x   x   x

22. The wh**ale** had a **kni**f**e**, a ba**dge**, a lim**b**, and a com**b** in its stoma**ch**.
     x x   x x   x x   x   x   x

23. I g**u**arante**e** that this cream wil**l** remov**e** the **wr**inkl**e**s on your for**e**h**e**ad.
    x   x   x   x   x   x   x   x x

24. My **kn**uckl**e**s ac**he** from **kno**cking so hard on the do**o**r.
    x x   x   x x   x x   x

25. He ne**e**ds dis**c**iplin**e** beca**u**s**e** he do**e**sn't list**e**n.
     x   x   x   x x   x   x

26. Do y**ou** remember the **ch**orus and the r**h**ythm of the hym**n**?
    x   x   x   x

27. We lov**e** to wa**l**k and ta**l**k along the ca**l**m river in autum**n**.
    x   x   x   x   x   x

28. He wants a rece**ip**t for the an**ch**or he bo**ugh**t.
          x x   x   x x x

29. My tong**ue** is num**b** beca**u**s**e** of al**l** the **ch**lorin**e** in the po**o**l.
       x x   x   x x   x   x   x   x

30. I sa**w** a g**h**ost wh**e**n I climb**ed** to the top of the cas**t**l**e**.
    x   x   x   x   x x

Pronunciation of *GH*

Sometimes **gh** *is not pronounced in words.*

ni**gh**t	si**gh**	cau**gh**t	bri**gh**t	ou**gh**t
x	x	x	x	x

Sometimes **gh** *is pronounced as an* **f** *sound in words.*

lau**gh**	cou**gh**	enou**gh**	tou**gh**	rou**gh**
f	f	f	f	f

Listen carefully and repeat the following sentences.

1. The candleli**gh**t is bri**gh**t enou**gh**.
             x   x   f

2. The firefi**gh**ter needs his flashli**gh**t to go into the buildings.
        x   x

3. The drau**gh**t beer from that ni**gh**tclub made me feel li**gh**theaded.
        f   x   x

4. I had a ni**gh**tmare around midni**gh**t last ni**gh**t.
         x   x   x

5. How much does your granddau**gh**ter wei**gh**?
                      x   x

6. There is a water trou**gh** for the thorou**gh**breds near the old slei**gh**.
            f   x   x

7. The drou**gh**t has been tou**gh** for everybody.
       x   f

8. You prepare the dou**gh** and I will make the dou**gh**nuts.
           x   x

9. The moonli**gh**t and the sunli**gh**t shine throu**gh** the skyli**gh**t in my bedroom.
         x   x   x   x

10. I am nearsi**gh**ted and my husband is farsi**gh**ted.
          x   x

11. You ou**gh**t to go to bed early on a weekni**gh**t.
        x   x

12. You are ri**gh**t again, he si**gh**ed.
        x   x

13. I thou**gh**t you said you brou**gh**t a li**gh**ter to start the fire.
      x   x   x

14. That was a fri**gh**tening ei**gh**t-hour fli**gh**t.
         x   x   x

15. The man is changing the li**gh**tbulbs in the streetli**gh**ts.
                  x   x

16. Your dau**gh**ter is a thou**gh**tful and deli**gh**tful girl.
        x   x   x

17. Turn off the li**gh**ts in the house during the dayli**gh**t hours.
        x   x

18. He is a rou**gh** and tou**gh** fi**gh**ter.
        f   f   x

19. I mi**gh**t li**gh**ten my hair for the summer.
      x   x

20. Go strai**gh**t to the end of the hi**gh**way.
        x   x

21. The audience burst into lau**gh**ter.
                              f

22. There is a bri**gh**t spotli**gh**t on the top of the snowpl**ow**.
          x   x   x

23. The police did a thorou**gh** search in the nei**gh**bourhood toni**gh**t.
                    x   x   x

24. She has enou**gh** makeup to last her a lifetime.
          f

25. What is your hei**gh**t and wei**gh**t?
          x   x

26. My nei**gh**bour cau**gh**t a bad cold and he is cou**gh**ing a lot.
        x   x   f

27. All ri**gh**t, you can use my green highli**gh**ter.
        x   x

28. The li**gh**tning hit the li**gh**thouse and caused a lot of damage.
        x   x

29. I don't have a pen; I have a pencil thou**gh**.
                                          x

30. Althou**gh** they fi**gh**t often, they are good friends.
        x   x

Pronunciation of Contractions with *Who, What, Where, When, Why,* and *How*

When **who**, **what**, **where**, **why**, *and* **how** *are contracted with* **is**, *the* **'s** *must be firmly pronounced.*

who is	→	who**'s**
what is	→	what**'s**
where is	→	where**'s**
when is	→	when**'s**
why is	→	why**'s**
how is	→	how**'s**

Listen carefully and repeat the following sentences.

1. Where**'s** the bathroom?
2. What**'s** the date today?
3. How**'s** the weather in Chicago?
4. Who**'s** the guy with you?
5. When**'s** the next bus?
6. Why**'s** he leaving so early?
7. Where**'s** the beach?
8. What**'s** her name?
9. How**'s** the food?
10. When**'s** your birthday?
11. Why**'s** it so cold in the basement?
12. Who**'s** the boss?
13. Where**'s** my watch?
14. What**'s** the answer?
15. How**'s** that possible?
16. Who**'s** at the door?
17. When**'s** it over?
18. Why**'s** she crying?
19. Where**'s** the remote control?
20. What**'s** for supper?
21. How**'s** the water?
22. Who**'s** your doctor?
23. When**'s** a good time to meet?
24. Why**'s** the grass green?
25. Where**'s** my other shoe?
26. What**'s** new?
27. How**'s** Mike?
28. Who**'s** he talking to?
29. When**'s** he going to be here?
30. Why**'s** there a dent in my car?

Pronunciation of the Contraction 'LL

When the personal pronouns **I, you, he, she, it, we,** *and* **they** *are contracted with* **will,** *the double l is firmly pronounced.*

I will	→	I'll
you will	→	you'll
he will	→	he'll
she will	→	she'll
it will	→	it'll
we will	→	we'll
they will	→	they'll

Listen carefully and repeat the following sentences.

1. It'll be late when I get home.
2. I'm sure she'll be here in the morning.
3. We don't think he'll like it.
4. If you don't tell them, they'll never know.
5. They said that they'll try to come Saturday night.
6. Hurry or we'll be late.
7. I'll call you later.
8. You'll be sick if you eat that.
9. We hope you'll receive it before the end of the week.
10. I think it'll be on special next week.
11. She said she'll meet us downtown.
12. I don't think he'll apply for the job.
13. They'll let us know the results next week.
14. You'll never guess what she did in class today.
15. I'll be home for Christmas.
16. He'll work in the basement and I'll work in the kitchen.
17. Be careful. It'll bite you.
18. She said that she'll be okay.
19. We'll never give up.
20. He'll spend the summer with friends in Calgary.
21. It'll give us the opportunity to meet and discuss this.
22. He said he'll be back in a few days.
23. Don't worry. I'll never tell anyone your secret.
24. I wonder if they'll notice the dent in their car.
25. Diana didn't bring her lunch today, so I'll give half my sandwich to her.
26. He'll make supper and she'll make dessert.
27. Count on us, we'll be there.
28. I'm certain that you'll win the race.
29. Do you know if it'll rain again tomorrow?
30. I have a surprise for you and it'll make you very happy.

Pronunciation of Negative Contractions

The following negative words can be expressed using contractions. The **n't** *sound must be firmly pronounced.*

are not	→	are**n't**	has not	→	has**n't**
were not	→	were**n't**	have not	→	have**n't**
do not	→	do**n't**	will not	→	wo**n't**
does not	→	does**n't**	could not	→	could**n't**
did not	→	did**n't**	would not	→	would**n't**
was not	→	was**n't**	should not	→	should**n't**
is not	→	is**n't**	had not	→	had**n't**

Listen carefully and repeat the following sentences.

1. Jennifer is**n't** my cousin.
2. It does**n't** matter.
3. We do**n't** speak Japanese at home.
4. They were**n't** in school yesterday.
5. You would**n't** be late for school if you got up earlier.
6. We had**n't** eaten, so we stopped for a pizza.
7. You should**n't** say that in class.
8. It did**n't** break when I dropped it.
9. She could**n't** sleep, so she turned on the TV.
10. He was**n't** at church this morning.
11. They have**n't** been here before.
12. You wo**n't** regret it.
13. The flowers are**n't** for you.
14. John and Jim were**n't** at the meeting.
15. The mailman has**n't** come yet.
16. Mary would**n't** mind if I borrowed her book.
17. The dogs did**n't** bark when you rang the bell.
18. She has**n't** called yet.
19. I do**n't** remember your phone number.
20. Mark does**n't** drink or smoke.
21. I had**n't** noticed that you were wearing my shoes.
22. It should**n't** be a problem.
23. You have**n't** touched your food.
24. They do**n't** play hockey together.
25. He was**n't** on the bus after school.
26. We wo**n't** be able to visit you.
27. I could**n't** believe what he was saying.
28. Those customers did**n't** leave a tip.
29. It was**n't** very funny.
30. He does**n't** work very hard in class.

Pronunciation of *Can* and *Can't*

Can and **can't** are opposites. The **n** in **can** must be firmly pronounced, as well as the **'t** in the negative contraction **can't**, to be able to distinguish between the affirmative and negative message.

I ca**n** hear you.   →   I can**'t** hear you.

Listen carefully and repeat the following sentences.

1. My computer has a problem. I can**'t** connect to the Internet.
2. Ca**n** you come with me tonight?
3. I have to clean my aquarium because I can**'t** see the fish.
4. He can**'t** tie his shoes.
5. We ca**n** order something for supper if you want.
6. Linda can**'t** find her keys.
7. I can**'t** skate very well.
8. You ca**n** use my cell phone if you need to make a call.
9. My boyfriend ca**n** cook.
10. I can**'t** pronounce this word.
11. He ca**n** speak several languages.
12. My aunt can**'t** work because of her illness.
13. We ca**n** see many bright stars in the sky at night.
14. I can**'t** open the door. It's stuck.
15. You ca**n** try.
16. It can**'t** be true.
17. I can**'t** believe you said that.
18. Ca**n** you help me with my homework?
19. You can**'t** drink and drive. It's against the law.
20. I can**'t** tell you.
21. Ca**n** you touch your toes?
22. I ca**n** sing, you can**'t**.
23. You can**'t** always get what you want.
24. I can**'t** talk right now. I'm busy.
25. Ca**n** you stay for a coffee?
26. I can**'t** remember your name.
27. We can**'t** see the difference.
28. You ca**n** call me tonight if you want.
29. I can**'t** understand you.
30. She can**'t** draw.

Pronunciation of Words Ending in *CT*

The letter combination **ct** *must be pronounced at the end of words.*

conne**ct**   subje**ct**   prote**ct**   inspe**ct**   dire**ct**

Listen carefully and repeat the following sentences.

1. There is a defe**ct** in my jacket.
2. She wants to improve every aspe**ct** of her life.
3. We will conta**ct** you if you are chosen for this project.
4. I predi**ct** that they will offer you a contra**ct**.
5. You have to subtra**ct** this, then dedu**ct** that.
6. Do you like abstra**ct** art?
7. It's not a good idea to fire the archite**ct**.
8. This anti-virus will dete**ct** and remove the virus.
9. They say that opposites attra**ct**.
10. Can you identify the subje**ct** and obje**ct** in each sentence?
11. The hospital uses a strong produ**ct** to disinfe**ct** everything.
12. If two things are not the same they are distin**ct**.
13. I expe**ct** that the landlord will evi**ct** the tenants.
14. The police will inspe**ct** the exa**ct** location of the crime.
15. That inse**ct** is extin**ct**.
16. I suspe**ct** that he will retra**ct** or corre**ct** his statement.
17. They will ere**ct** a new skyscraper in this distri**ct**.
18. It is a fa**ct** that we will ele**ct** a new president.
19. My school will sele**ct** a stri**ct** principal next year.
20. People a**ct** and rea**ct** better if you treat them with respe**ct**.
21. My dentist wants to extra**ct** my back tooth.
22. Your first instin**ct** is usually corre**ct**.
23. What diale**ct** do your people speak?
24. Can you dire**ct** me to the post office?
25. You always contradi**ct** what I say.
26. We want to colle**ct** money for the baby shower.
27. He admits that he is an extreme sports addi**ct**.
28. We will sell the truck and buy a compa**ct** car.
29. She was rewarded for her superior condu**ct**.
30. How did that crisis affe**ct** her?

Pronunciation of Words Ending in *ST*

The letter combination **st** *must be firmly pronounced at the end of words.*

dent**is̲t̲**   we**s̲t̲**   ins**is̲t̲**   ex**is̲t̲**   fir**s̲t̲**

Listen carefully and repeat the following sentences.

1. My team lo**s̲t̲** the game.
2. Do you see the ne**s̲t̲** in the tree?
3. I like to eat toa**s̲t̲** in the morning.
4. Mo**s̲t̲** of us like milk.
5. What is your la**s̲t̲** name?
6. I want to re**s̲t̲** on my bed.
7. My dent**is̲t̲** is very good.
8. He is fir**s̲t̲** in line.
9. We have a te**s̲t̲** tomorrow.
10. You mu**s̲t̲** try hard.
11. Look at all the du**s̲t̲** on the table.
12. The sun will rise in the ea**s̲t̲**.
13. The sun will set in the we**s̲t̲**.
14. It will not co**s̲t̲** a lot.
15. He has a ca**s̲t̲** on his left arm.
16. I do not tru**s̲t̲** her.
17. Make a li**s̲t̲** of the items you need.
18. You are the wor**s̲t̲** driver.
19. Tell me about your pa**s̲t̲**.
20. A snail is not very fa**s̲t̲**.
21. I ju**s̲t̲** had a coffee.
22. I ins**is̲t̲** that you stay for dinner.
23. We live near the coa**s̲t̲**.
24. He is a famous arti**s̲t̲**.
25. You make the be**s̲t̲** chocolate cake.
26. Can you ass**is̲t̲** me with this?
27. Did you see a gho**s̲t̲**?
28. The police will arre**s̲t̲** him.
29. Do angels ex**is̲t̲**?
30. He has a tattoo on his che**s̲t̲**.

Pronunciation of Contractions 'S and 'VE with the Present Perfect and Present Perfect Progressive Tenses

Contractions are often used with the present perfect and present perfect progressive tenses. The ending of these contractions must be firmly pronounced.

I have	→	I**'ve**
you have	→	you**'ve**
he has	→	he**'s**
she has	→	she**'s**
it has	→	it**'s**
we have	→	we**'ve**
they have	→	they**'ve**

Listen carefully and repeat the following sentences.

1. They**'ve** known each other for a long time.
2. I**'ve** been to Europe several times.
3. He told me that he**'s** taken the train before.
4. I think she**'s** had enough.
5. We**'ve** been waiting to see the doctor for over four hours.
6. They**'ve** lived in that house for ten years.
7. I**'ve** left several messages on his answering machine.
8. It**'s** been a long day.
9. He**'s** tried to talk to her more than once.
10. You**'ve** been a good friend to me.
11. She**'s** given a lot of money to charities.
12. They**'ve** been seeing a marriage counsellor for a few months.
13. It**'s** been raining for two days.
14. I**'ve** been trying to lose weight for a long time.
15. Do you know where they**'ve** gone?
16. We**'ve** eaten there once or twice.
17. He**'s** been working on it for several weeks.
18. They**'ve** stolen all the money.
19. You**'ve** gone too far.
20. We**'ve** calculated it twice but we can't find the mistake.
21. She**'s** been watching TV in her room all night.
22. They**'ve** worked together before.
23. Thank you, I**'ve** seen and heard enough.
24. We**'ve** been dancing all night.
25. He**'s** read every book about it.
26. I think she**'s** given up.
27. We**'ve** already done our homework.
28. I**'ve** learned a lot from them.
29. He**'s** grown so much over the years.
30. She said that she**'s** never met your brother.

Pronunciation of 'D

Pronouns that are contracted with **'d** *stem from* **would** *or* **had***. The* **d** *must be firmly pronounced.*

I would	→	I'**d**	I had	→	I'**d**
you would	→	you'**d**	you had	→	you'**d**
he would	→	he'**d**	he had	→	he'**d**
she would	→	she'**d**	she had	→	she'**d**
it would	→	it'**d**	it had	→	it'**d**
we would	→	we'**d**	we had	→	we'**d**
they would	→	they'**d**	they had	→	they'**d**

Listen carefully and repeat the following sentences.

1. I'**d** like to know who made this mess.
2. He'**d** had enough.
3. They'**d** like to come for dinner tonight.
4. She'**d** known the truth the whole time.
5. We'**d** prefer to stay home tonight.
6. You'**d** better not be late for class again.
7. I'**d** like to see you tomorrow.
8. It'**d** be hard to refuse that offer.
9. You'**d** better hurry up.
10. They'**d** rather not attend the wedding.
11. I'**d** love to have this recipe.
12. I'm sure he'**d** want to know you were here.
13. We'**d** better leave now.
14. She'**d** already gone to bed when we arrived.
15. I'**d** be happy to help you.
16. It'**d** been four years since we last saw him.
17. You'**d** better have a good excuse.
18. We'**d** like to invite you to our pool party.
19. They'**d** been to Mexico before.
20. He'**d** seen her picture in the newspaper several times.
21. I'**d** save a piece for your father if I were you.
22. I think he'**d** be pleased with the results.
23. It'**d** be better if you sent it by e-mail.
24. I wish I'**d** known that you were in town last weekend.
25. She'**d** like to know what is in the box.
26. I'**d** like to know your name.
27. We'**d** rather be on the beach right now.
28. They'**d** rather not go.
29. She'**d** done all the work by herself.
30. He'**d** never do that.

Pronunciation of Words Containing the *W* Sound

*The pronunciation of **w** can be challenging for many students as this sound does not exist in all languages; therefore it must be learned and practiced.*

winter   to**w**el   **w**ash   **w**orld   **w**eekend

Listen carefully and repeat the following sentences.

1. You **w**ill find it on the **W**orld **W**ide **W**eb.
2. It **w**on't **w**ork **w**ithout the **w**hite **w**ire.
3. **W**e **w**ish you **w**ell, **W**illy.
4. **W**orkaholics **w**ork on **w**eekends.
5. **W**ake up! **W**e **w**ant **w**affles.
6. I need **w**arm **w**ater to **w**ipe the **w**allpaper on the **w**all.
7. There **w**ere many **w**idows and **w**idowers after **W**orld **W**ar I.
8. **W**ow! **W**hat a **w**onderful **w**edding.
9. **W**hich **w**ay, east or **w**est?
10. My **w**ife **w**hispers **w**ords of **w**isdom **w**henever **w**e **w**alk in the **w**oods.
11. Spiders **w**eave **w**ebs.
12. The **w**ater slides **w**ere **w**et and **w**ild.
13. **W**hy do you **w**ant a to**w**el?
14. **W**here is the **w**ashroom?
15. The **w**itch **w**anted **w**hiskey but I only had **w**ater.
16. I **w**ant **w**hite **w**ine **w**ith my supper.
17. **W**ayne **w**orries **w**hen I **w**ork late.
18. **W**e **w**ent to **W**ashington for a **w**eek.
19. The **w**eather **w**as good on **W**ednesday.
20. **W**arren **w**histles **w**hile he **w**orks in the **w**arehouse.
21. **W**ait in the **w**aiting room **w**hile I **w**ax your car.
22. The **w**arm **w**eather made the **w**ater in the **w**ell **w**arm.
23. **W**here **w**ere **w**e on **W**ednesday **w**hen **W**endy **w**as in **W**yoming?
24. I **w**onder if the **w**oman **w**ants **w**atermelon.
25. The **w**eird **w**oman ble**w** her **w**histle **w**hen the **w**alrus **w**addled into the **w**ater.
26. **W**henever I **w**ork out **w**ith **w**eights, I feel **w**eak.
27. The **w**inner **w**ill **w**in a **w**atch.
28. **W**e can have **w**hatever **w**e **w**ant **w**henever **w**e **w**ant.
29. There is a **w**asp on the **w**indow.
30. Don't **w**aste the **w**indshield **w**asher fluid.

Pronunciation of *OI* and *OY*

The letter combinations **oi** *and* **oy** *have the same pronunciation in many words.*

enj**oy**   ch**oi**ce   j**oy**   b**oi**l   cowb**oy**

Listen carefully and repeat the following sentences.

1. Is there a pearl in the **oy**ster?
2. She is paran**oi**d that the picture will appear in the tabl**oi**d.
3. My dog is my l**oy**al friend.
4. I have to put **oi**l in my car.
5. That boy ann**oy**s everybody in his class.
6. What is that horrible n**oi**se?
7. We used a wooden duck as a dec**oy**.
8. I have an app**oi**ntment at the empl**oy**ment office.
9. The t**oy**s are all over the floor.
10. I need some c**oi**ns for the vending machine.
11. Did the aster**oi**d hit the earth?
12. We will add some new s**oi**l to the vegetable garden.
13. I wrote a v**oi**d check for my new empl**oy**er.
14. He really enj**oy**ed that sirl**oi**n steak.
15. I need aluminium f**oi**l to wrap the leftovers.
16. Please j**oi**n us for breakfast.
17. Do you want me to br**oi**l or b**oi**l the potatoes?
18. He did everything to av**oi**d the accident.
19. This cake is so m**oi**st.
20. I prefer to use a ballp**oi**nt pen.
21. She was disapp**oi**nted with her final mark.
22. Mark wants to be a cowb**oy** when he grows up.
23. I put **oi**ntment on the cut on my finger.
24. She dropped her keys in the t**oi**let.
25. There is a lot of m**oi**sture in the basement.
26. Is that a p**oi**sonous snake?
27. I didn't recognize your v**oi**ce on the phone.
28. I spilled my coffee on my book and destr**oy**ed it.
29. You have to make a ch**oi**ce today.
30. Did you attend the r**oy**al wedding?

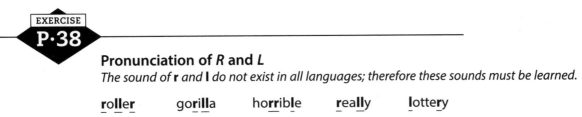

Pronunciation of *R* and *L*

*The sound of **r** and **l** do not exist in all languages; therefore these sounds must be learned.*

roller   gorilla   horrible   really   lottery

Listen carefully and repeat the following sentences.

1. Little rabbits like lots of leafy lettuce daily.
2. I really like relish.
3. Late last night, Larry learned a valuable lesson.
4. Our specialist in labour relations won the lottery.
5. Like Laura and Roy, Robert and Lenny really like round lollipops.
6. Are you ready for the election?
7. Read the letter out loud.
8. That was a horrible horror film about caterpillars.
9. Let Randy light the old oil lantern.
10. Lenny lost his luggage at the airport.
11. I always make lemonade with real lemons.
12. Big rabbits raise little rabbits that run and leap all around the rivers and lakes.
13. Leave my red ruler on the table.
14. Rake the leaves right now, Larry.
15. The gorilla left the last vanilla wafer for Leo the lion.
16. The Rolls-Royce that Lucy rented runs really well.
17. The lovely Russian lady wore a large, red raincoat to the rally.
18. My landlord asked for the rent that was late.
19. I will borrow the yellow roller from Laura.
20. Lily really looks like Rory.
21. I regularly look in my rearview mirror.
22. Rick rolls round rocks on the road.
23. Roll the yellow barrel down the hill.
24. Can I borrow your ballerina slippers tomorrow?
25. Hello Harry, hurry or we will miss the ferry.
26. I have allergies and I need a referral from my doctor to see a specialist.
27. Stir in the curry.
28. It's not a terrible error, Mr. Murry, your account is really in arrears.
29. Derrick is blind and he reads Braille.
30. I want four eggrolls and a bowl of rice.

Pronunciation of Words Ending in *ABLE*

*Words ending with the suffix **able** have the meaning of to be able or capable of.*

cap**able**   favor**able**   avail**able**   desir**able**   advis**able**

Listen carefully and repeat the following sentences.

1. I have a new port**able** computer.
2. Be careful because gasoline is flamm**able**.
3. Bathing suits are not exchange**able**.
4. We are unable to avoid the inevit**able**.
5. Are these items tax**able**?
6. The horses were excit**able** and uncontroll**able** during the parade.
7. Their business was very profit**able** last year.
8. Many road accidents are avoid**able**.
9. Extra charges may be applic**able**.
10. I don't think this decision is appeal**able**.
11. All your goals are achiev**able** in life.
12. I prefer dispos**able** contact lenses.
13. His medical condition is cur**able** and oper**able**.
14. It will en**able** you to live an enjoy**able** and comfort**able** life.
15. You are not employ**able** if you have no skills.
16. Is my bike fix**able**?
17. It is prefer**able** if you wear a more fashion**able** dress to the event.
18. Her behavior in class is unbear**able**, intoler**able**, and deplor**able**.
19. That is a reason**able** and prob**able** forecast.
20. Be careful, that vase is break**able** and irreplace**able**.
21. I prefer this car because it is afford**able** and has adjust**able** seats.
22. Are the two of you **able** to come to an amic**able** agreement?
23. It's not accept**able** if the city doesn't have a consider**able** amount of drink**able** water avail**able**.
24. It is desir**able** for a manager to be approach**able**.
25. They said that everything in the store is negoti**able**.
26. My new puppy is hugg**able**, lov**able**, and ador**able**.
27. It is admir**able** that you give nonperish**able** food items to charit**able** organizations.
28. If you are not **able** to swallow your pill, it is advis**able** that you buy chew**able** tablets.
29. It is favor**able** to have a reli**able** and depend**able** partner.
30. Are recharge**able** batteries biodegrad**able**?

Pronunciation of Words Ending in *STS* and *SKS*

*The letter combinations **sts** and **sks** at the end of nouns and verbs are difficult to pronounce for nonnative speakers. Try saying the word without the final **s** a few times then add the final **s** separately.*

ne**sts**   assi**sts**   di**sks**   che**sts**   a**sks**

Listen carefully and repeat the following sentences.

1. He has a collection of African ma**sks** on his wall.
2. I participate in all the conte**sts** at school.
3. Do you believe in gho**sts**?
4. She tru**sts** you.
5. I had two te**sts** at school today.
6. Elephants and walruses have tu**sks**.
7. Do you know if Santa Claus really exi**sts**?
8. My teacher assi**sts** all the students in my class.
9. Most denti**sts** agree that this product is better.
10. The exam consi**sts** of many difficult questions.
11. You know what your ta**sks** are, so you can begin.
12. A chef always has many whi**sks** in his kitchen.
13. Our fore**sts** are in danger.
14. My mother du**sts** the furniture every week.
15. There are two ne**sts** in the tree.
16. She a**sks** the same question every day.
17. It co**sts** a fortune.
18. I made several li**sts** for our camping trip.
19. He inve**sts** all his money in gold.
20. She insi**sts** that we attend the meeting.
21. Do we have enough for all the gue**sts**?
22. This is a long movie and it la**sts** for four hours.
23. We put the new po**sts** for the fence in the ground yesterday.
24. I really like to talk to arti**sts**.
25. We have new de**sks** at school.
26. None of the scienti**sts**, biologi**sts**, astrologi**sts**, or analy**sts** could explain it.
27. My father is a fireman and he ri**sks** his life to save others.
28. There are many treasure che**sts** at the bottom of the ocean.
29. I don't eat the cru**sts** on sandwiches.
30. My grandfather re**sts** every afternoon before supper.

Pronunciation of Words Containing _PH_
The letter combination **ph** _is pronounced as_ **f** _in most words._

hy**ph**en   **ph**armacy   gra**ph**   sym**ph**ony   pam**ph**let

Listen carefully and repeat the following sentences.

1. Did you read her autobiogra**ph**y?
2. Look at the dol**ph**ins leading the ship.
3. The men are putting new as**ph**alt on the road.
4. Can you say the al**ph**abet backwards?
5. Some people have claustro**ph**obia in elevators.
6. Can I have your autogra**ph**?
7. I was not very good in geogra**ph**y in school.
8. Our team won the tro**ph**y this year.
9. We love the atmos**ph**ere in Montreal.
10. She is a very so**ph**isticated **ph**iloso**ph**er.
11. You should ask the **ph**armacist at the **ph**armacy.
12. Jose**ph** wrote the last paragra**ph**.
13. Mr. Mur**ph**y is a **ph**otogra**ph**er in **Ph**iladel**ph**ia.
14. Do you have any **ph**obias?
15. It's not a catastro**ph**e if I'm 10 minutes late.
16. We received your pam**ph**let in the mail.
17. My ne**ph**ew plays the saxo**ph**one.
18. I can't find my head**ph**ones.
19. We visited an or**ph**anage during our mission.
20. Is there a bibliogra**ph**y in the book?
21. He teaches the art of calligra**ph**y.
22. Many old people suffer from em**ph**ysema.
23. I wish to em**ph**asize the importance of your presence in each class.
24. Did he fail the polygra**ph** test?
25. I need to make a **ph**otocopy of this.
26. Lynn goes to **ph**ysiotherapy twice a week.
27. We are in **ph**ase four of the project.
28. Shawn is a gra**ph**ic artist.
29. We love to listen to a live sym**ph**ony.
30. Record the information on a gra**ph**.

Pronunciation of Homophones (1)

*Many words are pronounced the same even though they are not spelled
the same and have different meanings.*

blue	blew		mail	male	
buy	by	bye	pail	pale	
cell	sell		patients	patience	
die	dye		piece	peace	
do	due	dew	pour	poor	
eight	ate		red	read	
fair	fare		sail	sale	
flour	flower		see	sea	
great	grate		sent	scent	cent
guest	guessed		sun	son	
here	hear		their	there	they're
knew	new		threw	through	
knight	night		which	witch	
knot	not		whole	hole	
made	maid		won	one	

Use your dictionary to find the meanings of these word pairs, then listen carefully and repeat
the following sentences.

1. see _____   sea _____

   I **see** you.   The ship sank to the bottom of the **sea**.

2. pour _____   poor _____

   Pour me a glass of wine, please.   **Poor** Mary, she lost her job.

3. eight _____   ate _____

   They have **eight** children.   I **ate** your banana.

4. won _____   one _____

   I can't believe I **won**.   Do you want **one**?

5. sun _____   son _____

   The **sun** is strong today.   How is your **son**?

6. mail _____   male _____

   Is there any **mail**?   Is your dog a **male** or female?

7. whole _____   hole _____

   It's the best in the **whole** world.   You have a **hole** in your sock.

8. die _____   dye _____

   Put the fish in water or it will **die**.   Did you **dye** your hair?

9. sail _____   sale _____

   They have a **sail** boat.   It's on **sale** this week.

10. knew _____   new _____

   Nobody **knew** the answer.   I have a **new** job.

11. knight _____   night _____

   He is a fearless **knight**.   It was a dark and stormy **night**.

12. which _____   witch _____

   Which way should we go?   There is a **witch** in your closet.

13. made _____   maid _____

   I **made** it myself.   When is the **maid** coming?

14. here _____   hear _____

   Come **here**.   I can't **hear** you.

15. pail _____   pale _____

   The sponge is in the **pail**.   You look very **pale** today.

16. cell _____   sell _____

   A **cell** is microscopic.   Do you want to **sell** your house?

   The prisoner was locked in his **cell**.

17. piece _____   peace _____

   I had a **piece**, thank you.   I love **peace** and quiet.

18. knot _____   not _____

   Can you undo the **knot** in the rope?   It's **not** true.

19. flour _____   flower _____

   I need three cups of **flour**.   He picked a **flower** for you.

20. red _____   read _____

   Why is your face **red**?   She **read** it to me.

21. fair _____   fare _____

   It's not **fair**.   How much is the bus **fare**?

22. blue _____   blew _____

   My favourite colour is **blue**.   The wind **blew** all night.

23. threw _____   through _____

   He **threw** the ball for the dog.   I will read **through** your material tonight.

24. patients _____   patience _____

   A doctor has many **patients**.   You need **patience** to be a doctor.

25. guest_____   guessed_____

   Who is your **guest** this evening?   She **guessed** most of the answers on the test.

26. great _____   grate _____

   Mr. Paterson is a **great** boss.   I have to **grate** the cheese for the pizza.

27. do _____   due _____   dew _____

   Do your homework.   Your payment is **due**.   There is **dew** on the ground.

28. buy _____   by _____   bye_____

   Don't **buy** that.   He went **by** train.   I'm leaving now, **bye**.

29. sent _____   scent _____   cent _____

   I **sent** it already.   What a lovely **scent**.   He found a **cent**.

30. their _____   there _____   they're _____

   They built **their** house.   Don't go **there**.   **They're** in the pool.

Pronunciation of Homophones (2)
Many words are pronounced the same even though they are not spelled the same and have different meanings.

be	bee	moose	mousse
bear	bare	morning	mourning
beet	beat	mussels	muscles
berry	bury	none	nun
break	brake	pain	pane
cereal	serial	plane	plain
choose	chews	right	write
dear	deer	road	rode
flea	flee	so	sew
heal	heel	stair	stare
heard	herd	steel	steal
I	eye	tea	tee
I'll	aisle	weather	whether
know	no	weight	wait
meet	meat	would	wood

Use your dictionary to find the meanings of these word pairs, then listen carefully and repeat the following sentences.

1. plane_____   plain _____

   The **plane** will leave soon.   I want a sandwich on **plain** white bread.

2. bear_____   bare_____

   We saw a big black **bear**.   He touched the fire with his **bare** hands.

3. stair_____   stare _____

   The bottom **stair** is broken.   Don't **stare** at me.

4. right _____   write _____

   I think you are **right**.   I will **write** it in my agenda.
   He wears the ring on his **right** hand.

5. know_____   no _____

   We don't **know** them.   She said, "**No**."

6. so _____   sew _____

   I am **so** hungry.   Can you **sew** my pants?

7. break_____   brake_____

   Don't **break** my glasses.   Step on the **brake** to stop a car.

8. road _____   rode _____

The **road** is wet and slippery.   I **rode** my horse yesterday.

9. pain _____   pane _____

She takes medication for **pain**.   I broke the **pane** of glass.

10. heal _____   heel _____

Can the doctors **heal** you?   The **heel** on my shoe fell off.

11. weight _____   wait _____

What is the **weight** of your truck?   Please **wait** downstairs.

12. meet _____   meat _____

I want to **meet** your mother.   Do you eat **meat**?

13. flea _____   flee _____

I saw a **flea** on my cat.   They will **flee** the country tonight.

14. moose _____   mousse _____

Did you ever see a **moose**?   I love chocolate **mousse**.

15. heard _____   herd _____

I **heard** you the first time.   The **herd** of horses ran wild in the valley.

16. none _____   nun _____

We have **none** left.   My sister is a **nun**.

17. beet _____   beat _____

Did you ever taste **beet** soup?   She **beat** everybody in both competitions.

18. berry _____   bury _____

I put a **berry** on my ice cream cone.   My dog likes to **bury** his bones in the yard.

19. mussels _____   muscles _____

Do you like to eat **mussels**?   I went to the gym and my **muscles** are sore.

20. choose _____   chews _____

You can **choose** the colour.   My friend **chews** gum all the time.

21. be _____   bee _____

She will **be** a big star someday.   The **bee** stung me.

22. I'll _____   aisle _____

I'll have a coffee please.   The peas are in **aisle** four.

23. I _____ eye _____

I will call you later. He has a glass **eye**.

24. tea _____ tee _____

Don't put sugar in my **tea**. I need a **tee** to go golfing.

25. weather _____ whether _____

The warm **weather** is coming. Do you know **whether** she is coming?

26. steel _____ steal _____

The price of **steel** is rising. Don't **steal** from your employer.

27. dear _____ deer _____

You are a **dear** friend to me. The **deer** ate everything in my garden.

28. morning _____ mourning _____

I get up early every **morning**. She is **mourning** for her husband.

29. would _____ wood _____

She **would** like to work here. We need **wood** for the winter.

30. cereal _____ serial _____

I usually eat **cereal** for breakfast. Every bank note has a **serial** number.

Pronunciation of Homophones (3)

Many words are pronounced the same even though they are not spelled the same and have different meanings.

air	heir	in	inn
allowed	aloud	kernel	colonel
aunt	ant	knows	nose
border	boarder	need	knead
caller	collar	our	hour
clothes	close	pause	paws
coarse	course	pear	pair
complements	compliments	pray	prey
feet	feat	roll	role
ferry	fairy	seller	cellar
flu	flew	tow	toe
foreword	forward	waist	waste
hair	hare	weak	week
higher	hire	weigh	way
horse	hoarse	where	wear

Use your dictionary to find the meanings of these word pairs, then listen carefully and repeat the following sentences.

1. pear_____   pair _____

   I had a **pear** during my break.   I need a new **pair** of shoes.

2. hair _____   hare_____

   Your **hair** is gorgeous.   Is it a rabbit or a **hare**?

3. where _____   wear _____

   Where are you going?   I don't want to **wear** this today.

4. waist _____   waste_____

   What size is your **waist**?   Don't **waste** food.

5. clothes _____   close _____

   All my **clothes** are dirty.   Please **close** the door.

6. roll_____   role _____

   The kids like to **roll** down the hill.   What **role** did he play in the movie?

7. seller _____   cellar _____

   Are you a buyer or **seller**?   The wine is in the **cellar**.

8. our _____   hour_____

   Where did we park **our** car?   I was stuck in traffic for an **hour**.

9. need _____

   Do you **need** any help?

   knead _____

   Knead the dough 10 times.

10. higher _____

    I can jump **higher** than you.

    hire _____

    My boss will **hire** a student for the summer.

11. weak _____

    I feel tired and **weak**.

    week _____

    I am on vacation for a **week**.

12. in _____

    Put the milk **in** the fridge.

    inn _____

    We stayed at a beautiful **inn**.

13. ferry _____

    I took a **ferry** for the first time.

    fairy _____

    Do you believe in the tooth **fairy**?

14. border _____

    He works as a **border** patrol officer.

    boarder _____

    I have a new **boarder** in my house.

15. pray _____

    We will **pray** for you.

    prey _____

    The lion hunted its **prey** all night.

16. aunt _____

    My **aunt** is a nurse.

    ant _____

    There is an **ant** on your foot.

17. flu _____

    He is in bed with the **flu**.

    flew _____

    The helicopter **flew** over my house.

18. weigh _____

    How much do you **weigh**?

    way _____

    Do you know the **way** to the mall?

19. knows _____

    Nobody **knows** her name.

    nose _____

    She has a big **nose**.

20. tow _____

    Can you call a **tow** truck please?

    toe _____

    I wear a ring on my big **toe**.

21. kernel _____

    I ate the last **kernel** on the cob.

    colonel _____

    He was promoted to **colonel** last year.

22. coarse _____

    I used **coarse** salt to make this.

    course _____

    I'm so happy I passed that **course**.

23. air _____

    I love the fresh morning **air**.

    heir _____

    He is **heir** to the throne.

24. foreword _____

    Did you read the **foreword**?

    forward _____

    Be brave and go **forward**.

25. caller _____

    The tenth **caller** will win a prize.

    collar _____

    Put the **collar** on the cat.

26. allowed _____

    You are not **allowed** to do that.

    aloud _____

    Don't read **aloud** in the library.

27. feet _____

    My **feet** hurt.

    feat _____

    That is an amazing **feat** of engineering.

28. complements _____

    That color **complements** your hair.

    compliments _____

    Thanks for those lovely **compliments**.

29. pause _____

    We will take a short **pause**.

    paws _____

    The dog's **paws** are dirty.

30. horse _____

    The **horse** is running in the field.

    hoarse _____

    Your voice is a little **hoarse**.

Pronunciation of Difficult Words (1)

Many words are difficult to pronounce and need to be practiced.

accommodate	mayonnaise
anxious	miscellaneous
ashamed	murderer
association	musician
cabbage	obey
cinnamon	owe
conscientious	paw
crutches	polish
delicious	Polish
drawer	recipe
entrepreneurial	representative
idea	sew
iron	spinach
issue	usually
knowledgeable	wasp

Use your dictionary to find the meaning of these difficult words, then listen carefully and repeat the following sentences.

1. musician _____

   He is a talented **musician**.

2. usually _____

   We **usually** have lunch together.

3. crutches _____

   Where are my **crutches**?

4. wasp _____

   There is a **wasp** in the house.

5. owe_____

   You **owe** me a lot of money.

6. iron _____

   Don't forget to unplug the **iron**.

7. ashamed_____

   I was **ashamed** of you last night.

8. Polish _____

   We have many **Polish** friends.

9. accommodate _____

   We can **accommodate** you.

10. mayonnaise _____

    Do you want mustard or **mayonnaise?**

11. idea _____

    That is a very good **idea**.

12. sew _____

    Can you **sew** my pants?

13. spinach _____

    Do you like **spinach** salad?

14. drawer _____

    Put the socks in the top **drawer**.

15. anxious _____

    We are **anxious** to see you.

16. cinnamon _____

    Do you like apples and **cinnamon**?

17. recipe _____

    Can I have your **recipe**?

18. polish _____

    Please **polish** the furniture.

19. paw _____

    My cat has one white **paw**.

20. obey _____

    Please **obey** the speed limit.

21. cabbage _____

    The **cabbage** is from my garden.

22. entrepreneurial _____

    He has good **entrepreneurial** skills.

23. murderer _____

    The judge sent the **murderer** to jail.

24. issue _____

I didn't read that **issue**.

25. conscientious _____

He made a **conscientious** effort.

26. association _____

Which **association** do you belong to?

27. delicious _____

The meal was **delicious**.

28. representative _____

Who is your **representative**?

29. knowledgeable _____

She is **knowledgeable** about many things.

30. miscellaneous _____

Put that in the **miscellaneous** file.

_____

Pronunciation of Difficult Words (2)

Many words are difficult to pronounce and need to be practiced.

actually	materialistic
antibiotics	microwave
busy	parentheses
chipmunk	prerogative
citizenship	pronunciation
enthusiasm	recognize
especially	refrigerator
exaggeration	regularly
extinguisher	squirrel
extraordinary	statistics
fictitious	studying
guarantee	sweat
huge	tiny
intuition	tuition
itinerary	unusual

Use your dictionary to find the meaning of these difficult words, then listen carefully and repeat the following sentences.

1. tuition_____

   Did you pay your **tuition** fees?

2. squirrel _____

   The **squirrel** is eating the peanuts.

3. extraordinary _____

   He is an **extraordinary** person.

4. tiny _____

   It's just a **tiny** little bug.

5. enthusiasm_____

   I can't contain my **enthusiasm**.

6. exaggeration _____

   That is a big **exaggeration**.

7. unusual_____

   That is very **unusual**.

8. studying _____

   Be quiet, I'm **studying**.

9. busy _____

    Are you **busy** today?

10. parentheses _____

    Put the definition in **parentheses**.

11. intuition _____

    She has great **intuition**.

12. regularly _____

    I go to the gym **regularly**.

13. chipmunk _____

    The **chipmunk** is sitting in my hand.

14. huge _____

    That is a **huge** cat.

15. especially _____

    I **especially** like the black Corvette.

16. itinerary _____

    Is my **itinerary** ready?

17. recognize _____

    I didn't **recognize** you.

18. microwave _____

    Put it in the **microwave** oven.

19. statistics _____

    We are looking at **statistics** all week.

20. materialistic _____

    Some people are very **materialistic**.

21. pronunciation _____

    Your **pronunciation** is improving.

22. prerogative _____

    It's your **prerogative**.

23. fictitious _____

    He writes **fictitious** stories.

24. sweat _____

    There is **sweat** on your forehead.

25. citizenship _____

    Did you bring your **citizenship** papers?

26. refrigerator _____

    Put the eggs in the **refrigerator**.

27. extinguisher _____

    Do you have a fire **extinguisher**?

28. actually _____

    Actually, I like rainy days.

29. guarantee _____

    Can you provide me with a written **guarantee**?

30. antibiotics _____

    He is taking **antibiotics** for the infection.

Pronunciation of Difficult Words (3)

Many words are difficult to pronounce and need to be practiced.

accidentally	magnificent
arctic	man
awkward	mansion
choir	men
deodorant	miniature
deteriorated	participate
espresso	privilege
facade	publicity
jewelry	recommendation
leisure	schedule
length	synonym
lengthen	weird
lengthened	woman
lengthening	women
lower	yolk

Use your dictionary to find the meaning of these difficult words, then listen carefully and repeat the following sentences.

1. man_____

   He is a nice **man**.

2. woman _____

   She is a beautiful **woman**.

3. length_____

   I don't like the **length** of my hair.

4. lengthening _____

   She is **lengthening** my hair.

5. recommendation_____

   My boss gave me a good **recommendation**.

6. leisure_____

   What do you do in your **leisure** time?

7. magnificent _____

   What a **magnificent** day!

8. deodorant _____

   Please wear your **deodorant** today.

9. lower_____

   Can you **lower** the volume on the TV?

10. deteriorated _____

   The house has **deteriorated** over the years.

11. men _____

   They are nice **men**.

12. women _____

   They are beautiful **women**.

13. lengthen_____

   She can **lengthen** my hair.

14. lengthened_____

   Yesterday, she **lengthened** my hair.

15. espresso _____

   Do you prefer regular coffee or **espresso**?

16. awkward_____

   It was an **awkward** situation.

17. choir _____

   I sing in the church **choir**.

18. jewelry _____

   She wears a lot of **jewelry**.

19. miniature _____

   She has a **miniature** horse.

20. mansion _____

   Who lives in that big **mansion**?

21. privilege _____

   It is a **privilege** to know you.

22. publicity _____

   We need more **publicity**.

23. facade_____

   We want to redo the **facade** of our house.

24. arctic_____

   We felt the cold **arctic** breeze.

25. yolk_____

   The **yolk** is yellow.

26. synonym_____

   What is a **synonym** for the word happy?

27. participate _____

   Do you want to **participate**?

28. weird_____

   That's **weird**.

29. schedule_____

   Do you know your **schedule** for next week?

30. accidentally _____

   I dropped it **accidentally**.

Pronunciation of Difficult Words (4)
Many words are difficult to pronounce and need to be practiced.

anticipated	intimidate
backache	licorice
binoculars	literature
carriage	mustache
concentration	oars
enormous	once
environment	particularly
headache	porcupine
hitchhiker	prejudice
illegitimately	pumpkin
imitate	soldier
immediate	stomachache
individuality	supposedly
individually	toothache
intimate	variety

Use your dictionary to find the meaning of these difficult words, then listen carefully and repeat the following sentences.

1. imitate _____

   She is trying to **imitate** me.

2. intimate _____

   They had an **intimate** conversation.

3. carriage_____

   The baby is in the **carriage**.

4. supposedly_____

   Supposedly, he will be there.

5. prejudice _____

   The letter was written without **prejudice**.

6. concentration_____

   You need to work on your **concentration**.

7. individually_____

   Each candy is wrapped **individually**.

8. environment _____

   We have to protect the **environment**.

9. headache _____

I have a **headache**.

10. backache _____

He needs painkillers for his **backache**.

11. intimidate _____

She is trying to **intimidate** me.

12. immediate _____

We need an **immediate** response.

13. variety _____

They sell a **variety** of books.

14. literature _____

She teaches English **literature**.

15. anticipated _____

The results were much **anticipated**.

16. mustache _____

You look good with a **mustache**.

17. individuality _____

Individuality is important.

18. soldier _____

Her brother is a **soldier**.

19. toothache _____

She has a bad **toothache**.

20. stomachache _____

I had a **stomachache** after lunch.

21. pumpkin _____

I bought a **pumpkin** for Halloween.

22. once _____

I only met him **once**.

23. licorice _____

Do you like black **licorice**?

24. binoculars_____

Bring your **binoculars** to the concert.

25. porcupine_____

We saw a **porcupine** in the woods.

26. hitchhiker_____

The **hitchhiker** wanted a ride to the city.

27. enormous_____

The Titanic was **enormous**.

28. illegitimately_____

She terminated her employee **illegitimately**.

29. oars_____

Put the **oars** in the boat.

30. particularly_____

I **particularly** like the white kitten.

Pronunciation of Difficult Words (5)
Many words are difficult to pronounce and need to be practiced.

anonymity	necessary
autonomous	obvious
bury	occasionally
confidentiality	phenomenon
daiquiri	photographer
dandelion	physiotherapist
debut	possession
envelope	prescription
ethnicity	probably
lawyer	remuneration
liar	suit
magnifying glass	suite
mirror	uncomfortable
mischievous	Worcestershire
necessarily	world

Use your dictionary to find the meaning of these difficult words, then listen carefully and repeat the following sentences.

1. remuneration _____

    You will receive fair **remuneration**.

2. occasionally _____

    I **occasionally** go in the pool.

3. possession _____

    It is my favorite **possession**.

4. suit _____

    That is a nice black **suit**.

5. confidentiality _____

    We respect **confidentiality**.

6. prescription _____

    You need a **prescription** from a doctor.

7. daiquiri _____

    I want a strawberry **daiquiri**.

8. lawyer _____

    That man is a **lawyer**.

9. world _____

    He is the richest man in the **world**.

10. photographer_____

    She wants to be a **photographer**.

11. uncomfortable _____

    This chair is very **uncomfortable**.

12. ethnicity _____

    What is your **ethnicity**?

13. autonomous_____

    Is your grandmother still **autonomous**?

14. suite _____

    We rented a nice **suite** at the hotel.

15. anonymity _____

    He prefers the computer for **anonymity**.

16. envelope_____

    I forgot to put a stamp on the **envelope**.

17. necessary _____

    I don't think it's **necessary**.

18. liar_____

    That man is a **liar**.

19. obvious_____

    It's **obvious** that she likes him.

20. physiotherapist _____

    My brother is a **physiotherapist**.

21. dandelion_____

    A **dandelion** is yellow.

22. mirror _____

    Stop looking at yourself in the **mirror**.

23. magnifying glass _____

    I need a **magnifying glass** to read your writing.

24. probably _____

I will **probably** stay home tonight.

25. necessarily _____

We don't **necessarily** have to do it.

26. debut _____

She made her **debut** in 2010.

27. Worcestershire _____

Did you buy the **Worcestershire** sauce?

28. bury _____

The dog will **bury** the bone.

29. phenomenon _____

What a strange **phenomenon**.

30. mischievous _____

She has a **mischievous** smile.

Pronunciation of Difficult Words (6)
Many words are difficult to pronounce and need to be practiced.

accomplishment	dehumidifier
affidavit	juror
anemone	lasagne
ask	official
ballet	orangutan
bologna	penguin
bouquet	phlegm
brewery	pseudonym
buffet	sensitivity
cocoa	specific
cologne	strength
conscience	strengthen
conscientious	strengthened
conscious	strengthening
courageous	vehicle

Use your dictionary to find the meaning of these difficult words, then listen carefully and repeat the following sentences.

1. strength _____

   This rope doesn't have much **strength**.

2. strengthening _____

   He is **strengthening** the rope.

3. conscious _____

   He was not **conscious** after he fell.

4. sensitivity _____

   The article was written with the right amount of **sensitivity**.

5. courageous _____

   That was a **courageous** act of bravery.

6. phlegm _____

   Her throat was congested with **phlegm**.

7. juror _____

   One **juror** was undecided.

8. ask_____

   Ask your teacher.

9. pseudonym _____

   Why did you use a **pseudonym**?

10. ballet_____

   She is a **ballet** dancer.

11. strengthen _____

   Can you **strengthen** the rope?

12. strengthened _____

   I **strengthened** the rope for you.

13. conscience _____

   It will affect your **conscience**.

14. accomplishment _____

   That was an incredible **accomplishment**.

15. official_____

   That is our **official** logo.

16. penguin _____

   A **penguin** can't fly.

17. orangutan _____

   An **orangutan** is not a good house pet.

18. conscientious_____

   She made a **conscientious** effort.

19. affidavit _____

   The lawyer issued an **affidavit**.

20. bouquet _____

   What a beautiful **bouquet** of flowers.

21. bologna _____

   I want a **bologna** sandwich.

22. lasagne_____

   She made a vegetarian **lasagne**.

23. buffet _____

   They have a wonderful lunch **buffet**.

24. cologne _____

    I love the **cologne** you are wearing.

25. vehicle _____

    You need a new **vehicle**.

26. dehumidifier _____

    Did you empty the **dehumidifier**?

27. anemone _____

    Can an **anemone** be blue?

28. brewery _____

    He works at the local **brewery**.

29. cocoa _____

    I think I will have a hot **cocoa**.

30. specific _____

    Please be more **specific**.

Answer Key

1   *To Be*: Present Tense

1-1   1. The girl is pretty.   2. I am ready.   3. She is my friend.   4. They are twins.   5. The flowers are yellow.   6. The flashlight is in the tent.   7. The fridge and counter in the kitchen are dirty.   8. I am tired today.   9. We are busy.   10. The toys are in the basement.   11. The ribbons in my hair are pink.   12. The kitchen is very small.   13. The vacuum is in the closet.   14. He is nice.   15. The microwave oven is in the kitchen.   16. The toy is on the floor.   17. I am sick today.

1-2   1. is   2. are   3. is   4. are   5. are   6. are   7. are   8. are   9. is   10. are   11. is   12. is   13. are   14. is   15. is   16. are   17. is   18. is   19. am   20. is   21. is   22. is   23. is   24. is   25. are   26. is   27. is   28. is   29. is   30. is   31. is   32. is   33. is   34. is

2   *To Be*: Present Tense: Negative Form

2-1   1. The cheese is not on the table. The cheese isn't on the table.   2. She is not my sister. She isn't my sister.   3. My neighbors are not Spanish. My neighbors aren't Spanish.   4. My sister-in-law is not Italian. My sister-in-law isn't Italian.   5. Diane is not pregnant. Diane isn't pregnant.   6. The limes are not sour. The limes aren't sour.   7. The bus is not empty. The bus isn't empty.   8. The kids are not early for class today. The kids aren't early for class today.   9. The drawers are not empty. The drawers aren't empty.   10. It is not a nice city. It isn't a nice city.

2-2   1. isn't   2. aren't   3. isn't   4. aren't   5. isn't   6. isn't   7. aren't   8. aren't   9. aren't   10. isn't   11. isn't   12. isn't   13. aren't   14. aren't   15. isn't   16. isn't   17. isn't   18. aren't   19. isn't   20. aren't   21. aren't   22. isn't   23. aren't   24. isn't   25. isn't   26. isn't   27. am not   28. isn't   29. isn't   30. isn't   31. aren't   32. aren't   33. isn't   34. isn't

3   *To Be*: Present Tense: Question Form

3-1   1. Are the wheels in the garage?   2. Is the sharpener on my desk?   3. Are the toothbrush and toothpaste in the bathroom?   4. Is my bathing suit on the clothesline?   5. Am I in your English class?   6. Is it cold outside?   7. Is he a policeman in the city?   8. Are the coats on the floor?   9. Are Johanne and Véronique in a meeting?   10. Are the toys in the box downstairs?   11. Are the cow and calf brown?   12. Is the orange juice sweet?   13. Are the frogs in the pond?   14. Is the goldfish in the bowl?   15. Are you serious?   16. Is Marie French?

3-2   1. Is   2. Are   3. Are   4. Is   5. Are   6. Is   7. Are   8. Is   9. Are   10. Are   11. Is   12. Am   13. Are   14. Is   15. Is   16. Are   17. Are   18. Is   19. Are   20. Are   21. Are   22. Is   23. Are   24. Is   25. Is   26. Are   27. Are   28. Is   29. Is   30. Is   31. Are   32. Am

4   *To Be:* Past Tense

4-1   1. He was my roommate.   2. It was in my pocket.   3. The snake was in the garden.   4. The diapers were in the bag.   5. Lisa was sick.   6. The kids were in the pool.   7. The bucket was full of minnows.   8. The washer and dryer were in the laundry room.   9. I was in my office.   10. The pencil was on the floor.   11. Sorry that I was late.   12. The flowers were for Jennifer.   13. My grandmother was in the hospital.   14. The exam was easy.   15. The crust was very thick.   16. The farm was very far.

4-2   1. was   2. were   3. was   4. were   5. was   6. was   7. was   8. was   9. were   10. were   11. was   12. was   13. were   14. was   15. were   16. was   17. were   18. was   19. were   20. was   21. were   22. was   23. were   24. was   25. were   26. was   27. was   28. were   29. was   30. was   31. were   32. were

5   *To Be:* Past Tense: Negative Form

5-1   1. The dress was not blue. The dress wasn't blue.   2. The couch in the living room was not dirty. The couch in the living room wasn't dirty.   3. They were not very fast. They weren't very fast.   4. It was not a good joke. It wasn't a good joke.   5. The raccoons were not in the tree. The raccoons weren't in the tree.   6. The slippers were not purple. The slippers weren't purple.   7. We were not at the play last night. We weren't at the play last night.   8. The plates were not in the dishwasher. The plates weren't in the dishwasher.   9. Karen was not a waitress for three years. Karen wasn't a waitress for three years.   10. My name was not on the list. My name wasn't on the list.

5-2   1. weren't   2. wasn't   3. wasn't   4. weren't   5. weren't   6. wasn't   7. wasn't   8. weren't   9. weren't   10. wasn't   11. wasn't   12. wasn't   13. wasn't   14. wasn't   15. weren't   16. wasn't   17. weren't   18. wasn't   19. weren't   20. wasn't   21. wasn't   22. wasn't   23. weren't   24. wasn't   25. wasn't   26. wasn't   27. weren't   28. wasn't   29. wasn't   30. wasn't   31. wasn't   32. wasn't

6   *To Be:* Past Tense: Question Form

6-1   1. Was it free?   2. Was the airplane very low in the sky?   3. Was the mall empty?   4. Were they in kindergarten together?   5. Was it bitter?   6. Were you angry at Susan?   7. Was the recipe easy?   8. Were the nail clippers in the drawer?   9. Were the curtains velvet?   10. Was the tablecloth dirty?   11. Was it enough?   12. Was she a flight attendant when she was young?   13. Were the ashtrays full?   14. Was the lady thin?   15. Was Claude seasick on the ship?   16. Were the crutches behind the door?

6-2   1. Was   2. Were   3. Was   4. Were   5. Was   6. Were   7. Was   8. Were   9. Was   10. Was   11. Was   12. Was   13. Were   14. Was   15. Were   16. Was   17. Were   18. Was   19. Were   20. Were   21. Was   22. Was   23. Were   24. Was   25. Was   26. Was   27. Was   28. Was   29. Was   30. Was   31. Were   32. Was   33. Was   34. Were   35. Were   36. Was   37. Was   38. Were   39. Was

7   Exceptional Uses with the Verb *To Be*

7-1   1. My daughter is afraid of the dark.   2. Is Jason right?   3. She wasn't hungry for breakfast this morning.   4. Please open the windows. I am very hot.   5. I am not ashamed of the size of my shoes.   6. Cathy was thirty-three years old on her last birthday.   7. We were very thirsty after the race.   8. You are wrong again.   9. I am not right all the time.   10. Are you scared of thunder?   11. He wasn't afraid of the lightning.   12. I was cold this morning.   13. Are the guests hungry?   14. My mother and father were ashamed of my behavior.   15. Is your son scared of spiders?   16. I am not eighteen years old.   17. Bill is happy because he is right.   18. I am cold because of the snowballs in my pocket.

7-2   1. wasn't   2. Were   3. isn't   4. were   5. is   6. was   7. isn't   8. am   9. isn't   10. is   11. Was   12. is   13. Are   14. Was   15. Was   16. weren't   17. isn't   18. Were   19. wasn't   20. aren't   21. is   22. Was   23. aren't   24. am   25. are   26. Were   27. wasn't   28. is   29. isn't   30. was   31. is   32. Is   33. wasn't   34. are

8 Adjectives

8-1 1. The cute little house is for sale.   2. It is a very sharp knife.   3. He is a tall, handsome man.   4. It was a cold, windy day yesterday.   5. I want a black leather jacket.   6. They drink prune juice every morning.   7. The big, green bug is in my shoe.   8. Elizabeth is a French teacher.   9. The ugly, hairy spider is in the kitchen.   10. Canada is a big, beautiful country.   11. The English test was hard.   12. He was a nice policeman.   13. Look at the beautiful white snow.   14. The little green frog is in the pond.   15. It was a huge whale.

8-2 1. It was a long, hard winter.   2. I need a new silver watch.   3. My right hand is sore.   4. I want the round balloons.   5. We like to watch old movies.   6. Look at the bright stars in the sky.   7. I like BBQ chips.   8. They want chocolate cake for dessert.   9. I love Mexican food.   10. He is a wealthy lawyer.   11. You draw funny pictures.   12. It was a long, boring meeting.   13. My left knee is swollen.   14. The kids like junk food.   15. We like to make rhubarb pies.   16. I hate strawberry yogurt.   17. We wear white shoes to school.   18. They are identical twins.

9 To *Have*: Present Tense

9-1 1. He has a bad attitude.   2. The cat has white paws.   3. I have a peanut butter sandwich for lunch today.   4. Maria has a red velvet skirt.   5. We have a nice landlord.   6. Jessica has a terrible headache.   7. We have a good housekeeper.   8. She has a lot of dandruff.   9. Tony has very good skills.   10. The milk has a weird taste.   11. The house has a green roof.   12. It has a short tail.   13. We have a day off next week.   14. I have a warm sleeping bag.   15. My sister has purple eye shadow.   16. You have a nice smile.

9-2 1. have 2. has 3. has 4. have 5. has 6. have 7. has 8. has 9. has 10. have 11. has 12. has 13. has 14. have 15. have 16. has 17. has 18. has 19. have 20. have 21. has 22. have 23. has 24. have 25. has 26. have 27. has 28. has 29. has 30. have 31. has 32. has

10 To *Have*: Present Tense: Negative Form

10-1 1. My cat does not have fleas. My cat doesn't have fleas.   2. We do not have a satellite dish on the roof. We don't have a satellite dish on the roof.   3. I do not have a surprise for you. I don't have a surprise for you.   4. Jimmy does not have a fast snowmobile. Jimmy doesn't have a fast snowmobile.   5. We do not have many good books about antique jewelry. We don't have many good books about antique jewelry.   6. She does not have a lot of customers. She doesn't have a lot of customers.   7. My brother-in-law does not have a screwdriver. My brother-in-law doesn't have a screwdriver.   8. The clown does not have a big red nose. The clown doesn't have a big red nose.   9. I do not have long straight hair and bangs. I don't have long straight hair and bangs.   10. She does not have fantastic news. She doesn't have fantastic news.

10-2 1. don't 2. doesn't 3. doesn't 4. doesn't 5. don't 6. doesn't 7. don't 8. don't 9. don't 10. doesn't 11. don't 12. doesn't 13. doesn't 14. don't 15. doesn't 16. doesn't 17. don't 18. doesn't 19. don't 20. doesn't 21. don't 22. doesn't 23. doesn't 24. don't 25. doesn't 26. don't 27. don't 28. don't 29. don't 30. don't 31. don't 32. don't 33. doesn't 34. doesn't

11 To *Have*: Present Tense: Question Form

11-1 1. Do you have a pink eraser?   2. Does he have my phone number?   3. Do they have everything they need?   4. Do we have the same scarf?   5. Do I have rights?   6. Does Marissa have green flip-flops?   7. Do you have a huge turkey for Thanksgiving?   8. Do they have a lease until next year?   9. Does it have a funny taste?   10. Do you have two important appointments today?   11. Does the dove have white wings?   12. Do we have a day off next week?   13. Does David have a virtual reality headset?   14. Does Juanita have a good recipe for meat loaf?   15. Do we have a tight deadline for the project?   16. Do they have a big celebration on Christmas Eve?

11-2 1. Do 2. Do 3. Does 4. Do 5. Does 6. Do 7. Does 8. Do 9. Does 10. Does 11. Do 12. Do 13. Does 14. Do 15. Does 16. Does 17. Does 18. Does 19. Do 20. Do 21. Does 22. Do 23. Does 24. Do 25. Does 26. Do 27. Do 28. Do 29. Do 30. Do 31. Do 32. Does

12 The Simple Present Tense

12-1 1. He smokes American cigarettes. 2. Karen blushes when she sees that boy. 3. I love caramel apple cake. 4. He cries like a baby. 5. It amazes me. 6. It jumps very high. 7. He kisses all the girls in school. 8. My cats scratch the furniture. 9. They help many people in the village. 10. The knights guard the king and castle in the kingdom. 11. He never flushes the toilet.

12-2 1. explains 2. whisper 3. crushes 4. buys 5. do 6. earn 7. works 8. manages 9. carry 10. owe 11. eats 12. fears 13. follow 14. work 15. drinks 16. pushes 17. spoils 18. dreams 19. drives 20. does 21. goes 22. own 23. obey 24. melts

13 The Simple Present Tense: Negative Form

13-1 1. My husband does not snore every night. My husband doesn't snore every night. 2. I do not believe your story about the giant monkeys. I don't believe your story about the giant monkeys. 3. Nancy and Yvan do not collect coins. Nancy and Yvan don't collect coins. 4. She does not speak several foreign languages. She doesn't speak several foreign languages. 5. It does not dislike fish. It doesn't dislike fish. 6. Ron does not swear and yell in class. Ron doesn't swear and yell in class. 7. Sara does not sell sewing machines. Sara doesn't sell sewing machines. 8. I do not trust you. I don't trust you. 9. We do not eat meat. We don't eat meat.

13-2 1. doesn't 2. don't 3. don't 4. doesn't 5. don't 6. doesn't 7. doesn't 8. don't 9. doesn't 10. don't 11. doesn't 12. doesn't 13. don't 14. don't 15. doesn't 16. don't 17. doesn't 18. don't 19. doesn't 20. doesn't 21. doesn't 22. don't 23. doesn't 24. doesn't 25. don't 26. don't 27. doesn't 28. doesn't 29. don't 30. doesn't

14 The Simple Present Tense: Question Form

14-1 1. Does she skate in the morning? 2. Do they boil the vegetables? 3. Does he sleep in the afternoon? 4. Do the boys play chess at night? 5. Do you pay the mortgage on time? 6. Does she read the English newspaper? 7. Do they drive to work together? 8. Does it cost $20 to travel by train to the city? 9. Does she scream when she watches horror movies? 10. Does she want a new hobby? 11. Does the king wear a red velvet crown? 12. Does Bobby play with toy soldiers? 13. Do you put salt and pepper in the dough? 14. Does Jackie touch everything in my office? 15. Do you see the fox in the woods?

14-2 1. Does 2. Do 3. Does 4. Do 5. Do 6. Does 7. Do 8. Does 9. Do 10. Do 11. Does 12. Do 13. Does 14. Does 15. Do 16. Does 17. Does 18. Do 19. Do 20. Does 21. Does 22. Do 23. Does 24. Do 25. Does 26. Do 27. Do 28. Does

15 Possessive Adjectives

15-1 1. She visits her relatives every summer. 2. We hide our money under the carpet in the master bedroom. 3. They keep their jewels in a jewelry box. 4. I wash my stairs with a sponge. 5. He passes all his exams. 6. She dresses her dolls in pink. 7. I open my mail after breakfast. 8. He bites his nails. 9. We rent our apartment. 10. It licks its paws. 11. I burn my marshmallows. 12. Jeff takes his pills in the morning. 13. The boys forget their homework every day. 14. He wipes his nose on his sleeve. 15. She dyes her hair. 16. The sailors believe their new submarine is better.

15-2 1. their 2. her 3. our 4. my 5. her 6. your 7. my 8. its 9. our 10. his 11. their 12. my 13. their 14. his 15. our 16. his 17. my 18. her 19. their 20. my 21. her 22. your 23. our 24. her 25. his 26. my

16 The Simple Past Tense

16-1 1. I used my hair dryer to dry my hair. 2. We tried a new recipe last night. 3. Thomas answered the phone. 4. I noticed that your sweater was inside out. 5. The car landed upside down in the ditch. 6. She shared her snack with her friends at school yesterday. 7. The minimum wage increased last year. 8. Suzanne lied about her age. 9. My company signed the lease for our building for another three years. 10. The teacher challenged her students and rewarded them for their hard work. 11. The eel killed the toad.

16-2 1. accepted 2. joined 3. moved 4. knocked 5. described 6. proved 7. denied 8. borrowed 9. watched 10. used 11. tidied 12. rained 13. painted 14. avoided 15. pushed 16. married 17. pleased 18. destroyed 19. served 20. obtained 21. arrested 22. ordered 23. decided 24. expected

17 The Simple Past Tense with Irregular Verbs: 1

17-1 1. She blew on her soup because it was hot. 2. The house shook a lot during the earthquake. 3. They took the plane and spent their honeymoon overseas. 4. I always felt sick when I was pregnant. 5. He tore his pants when he fell. 6. We bought a nice gift for our grandparents in Ireland. 7. The kids slid down the mountain on their new toboggan. 8. I did the dishes after supper. 9. I cut my finger on the sharp saw. 10. You broke my favorite cup. 11. Your dog bit my ankle. 12. Karen found a purse at the beach. 13. I taught math at the high school last year.

17-2 1. spoke 2. began 3. gave 4. hung 5. saw 6. sat 7. stole 8. paid 9. drew 10. swore 11. dug 12. held 13. shot 14. heard 15. left 16. saw

18 The Simple Past Tense with Irregular Verbs: 2

18-1 1. We withdrew enough money for the whole month. 2. I caught a bullfrog and four tadpoles in the pond. 3. Salina rode a horse for the first time yesterday. 4. Robert, Claire, and Daniel built a huge sand castle on the beach. 5. Brandon bent the hanger to open the car door. 6. I drove to the post office to buy some stamps and envelopes. 7. The hunter forgot his rifle in the woods. 8. You woke your grandmother when you knocked on the window. 9. The sheep and lamb slept on the hay in the barn. 10. I had a bagel with bacon, tomato, cheese, and lettuce for lunch. 11. Camilie understood what the teacher taught in class today. 12. My mother froze the vegetables for the winter. 13. Dimitri lent the shovel to his neighbor. 14. The red team beat the blue team. 15. Laurent came to help us with the inventory in the warehouse.

18-2 1. brought 2. cost 3. rose 4. won 5. grew 6. put 7. meant 8. shut 9. chose 10. forgave 11. thought 12. lost 13. hurt 14. kept 15. sent 16. drank

19 The Simple Past Tense with Irregular Verbs: 3

19-1 1. She sang on Monday, Wednesday, and Friday at the concert in Montreal. 2. The house was dark because of the power failure, so we lit the candles. 3. The car spun out of control on the ice. 4. I read the newspaper in the evening on Saturday and Sunday. 5. My son fought at school on Tuesday and Thursday last week. 6. The phone rang in the middle of the night. 7. I knew that he was guilty of the crime. 8. She met Sara at the liquor store. 9. Sorry, but I ate all the icing on your cake when you went to the bathroom. 10. I got a big raise at work last month. 11. We sold our parrot because he was too noisy. 12. Alexandre threw the papers in the fire. 13. My pants fit me last year. 14. Carmen ran and hid under the bed. 15. We fed meat to the fox.

19-2 1. dealt 2. said 3. swept 4. made 5. stuck 6. hit 7. became, quit 8. wore 9. led 10. flew 11. wrote 12. swam 13. wept 14. told 15. stood 16. gave

20 The Simple Past Tense: Negative Form

20-1 1. They did not watch the hockey game on their new big-screen TV. They didn't watch the hockey game on their new big-screen TV. 2. I did not forget to tell him. I didn't forget to tell him. 3. She did not waste my valuable time. She didn't waste my valuable time. 4. Marcia did not report her income. Marcia didn't report her income. 5. I did not shake the bottle of medicine. I didn't shake the bottle of medicine. 6. My uncle did not shave his head. My uncle didn't shave his head. 7. He did not apologize to his friend. He didn't apologize to his friend. 8. We did not find clams and mussels in the sand on the beach. We didn't find clams and mussels in the sand on the beach. 9. The police did not read the man his rights. The police didn't read the man his rights. 10. It did not scratch my skin. It didn't scratch my skin.

20-2 1. He didn't prevent the accident. 2. She didn't express her opinion. 3. The movie didn't last three hours. 4. They didn't go to see their granddaughter and grandson. 5. They didn't save a lot of money for their trip to Greece. 6. Patricia didn't lose her mittens, scarf, and hat at school. 7. Sonia didn't translate the letter. 8. I didn't buy a gift for her. 9. Mario didn't find a black leather wallet in the snow. 10. We

didn't put the leftovers in plastic bags.   11. I didn't tear my pantyhose.   12. I didn't know you were there.
13. He didn't deposit his pay in his savings account.   14. The plumber didn't fix the pipes, shower, and toilet in the bathroom upstairs.   15. I didn't clean the litter box and brush the cat this morning.   16. I didn't read my horoscope today.   17. The wind didn't bend the antenna.   18. Laura didn't grow two inches and gain ten pounds last year.

21   The Simple Past Tense: Question Form

21-1   1. Did you see the beautiful rainbow?   2. Did he offend you when he said that?   3. Did Jessica find a starfish on the beach?   4. Did the squirrel eat the peanuts?   5. Did he shoot a deer last weekend?   6. Did I indicate my overtime hours on my timesheet?   7. Did they remain friends after the argument?   8. Did Luke break the remote control for the TV?   9. Did she change her mind?   10. Did Brandon cheat when we played cards?   11. Did they weigh the fish on the scale?   12. Did you put garlic in the salad?   13. Did the people elect a new president?   14. Did he escape from prison?   15. Did it sleep under your bed?

21-2   1. Did you take a picture of the sunset?   2. Did she lock the safe?   3. Did they attend the funeral?   4. Did Barry order seafood?   5. Did the chipmunk climb the tree?   6. Did they ride the roller-coaster?   7. Did she make the earrings?   8. Did the divers find a treasure chest?   9. Did the baby blow bubbles in the bath?   10. Did they load the wagon?   11. Did the rattlesnake bite his arm?   12. Did the policeman put handcuffs on the thief?   13. Did she convince you?   14. Did you pick a flower for me?   15. Did it appear to be true?   16. Did you ask a question?   17. Did the maid iron my apron?   18. Did the dog lick my ice-cream cone?   19. Did she draw a picture of a mermaid?   20. Did Ravi lose his comb?

22   Prepositions: *In* and *On*

22-1   1. The garbage can is in the garage.   2. Do you see signs of life on the moon?   3. We will talk about it in the morning.   4. Mark moved here in 1997.   5. Don't throw your empty bottle on the ground.   6. We spent five days in Paris.   7. All the kids start school in September.   8. I will see you on Saturday.   9. They advertised it on the radio in California.   10. What do you have in your mouth?   11. I saw your picture in the newspaper in Ontario.   12. It's my birthday on Tuesday.   13. The bathroom is on the left.   14. We went for a ride on his motorcycle in the country.   15. She presented her project on trees.

22-2   1. on 2. in 3. in 4. on 5. on 6. in 7. on 8. on 9. in 10. on 11. on 12. on 13. in
14. in 15. on 16. in 17. in 18. in 19. in 20. in 21. on 22. in 23. on 24. in 25. on
26. in 27. on 28. in 29. on 30. in 31. on 32. on 33. on 34. in 35. on 36. in 37. on
38. on 39. in 40. in

23   *There Is* and *There Are*: Present Tense

23-1   1. There are many meatballs and red peppers in the sauce.   2. There is a whiteboard in my classroom.
3. There are rocks in my boot.   4. There is a signature on the letter.   5. There are gigantic footprints in the snow.   6. There is a fire hydrant at the corner of my street.   7. There are many caterpillars on the tree.   8. There is a black stallion in the field.   9. There are four piglets and three colts in the barn.
10. There is a quilt on my bed.   11. There are many seagulls on the beach.   12. There is a new keyboard in the box.   13. There are two sponges in the bucket.   14. There are many dirty plates in the sink.
15. There are six diamonds on my ring.   16. There are a few gray squirrels in the tree.

23-2   1. are 2. is 3. is 4. is 5. are 6. is 7. is 8. is 9. are 10. is 11. are 12. is 13. is
14. are 15. is 16. is 17. are 18. is 19. are 20. is 21. are 22. is 23. are 24. is 25. are
26. is 27. is 28. are 29. is 30. are

24   *There Is* and *There Are*: Present Tense: Negative Form

24-1   1. There is not a lot of shade in the backyard. There isn't a lot of shade in the backyard.   2. There are not three gold buttons on my coat. There aren't three gold buttons on my coat.   3. There are not two yellow folders on my desk. There aren't two yellow folders on my desk.   4. There is not a tricycle on the sidewalk. There isn't a tricycle on the sidewalk.   5. There is not a thermometer in the bathroom. There isn't a thermometer in the bathroom.   6. There are not three white rabbits in the cage. There aren't three white rabbits in the cage.   7. There is not a turtle on the log. There isn't a turtle on the log.   8. There are not many angels in the picture. There aren't many angels in the picture.   9. There is not a scarecrow in the field. There isn't a scarecrow in the field.   10. There are not many dimes and nickels in the wishing well. There aren't many dimes and nickels in the wishing well.   11. There are not five quarters and a penny in my back pocket. There aren't five quarters and a penny in my back pocket.

24-2 1. isn't 2. isn't 3. aren't 4. isn't 5. aren't 6. isn't 7. isn't 8. isn't 9. aren't 10. isn't
11. isn't 12. aren't 13. isn't 14. aren't 15. isn't 16. aren't 17. isn't 18. aren't 19. isn't
20. isn't 21. isn't 22. aren't 23. isn't 24. aren't 25. isn't 26. aren't 27. isn't 28. isn't
29. aren't 30. isn't 31. aren't

25 *There Is* and *There Are*: Present Tense: Question Form

25-1 1. Is there a vending machine in the cafeteria?   2. Are there enough life jackets in the boat?   3. Are there many skyscrapers in the city?   4. Is there a lifeguard at the pool?   5. Are there two owls in the tree?   6. Is there a diving board at the public pool?   7. Are there germs on my hands?   8. Is there a handle on my suitcase?   9. Is there a UFO in the sky?   10. Are there aliens in the UFO?   11. Are there candy canes on the Christmas tree?   12. Is there a ruler on my desk?   13. Are there enough place mats on the table? 14. Is there a measuring cup in the cupboard?   15. Is there a catfish in the pail?   16. Are there many hangers in the closet?   17. Is there a mirror in your purse?

25-2 1. Are 2. Is 3. Is 4. Are 5. Is 6. Is 7. Are 8. Is 9. Is 10. Are 11. Are 12. Are
13. Is 14. Is 15. Are 16. Are 17. Is 18. Is 19. Are 20. Is 21. Are 22. Are 23. Is
24. Are 25. Is 26. Are 27. Is 28. Is 29. Is 30. Are 31. Are 32. Is 33. Is 34. Are

26 *There Is* and *There Are*: Past Tense

26-1 1. There was rust on the knife.   2. There were rules to follow.   3. There was a big sale at the mall, so I bought a scarf and shoes.   4. There were many speed bumps on the road.   5. There were wet towels on the floor after he took his shower.   6. There was a hurricane in the southeast last week.   7. There were many stray cats in the alley.   8. There were beautiful fireworks in the sky last night.   9. There was a magnifying glass on the table.   10. There were two circles, three squares, and four triangles in the picture. 11. There was a diamond in her belly button.   12. There was a cork in the bottle of wine.   13. There were many straws in the cup on the counter in the kitchen.   14. There was a good story about you in the newspaper this morning.   15. There were a lot of dirty pots and pans in the sink.   16. There were many dimes, nickels, and quarters in my piggy bank.   17. There was gravy on my mashed potatoes but not on my meat.   18. There was a snowstorm in the northwest last night.

26-2 1. was 2. were 3. were 4. was 5. were 6. was 7. were 8. was 9. were 10. was 11. was
12. was 13. were 14. were 15. was 16. were 17. was 18. were 19. was 20. were 21. were
22. was 23. was 24. was 25. was 26. were 27. was 28. were 29. was 30. were 31. were
32. were 33. was 34. was

27 *There Is* and *There Are*: Past Tense: Negative Form

27-1 1. There was not a crack in my windshield. There wasn't a crack in my windshield.   2. There were not many shells and stones in the sand on the beach. There weren't many shells and stones in the sand on the beach. 3. There were not a lot of big heavy trucks on the bridge this morning. There weren't a lot of big heavy trucks on the bridge this morning.   4. There was not a peach in my lunch box. There wasn't a peach in my lunch box.   5. There were not two staplers on my desk in my office. There weren't two staplers on my desk in my office.   6. There was not a big brown beaver near the dam. There wasn't a big brown beaver near the dam. 7. There were not many wheelchairs in the hall in the hospital. There weren't many wheelchairs in the hall in the hospital.   8. There was not a wreath on the door. There wasn't a wreath on the door.   9. There were not many camels in the desert. There weren't many camels in the desert.   10. There was not a huge octopus in the boat. There wasn't a huge octopus in the boat.   11. There were not many fun games to play. There weren't many fun games to play.

27-2 1. wasn't 2. weren't 3. wasn't 4. weren't 5. wasn't 6. wasn't 7. weren't 8. wasn't 9. weren't
10. wasn't 11. wasn't 12. weren't 13. weren't 14. wasn't 15. weren't 16. wasn't 17. wasn't
18. wasn't 19. weren't 20. wasn't 21. weren't 22. weren't 23. weren't 24. weren't 25. wasn't
26. wasn't 27. weren't 28. wasn't 29. wasn't 30. wasn't 31. wasn't 32. weren't

28 *There Is* and *There Are*: Past Tense: Question Form

28-1 1. Were there many knights to guard the castle in the kingdom?   2. Was there a wooden outhouse behind our cottage in the country?   3. Was there a picture of a skull and bones on the bottle?   4. Were there many cigarette butts in the ashtray?   5. Was there a car in my blind spot?   6. Were there pink fuzzy dice on his rearview mirror?   7. Was there a splinter in his thumb?   8. Was there enough room on the bus for everybody?   9. Was there a rude boy in your class last year?   10. Were there two pretty blue bows in her hair?   11. Was there a Canada goose near the lake?   12. Was there a green carpet on the floor in the entrance?   13. Was there a lot of garlic in the butter?   14. Were there many people without a passport at the airport?   15. Were there many thorns on the rose?   16. Was there a garage sale last weekend?   17. Were there many people on the roller-coaster?   18. Was there a locksmith in the mall?

28-2 1. Were   2. Was   3. Was   4. Was   5. Was   6. Was   7. Was   8. Were   9. Were   10. Was   11. Was   12. Was   13. Were   14. Was   15. Was   16. Were   17. Were   18. Was   19. Were   20. Was   21. Were   22. Was   23. Was   24. Was   25. Was   26. Were   27. Was   28. Was   29. Were   30. Was   31. Was   32. Was   33. Were   34. Was

29 Prepositions: To and At

29-1 1. Please explain this to me.   2. The girls ate cake at the birthday party.   3. We saw Tony and his brother at the restaurant.   4. I sold my car to Mike.   5. I bought a muzzle for my dog at the pet store.   6. The funeral was at four o'clock.   7. We fed the apple cores to the raccoons.   8. I go to the gym daily.   9. We made a bonfire at the beach.   10. They drive to the city.   11. The elevator went to the basement.   12. We noticed that there was a policeman at the door.   13. He talked to the press after the meeting.   14. They gave the prize to my opponent.   15. Call me at 6:30 P.M.   16. We went to England and Spain last year.

29-2 1. at   2. at   3. to   4. at   5. at   6. to   7. to   8. at   9. at, at   10. to   11. to   12. to   13. at   14. to   15. to   16. at   17. to   18. at   19. to   20. at   21. to   22. at   23. to   24. to   25. at   26. to   27. at   28. at   29. to   30. at   31. to   32. at   33. at   34. to

30 The Present Progressive (Continuous) Tense

30-1 1. The wolf is howling at the moon.   2. Sheila is worrying now because her daughter is late.   3. It is cold. We are shivering and we have goose bumps.   4. They are crossing the lake in a canoe.   5. The mayor is discussing the enormous potholes on the roads.   6. She is pouring a soft drink for you.   7. The nuns are sewing clothes and knitting slippers for the children.   8. The policeman is wearing his bulletproof vest.   9. My great-grandfather is living in a retirement home.   10. They are suing the city.   11. We are looking at the Big Dipper and the Little Dipper with our binoculars.   12. Rollande is drinking water because she has the hiccups.   13. My stepfather is repairing the bleachers in the stadium.   14. It is snowing again.   15. The dog is barking and growling at the groundhog outside.

30-2 1. is dressing   2. are coughing   3. is tickling   4. am rewinding   5. is waving   6. is rubbing   7. is drooling   8. are sitting   9. are living   10. is delivering   11. are writing   12. is whispering   13. are breaking   14. is ringing   15. is winning   16. are rattling   17. is teasing   18. are annoying   19. is curling   20. are wasting   21. is juggling   22. is overflowing   23. is chewing   24. is putting   25. am sending   26. are surrounding   27. am leaving   28. is drawing   29. are melting   30. am giving

31 The Present Progressive (Continuous) Tense: Negative Form

31-1 1. He is not shouting at you. He isn't shouting at you.   2. They are not waiting downstairs for us. They aren't waiting downstairs for us.   3. The ship is not sinking. The ship isn't sinking.   4. The dog is not burying the bone in the sand. The dog isn't burying the bone in the sand.   5. We are not planting the seeds in the garden. We aren't planting the seeds in the garden.   6. I am not teaching in the elementary school this year. No contraction.   7. Mike is not stirring the paint with the paintbrush. Mike isn't stirring the paint with the paintbrush.   8. You are not wearing your seat belt. You aren't wearing your seat belt.   9. The crowd is not clapping and cheering. The crowd isn't clapping and cheering.

31-2 1. isn't joking   2. aren't praying   3. aren't dancing   4. am not making   5. isn't putting   6. aren't dripping   7. isn't wiggling   8. aren't walking   9. isn't squeezing   10. am not separating   11. aren't ending   12. isn't correcting   13. aren't complaining   14. isn't boring   15. isn't aiming   16. aren't solving   17. isn't working   18. am not starring   19. isn't winking   20. aren't freeing   21. isn't surrendering   22. aren't wrapping   23. isn't swallowing   24. isn't sharpening   25. isn't typing 26. aren't inviting

32 The Present Progressive (Continuous) Tense: Question Form

32-1   1. Are they talking about the newborn baby?   2. Is he hunting with a bow and arrow?   3. Is the saleslady offering you a good deal?   4. Is it walking backward or forward?   5. Are the employees adding their expenses for the business trip?   6. Is Mrs. Smith living in the suburbs?   7. Is Mr. Jones working in a gas station?   8. Is he slicing the pineapple?   9. Am I rocking the boat?   10. Is she sweating a lot?   11. Is my lip bleeding?   12. Are you bringing your compass when we go in the woods?   13. Are Bob and Tina on the beach enjoying the sunrise?   14. Am I eating your muffin?   15. Is Rosa making a cake for the surprise birthday party?

32-2   1. Is Tom spying on us?   2. Is he pushing the kids in the wheelbarrow?   3. Is the patient suffering a lot?   4. Is she cutting the crusty bread on the breadboard?   5. Is Jimmy throwing up in the bathroom? 6. Am I failing my science class?   7. Is Roger playing the bagpipes?   8. Are the children bursting the balloons?   9. Is the little boy showing me something?   10. Is the snail crawling on the tree?   11. Is Shane drawing a maple leaf?   12. Are the seals playing in the waves?   13. Are they swimming in the pool with their water wings?   14. Is Chris grating the cheese with the grater?   15. Are they kidding?   16. Is he shuffling the cards?   17. Is Grace sobbing in her bedroom?   18. Is the dog wagging its tail?

33 The Past Progressive (Continuous) Tense

33-1   1. The laboratory was testing the blood for leukemia and other diseases.   2. We were walking in the snow with our snowshoes.   3. The mechanic was lowering the car when it fell.   4. The girls were talking on the phone for two hours.   5. I was changing the lightbulb when I got a shock.   6. The kids were rolling down the mountain.   7. She was placing a wig on her head when I entered.   8. George was listening to music with his headphones.   9. Vance was covering his answers during the test.   10. We were buying a gift for the christening.   11. I was dropping a quarter in the tollbooth when he rammed the back of my car. 12. My daughter was blowing her nose.   13. The lights were glowing in the distance.   14. They were struggling to keep the files up-to-date.   15. We were dividing our time between the Grand Canyon and the casinos.

33-2   1. were blooming   2. was eating   3. was crushing   4. was warning   5. was welcoming   6. was putting   7. were wearing   8. were playing   9. were hiding   10. was reading   11. was wearing 12. was talking   13. were crying   14. was grieving   15. were weaving   16. was combing   17. was scolding   18. was working   19. were frightening   20. was gambling   21. were flying   22. was acting   23. were reaching   24. was sweeping   25. were hatching   26. was putting

34 The Past Progressive (Continuous) Tense: Negative Form

34-1   1. She was not getting chemotherapy treatments for lung cancer. She wasn't getting chemotherapy treatments for lung cancer.   2. My stomach was not growling in class this morning. My stomach wasn't growling in class this morning.   3. We were not driving on the wrong side of the road. We weren't driving on the wrong side of the road.   4. He was not smiling at you. He wasn't smiling at you.   5. It was not nipping my ankle. It wasn't nipping my ankle.   6. The collar was not choking the dog. The collar wasn't choking the dog.   7. Tania was not succeeding in her course and she quit. Tania wasn't succeeding in her course and she quit.   8. The guests were not eating the potato salad. The guests weren't eating the potato salad.   9. They were not joking. They weren't joking.

34-2   1. wasn't snipping   2. wasn't working   3. weren't overdoing   4. wasn't relying   5. wasn't carrying 6. weren't making   7. wasn't carving   8. wasn't coping   9. wasn't slurring   10. weren't diving 11. wasn't tasting   12. weren't feeding   13. wasn't cleaning   14. wasn't flapping   15. weren't distracting 16. wasn't dripping   17. wasn't wearing   18. weren't sitting   19. weren't jumping   20. weren't rotting 21. wasn't hovering   22. wasn't petting   23. weren't counting   24. wasn't wearing   25. wasn't breathing 26. weren't laughing

35 The Past Progressive (Continuous) Tense: Question Form

35-1 1. Were the police stopping everyone at the corner? 2. Was my yellow rubber duck floating in the bath? 3. Was the meat thawing on the counter? 4. Were the wounds on his body healing? 5. Was she hoping for a new nightgown for Christmas? 6. Was the ice cracking on the lake? 7. Was the beautiful peacock attracting a lot of attention? 8. Was she buying watermelon and corn on the cob for the picnic? 9. Were the actors rehearsing for the play? 10. Was it drifting on the sea? 11. Were they using matches to light the candles on the cake? 12. Were you swimming with goggles and a snorkel? 13. Was Réal grabbing the bull by the horns? 14. Was she taking vitamins during her pregnancy? 15. Was the housekeeper dusting the furniture?

35-2 1. Was she starting her car? 2. Were they begging us to stay for supper? 3. Were we closing the store early? 4. Were they walking barefoot on the pebbles? 5. Was the dog panting? 6. Were you scratching your elbow? 7. Was she measuring her waist and hips? 8. Was Danny daring me to jump in the lake? 9. Was it eating my peanut butter sandwich? 10. Were you ripping my sweater? 11. Was Gary omitting the details? 12. Was it following me? 13. Were the detectives investigating the crime? 14. Was he spitting on the sidewalk? 15. Were they raising goats? 16. Were you pretending to be a big ape? 17. Was I reading the right letter? 18. Was the ox pulling the cart?

36 Prepositions: *From* and *Of*

36-1 1. We gave her a beautiful bouquet of flowers. 2. I got a toothbrush from my dentist. 3. He is a member of the hockey hall of fame. 4. She sent me a postcard from Canada. 5. Peter is a man of many talents. 6. We heard voices from beyond the bushes. 7. He called me from a pay phone. 8. I need a cup of sugar for this recipe. 9. Is that guy from Mexico? 10. I work from Monday to Thursday. I don't work Friday. 11. Do you want a glass of beer? 12. She is a woman of value in our company. 13. The cat jumped from the couch to the window. 14. Open the gift from me.

36-2 1. of 2. of 3. from 4. of 5. from 6. of 7. of 8. from 9. of 10. of, from 11. of 12. of 13. from 14. of 15. from 16. from 17. of 18. of 19. of 20. from 21. of 22. from 23. from 24. from 25. of 26. from 27. of 28. from 29. from 30. of 31. of 32. from 33. of 34. from 35. of 36. from 37. of 38. from

37 Will: Future Tense

37-1 1. I will climb to the top of the lighthouse to see the ships. 2. You will become a rich and famous author. 3. The government will reduce taxes next year. 4. The fairy will grant you several wishes. 5. My mother will make a cherry pie. 6. We will study the brain in my science class. 7. They will enlarge the picture of the swordfish that they caught. 8. We will gather blueberries, strawberries, and raspberries to make jam. 9. He will hug and kiss you when he sees you. 10. Brad will introduce me to his parents tomorrow night. 11. We will ship the package to you this afternoon. 12. Mary will envy your friendship with Paul. 13. The government will ban tobacco in all public places. 14. She will pamper her new baby. 15. I will flip the pancakes now.

37-2 1. will calculate 2. will balance 3. will develop 4. will concentrate 5. will last 6. will postpone 7. will learn 8. will tame 9. will tell 10. will wonder 11. will order 12. will move 13. will miss 14. will bake 15. will continue 16. will be 17. will nod 18. will use 19. will get 20. will stimulate 21. will cause 22. will donate 23. will inform 24. will share

38 Will: Future Tense: Negative Form

38-1 1. He will not declare bankruptcy. He won't declare bankruptcy. 2. My neighbor will not trim his bushes. My neighbor won't trim his bushes. 3. John will not trim his sideburns. John won't trim his sideburns. 4. Anna will not go on a blind date. Anna won't go on a blind date. 5. You will not recognize me with my wig. You won't recognize me with my wig. 6. They will not allow you to stay overnight. They won't allow you to stay overnight. 7. We will not celebrate on New Year's Eve. We won't celebrate on New Year's Eve. 8. The man will not confess to the murder. The man won't confess to the murder. 9. I will not pawn my guitar. I won't pawn my guitar.

38-2 1. won't ruin 2. won't clog 3. won't issue 4. won't improve 5. won't guess 6. won't discuss 7. won't benefit 8. won't delay 9. won't compensate 10. won't allow 11. won't cure 12. won't purchase 13. won't listen 14. won't attempt 15. won't wear 16. won't sign 17. won't make 18. won't operate 19. won't betray 20. won't remove 21. won't have 22. won't live 23. won't mean 24. won't tolerate 25. won't hand 26. won't fail

39   *Will: Future Tense: Question Form*

39-1   1. Will the snow disappear in the spring?   2. Will your mother punish you for that?   3. Will the police accuse Sara?   4. Will you spell your last name for me?   5. Will she throw her old pajamas in the garbage?   6. Will he measure it with his brand-new tape measure?   7. Will Bobby show the judges his muscles?   8. Will it poison you with its fangs?   9. Will they mention it to their foreman?   10. Will the gardener spray the wasps and bees with poison?   11. Will they rescue the eagles on the island?   12. Will your boyfriend partake in the writing competition?   13. Will we travel a lot next year?   14. Will it kick me?   15. Will she buy a new ironing board and toaster for her apartment?

39-2   1. Will it arrive on time?   2. Will he publish his report?   3. Will they blame me?   4. Will we be in rush hour traffic?   5. Will our country ban the sale of ivory?   6. Will Sheila stick the magnet on the fridge?   7. Will you close your mouth when you eat?   8. Will we produce a lot of corn this year?   9. Will our company expand next year?   10. Will it rain tomorrow?   11. Will we trade our trailer for a boat?   12. Will he pause the movie for a few minutes?   13. Will I regret it?   14. Will it grind the coffee beans?   15. Will you require stitches in your knee?   16. Will the roof sag with all the snow on it?   17. Will they bid on the famous painting?   18. Will I gain weight if I eat this?   19. Will he respond?   20. Will I have enough time?

40   *Be Going To: Future Tense*

40-1   1. I am going to hurry because I don't want to miss my bus.   2. He drank too much, and now he is going to vomit.   3. You are going to dirty my floor with your muddy shoes.   4. The sun is going to shine all day today.   5. I am going to wait for you in the lobby downstairs.   6. We are going to sell our waterbed in our garage sale.   7. The kids are going to swim in the shallow end of the pool.   8. The adults are going to dive in the deep end of the pool.   9. You are going to injure your back if you lift that heavy box.   10. It is going to create problems in the office.   11. I am going to spread the jam on my toast.   12. My manager is going to check his schedule for next week.   13. You are going to be upset if the audience doesn't applaud.   14. He is going to surprise her with a diamond ring.   15. She is going to remove your name from the list.

40-2   1. are, assume   2. is, suggest   3. is, tighten   4. am, clip   5. are, observe   6. am, give   7. is, seem   8. are, remind   9. are, admit   10. is, be   11. is, ask   12. am, tap   13. are, commute   14. are, skip   15. am, put   16. is, marry   17. is, occur   18. are, charge   19. is, belong   20. is, vanish   21. am, buy   22. are, be

41   *Be Going To: Future Tense: Negative Form*

41-1   1. My company is not going to announce cutbacks for the new year. My company isn't going to announce cutbacks for the new year.   2. We are not going to submit the report in the morning. We aren't going to submit the report in the morning.   3. I am not going to withdraw all my money. No contraction.   4. They are not going to invest the funds in the stock market. They aren't going to invest the funds in the stock market.   5. This experience is not going to haunt me for the rest of my life. This experience isn't going to haunt me for the rest of my life.   6. Annie is not going to chill the wine before she serves it. Annie isn't going to chill the wine before she serves it.   7. The ostrich is not going to attack you. The ostrich isn't going to attack you.   8. You are not going to reuse the bags. You aren't going to reuse the bags.   9. He is not going to divorce his wife. He isn't going to divorce his wife.

41-2   1. aren't   2. isn't   3. aren't   4. aren't   5. aren't   6. isn't   7. am not   8. aren't   9. isn't   10. aren't   11. isn't   12. am not   13. isn't   14. aren't   15. aren't   16. am not   17. isn't   18. aren't   19. isn't   20. isn't   21. aren't   22. isn't   23. isn't   24. aren't   25. aren't   26. isn't   27. isn't   28. aren't

42   *Be Going To: Future Tense: Question Form*

42-1   1. Is he going to share this knowledge with the world?   2. Is she going to cooperate with us?   3. Are you going to provide me with a good explanation?   4. Are they going to immigrate to the United States in

August?   5. Is it going to turn green when I put it in water?   6. Is the immigration office going to process my file in July?   7. Are my parents going to supply me with my school supplies in September?   8. Am I going to drain the vegetables with this?   9. Are they going to complete the project in November or December?   10. Is she going to apply for a new job in October?   11. Are you going to scrub the bathtub now?   12. Are the cows and horses going to graze in the field?   13. Are you going to dip the apple in honey?   14. Are we going to store the snowblower in the garage during the summer?   15. Is the teacher going to talk about war and peace in history class today?

42-2   1. Is he going to promise to be good?   2. Are you going to wish for a car again?   3. Am I going to compete with you?   4. Is she going to rest on the couch?   5. Are you going to fake that you are sick?   6. Is he going to break the icicles with the shovel?   7. Is Sonia going to buy new oven mitts?   8. Is the insurance company going to assess the damage?   9. Are you going to cry?   10. Is it going to be sunny tomorrow?   11. Am I going to have a second interview?   12. Are we going to wait a long time at customs?   13. Is she going to sort the dirty laundry?   14. Is Bobby going to tidy his room?   15. Are we going to watch the scary movie about the werewolf?   16. Are they going to whistle the song?   17. Are they going to bring shrimp to the party tomorrow night?   18. Is it going to be good?

43 The Indefinite Articles: A and *An*

43-1   1. We saw a horrible accident this morning.   2. This is a one-way street.   3. My uncle has an ostrich on his farm.   4. He is an American citizen.   5. I wear a uniform to work.   6. There was an earthquake last night.   7. You are an excellent student.   8. I need a hammer to fix the roof.   9. It was a useful tool.   10. I have a red apple in my lunch bag.   11. We bought an oil painting at the market.   12. This is a busy airport.   13. Give me an example, please.   14. We played the game for an hour and a half.

43-2   1. an, a, a   2. a   3. an, a   4. an   5. a, an, a   6. an   7. an   8. a   9. a   10. an   11. a   12. an, a, an   13. a   14. an, a, an, a, an   15. a, a   16. an   17. an   18. an   19. a, a   20. an, a   21. a   22. an   23. a   24. an   25. an, a   26. an   27. a   28. an   29. a   30. an   31. an   32. a, a, an   33. a   34. an, a, a   35. a, an   36. an   37. a   38. an   39. a   40. an

44 Irregular Verbs Table

No exercises

45 The Present Perfect Tense

45-1   1. They have worked in Japan.   2. William has grown a lot since the last time I saw him.   3. My parents have been together for twenty years.   4. They have borrowed a lot of money from their friends.   5. She has taught English in many different schools.   6. You have offended everybody in the office.   7. I have heard that noise in my car several times.   8. He has cheated on every one of his tests.   9. We have tried to help them.   10. It has taken a long time.

45-2   1. has broken   2. have used   3. have seen   4. has made   5. has bitten   6. have offered   7. have flown   8. have suffered   9. have torn   10. has forgiven   11. have known   12. has accused   13. has started   14. have discussed   15. have warned   16. has helped   17. have chosen   18. has sung   19. have thanked   20. has climbed

46 The Present Perfect Tense: Negative Form

46-1   1. My teacher has not written two books. My teacher hasn't written two books.   2. I have not accepted the offer. I haven't accepted the offer.   3. They have not invented many fun games. They haven't invented many fun games.   4. The light has not attracted all the bugs. The light hasn't attracted all the bugs.   5. Joe and Lynn have not become rich and famous. Joe and Lynn haven't become rich and famous.   6. We have not found that he works very hard. We haven't found that he works very hard.   7. Cassandra has not waited a long time for the news. Cassandra hasn't waited a long time for the news.

46-2   1. haven't kept   2. hasn't noticed   3. haven't gone   4. hasn't convinced   5. hasn't built   6. haven't done   7. hasn't expressed   8. haven't wasted   9. haven't given   10. haven't solved   11. hasn't had   12. haven't asked   13. hasn't beaten   14. haven't escaped   15. hasn't fallen   16. hasn't forgotten

47 The Present Perfect Tense: Question Form

47-1 1. Have you shown your report card to your parents? 2. Has the teacher corrected all the exams? 3. Have I brought enough for everybody? 4. Has my dog chewed all the furniture? 5. Has it followed me to school often? 6. Have we wrapped all the gifts? 7. Has she blown out all the candles on the cake? 8. Have they apologized many times? 9. Has he drawn many beautiful pictures for her? 10. Have we benefited from that? 11. Has it hidden the peanuts? 12. Have I paid all the bills? 13. Has the sun risen? 14. Have I awoken the baby again?

47-2 1. Have you ironed the clothes? 2. Has he driven many miles? 3. Has Leora answered all the questions? 4. Have they fed the animals? 5. Has it occurred a few times? 6. Have I read that book before? 7. Have we invested all our money? 8. Have I parked here before? 9. Have you lost a lot of weight? 10. Has he managed the company alone? 11. Has Elvis left the building? 12. Has it disappeared? 13. Has Robin met many famous people? 14. Has George slept late many times?

48 The Past Perfect Tense

48-1 1. We had decided to stay home when they asked us to go out for dinner. 2. They had sold their boat when they bought the motorcycle. 3. He had expected to see you before you left. 4. I had had supper, so I only ate the dessert. 5. My grandmother had died when I was born. 6. The rain had stopped, so we went for a walk. 7. I had done the laundry when he brought me his dirty clothes. 8. She had seen the movie before, so she went to bed. 9. The teacher had explained the lesson twice, but we didn't understand. 10. We had passed all our exams, so we celebrated all night.

48-2 1. had thrown 2. had sung 3. had opened 4. had ordered 5. had swept 6. had worried 7. had ridden 8. had run 9. had completed 10. had finished 11. had rung 12. had rescued 13. had cut 14. had divorced

49 The Past Perfect Tense: Negative Form

49-1 1. He had not held a baby before today. He hadn't held a baby before today. 2. It had not arrived, so I called the store. It hadn't arrived, so I called the store. 3. I had not noticed that you were standing there. I hadn't noticed that you were standing there. 4. She had not paid the phone bill, so I paid it. She hadn't paid the phone bill, so I paid it. 5. They had not seen that movie before, and they really enjoyed it. They hadn't seen that movie before, and they really enjoyed it. 6. We had not flown before, so we were very nervous on the airplane. We hadn't flown before, so we were very nervous on the airplane. 7. You had not followed the instructions, and you made a mistake. You hadn't followed the instructions, and you made a mistake.

49-2 1. hadn't eaten 2. hadn't cleaned 3. hadn't rained 4. hadn't driven 5. hadn't hung 6. hadn't talked 7. hadn't bought 8. hadn't sent 9. hadn't had 10. hadn't borrowed 11. hadn't given 12. hadn't waited 13. hadn't smoked 14. hadn't drunk 15. hadn't started 16. hadn't made

50 The Past Perfect Tense: Question Form

50-1 1. Had he known that you were my brother? 2. Had they withdrawn all the money from their savings account? 3. Had you tried to ski before you bought the skis? 4. Had the play ended when she arrived? 5. Had you given him your phone number? 6. Had your aunt worn this dress before? 7. Had they tasted seafood before today? 8. Had Richard and Jennifer planned their vacation together? 9. Had Wade made coffee for everybody? 10. Had you had your breakfast before you went to school? 11. Had the teacher spoken to you before she called your parents? 12. Had it happened before? 13. Had you seen that woman before she came to your house? 14. Had they lived in Ontario before they moved to British Columbia?

50-2 1. Had she realized what she did? 2. Had you taken the wrong bus? 3. Had it seemed fair to everyone? 4. Had your boss brought his dog to work before today? 5. Had Tony been in the hospital before he had his operation? 6. Had they left the building before the fire started? 7. Had Jessica worked as a flight attendant before she became a nurse? 8. Had he taken the time to do it right? 9. Had they noticed where you put it? 10. Had you paid cash for it? 11. Had Maria found a new job before she quit her old job? 12. Had he played hockey before he joined our team? 13. Had you read the contract before you signed it? 14. Had it belonged to your grandmother before your mother gave it to you?

51 The Future Perfect Tense

51-1   1. She will have finished all the housework by lunch time.   2. I will have taken my shower by the time you arrive.   3. The flowers in my garden will have died by the end of October.   4. Mrs. Stacey will have taught for 30 years when she finally retires.   5. They will have eaten supper by the time we arrive.   6. The plane will have left by the time we arrive at the airport.   7. The girls will have completed their project by Saturday.   8. Chris will have found a new job by the end of the summer.   9. I will have started school by September.   10. Benjamin will have read the complete series by the time he finishes this book.   11. We will have spent all our money by the time we finish our vacation.

51-2   1. She'll have lost   2. He'll have had   3. We'll have received   4. Jesse will have left   5. They'll have elected   6. The birds will have flown   7. I'll have spoken   8. My mother-in-law will have been   9. You'll have learned   10. She'll have worked   11. They'll have completed   12. The lake will have frozen   13. We'll have driven   14. I'll have forgotten   15. The snow will have melted   16. They'll have seen

52 The Future Perfect Tense: Negative Form

52-1   1. We will not have been here for two hours by the time the bus arrives. We won't have been here for two hours by the time the bus arrives.   2. They will not have opened all the gifts by noon. They won't have opened all the gifts by noon.   3. You will not have convinced the judges by the time you finish your song. You won't have convinced the judges by the time you finish your song.   4. We will not have met the neighbors by the time we move. We won't have met the neighbors by the time we move.   5. My parents will not have discussed it by the weekend. My parents won't have discussed it by the weekend.   6. The kids will not have eaten by 5 o'clock. The kids won't have eaten by 5 o'clock.   7. He will not have become famous by the time he is 30 years old. He won't have become famous by the time he is 30 years old.

52-2   1. won't have chosen   2. won't have spoken   3. won't have prevented   4. won't have talked   5. won't have purchased   6. won't have helped   7. won't have shown   8. won't have brought   9. won't have sorted   10. won't have swept   11. won't have made   12. won't have gone   13. won't have completed   14. won't have sliced   15. won't have left   16. won't have postponed

53 The Future Perfect Tense: Question Form

53-1   1. Will we have signed all the necessary documents?   2. Will you have spoken to Bob before Friday?   3. Will Joanie have cleaned the basement before everybody arrives for the party?   4. Will they have saved enough money to visit their cousins in California?   5. Will it have been in the oven for four hours by 6 o'clock?   6. Will he have worked there long enough to get a bonus at the end of the year?   7. Will the kids have gone to bed by the time I arrive tonight?   8. Will you have eaten your dessert by the time I finish my meal?   9. Will she have finished her exams by May?   10. Will Dennis have written the report by Tuesday?   11. Will we have seen everything before we leave?   12. Will they have moved by July?   13. Will the rain have stopped by the morning?   14. Will the birds have flown south by November?

53-2   1. Will you have paid all the bills by the end of the month?   2. Will the game have started if we arrive at 7 o'clock?   3. Will the secretary have sent all the letters by next Thursday?   4. Will she have swept the bedrooms by the time I finish the dishes?   5. Will you have fed the baby before the movie starts?   6. Will we have caught many trout by sunset?   7. Will Wendy have begun her painting class by September?   8. Will I have met all the new students by the end of the day?   9. Will he have read the newspaper by the time I finish my book?   10. Will you have removed all the furniture by the time the painters come?   11. Will the mechanic have repaired the car by 6 o'clock?   12. Will you have forgotten about us by then?

REVIEW EXERCISES
54 Verb Tenses Review: 1

54-1   1. The kids were playing outside in the leaves.   2. Tommy had not played baseball until he started school.   3. Does your brother play football at the university?   4. She has played the piano at church many times.   5. Did you play with Bobby at school today?   6. Are they going to play with their friends at the park?   7. We play hockey on the street in the summer.   8. I will play games on my phone in the waiting room.   9. My cat isn't playing with the puppy.   10. They don't play hide and seek in the dark.   11. Kristy hasn't played with her dolls all week.   12. Were your sisters playing in the sandbox?   13. We won't play with water guns in the house, Mom.   14. My parents are playing cards with the neighbors.   15. Have you played with a yo-yo before?   16. Derek is not going to play the drums all night, I hope.   17. She will have played that song 50 times by tonight.   18. You played with fire and you got burned.   19. Are Jordan and Julien playing with their trucks?   20. Will he play the guitar for us?   21. They are going to play on the swings during recess.   22. We have not played checkers or chess in a long time.   23. Will you play dice with me later?

55 Verb Tenses Review: 2

55-1   1. Had you bought enough plates for all the guests?   2. I bought it at the garage sale down the street.   3. She isn't going to buy new clothes for the trip.   4. They had not bought butter before.   5. Are you buying that for me?   6. Jessica didn't buy balloons for the party.   7. I will buy my lunch in the cafeteria tomorrow.   8. Have you bought this kind of toothpaste?   9. My husband buys a lot of tools.   10. Rachel will have bought all her school books by next week.   11. Were they buying a new truck when you saw them?   12. We don't buy fur products.   13. Will Tony have bought furniture before he moves into his house?   14. My mother did not buy a lot of vegetables at the market.   15. Joseph is buying flowers for his girlfriend.   16. Did you buy the tickets?   17. Will they buy bagels and cheese?   18. We won't buy from that store again.   19. The boys had bought everything for their camping trip.   20. Sonia has not bought her wedding dress.   21. I am not going to buy new tires.   22. Did she buy the newspaper this morning?   23. Is your brother going to buy a new calculator?

56 Verb Tenses Review: 3

56-1   1. I was calling my friend.   2. Have they called you?   3. Sandy will call to make a complaint.   4. Do you call your mother every week?   5. He hasn't called me in over a month.   6. Did they call to confirm my appointment?   7. She will have called by Friday, I hope.   8. Are you calling me a chicken?   9. We called Monique to see if you were there.   10. Is Stacy going to call her brother overseas tonight?   11. I have called you several times since your wedding.   12. They hadn't called the fire department.   13. Will you call the plumber, please?   14. She was not calling the police.   15. I am not going to call you again.   16. Jack calls every day just to say hello.   17. I had called the doctor, but he was on vacation that week.   18. We are calling to congratulate you.   19. Will they have called before we leave next week?   20. Janice does not call him anymore.   21. He won't call too late.   22. I am calling to invite you to our annual barbecue.   23. It isn't calling to its baby.

57 Verb Tenses Review: 4

57-1   1. Were you sleeping in my bed?   2. We slept until dawn.   3. Mary hadn't slept at that hotel before.   4. Will they have slept enough by the time the plane lands?   5. I won't sleep in the car on the way to Nova Scotia.   6. Joe did not sleep all afternoon.   7. The girls hadn't slept in a tent before they went camping with Sandra.   8. Was it sleeping on my pillow?   9. We are not going to sleep if you are not home.   10. I didn't sleep all night.   11. She hasn't slept in days.   12. Is Mike sleeping in my sleeping bag?   13. He sleeps with the light on.   14. Did you sleep well last night?   15. Will the dog sleep in the dog house?   16. I was sleeping when you called.   17. Has he slept on the couch often?   18. Does a bear sleep all winter?   19. We have slept under the stars many times.   20. Crystal is sleeping with her favorite doll.   21. My cat doesn't sleep outside.   22. I will sleep until noon tomorrow.   23. Gerry will have slept 12 hours by 8 o'clock.

58 Verb Tenses Practice: 1

58-1   1. I ask the right questions.   2. I do not (don't) ask the right questions.   3. Do I ask the right questions?   4. I asked the right questions.   5. I did not (didn't) ask the right questions.   6. Did I ask the right questions?   7. I am asking the right questions.   8. I am not asking the right questions.   9. Am I asking the right questions?   10. I was asking the right questions.   11. I was not (wasn't) asking the right questions.   12. Was I asking the right questions?   13. I will ask the right questions.   14. I will not (won't) ask the right questions.   15. Will I ask the right questions?   16. I am going to ask the right questions.   17. I am not going to ask the right questions.   18. Am I going to ask the right questions?   19. I have asked the right questions.   20. I have not (haven't) asked the right questions.   21. Have I asked the right questions?   22. I had asked the right questions.   23. I had not (hadn't) asked the right questions.   24. Had I asked the right questions?   25. I will have asked the right questions.   26. I will not (won't) have asked the right questions.   27. Will I have asked the right questions?

58-2   1. You take the bus.   2. You do not (don't) take the bus.   3. Do you take the bus?   4. You took the bus.   5. You did not (didn't) take the bus.   6. Did you take the bus?   7. You are taking the bus.   8. You are not (aren't) taking the bus.   9. Are you taking the bus?   10. You were taking the bus.   11. You were not (weren't) taking the bus.   12. Were you taking the bus?   13. You will take the bus.   14. You will not (won't) take the bus.   15. Will you take the bus?   16. You are going to take the bus.   17. You are not (aren't) going to take the bus.   18. Are you going to take the bus?   19. You have taken the bus.   20. You have not (haven't) taken the bus.   21. Have you taken the bus?   22. You had taken the bus.   23. You had not (hadn't) taken the bus.   24. Had you taken the bus?   25. You will have taken the bus.   26. You will not (won't) have taken the bus.   27. Will you have taken the bus?

58-3   1. He cleans his car.   2. He does not (doesn't) clean his car.   3. Does he clean his car?   4. He cleaned his car.   5. He did not (didn't) clean his car.   6. Did he clean his car?   7. He is cleaning his car.   8. He is not (isn't) cleaning his car.   9. Is he cleaning his car?   10. He was cleaning his car.   11. He was not (wasn't) cleaning his car.   12. Was he cleaning his car?   13. He will clean his car.   14. He will not (won't) clean his car.   15. Will he clean his car?   16. He is going to clean his car.   17. He is not (isn't) going to clean his car.   18. Is he going to clean his car?   19. He has cleaned his car.   20. He has not (hasn't) cleaned his car.   21. Has he cleaned his car?   22. He had cleaned his car.   23. He had not (hadn't) cleaned his car.   24. Had he cleaned his car?   25. He will have cleaned his car.   26. He will not (won't) have cleaned his car.   27. Will he have cleaned his car?

58-4   1. She speaks on the phone.   2. She does not (doesn't) speak on the phone.   3. Does she speak on the phone?   4. She spoke on the phone.   5. She did not (didn't) speak on the phone.   6. Did she speak on the phone?   7. She is speaking on the phone.   8. She is not (isn't) speaking on the phone.   9. Is she speaking on the phone?   10. She was speaking on the phone.   11. She was not (wasn't) speaking on the phone.   12. Was she speaking on the phone?   13. She will speak on the phone.   14. She will not (won't) speak on the phone.   15. Will she speak on the phone?   16. She is going to speak on the phone.   17. She is not (isn't) going to speak on the phone.   18. Is she going to speak on the phone?   19. She has spoken on the phone.   20. She has not (hasn't) spoken on the phone.   21. Has she spoken on the phone?   22. She had spoken on the phone.   23. She had not (hadn't) spoken on the phone.   24. Had she spoken on the phone?   25. She will have spoken on the phone.   26. She will not (won't) have spoken on the phone.   27. Will she have spoken on the phone?

59   Verb Tenses Practice: 2

59-1   1. It eats bugs.   2. It does not (doesn't) eat bugs.   3. Does it eat bugs?   4. It ate bugs.   5. It did not (didn't) eat bugs.   6. Did it eat bugs?   7. It is eating bugs.   8. It is not (isn't) eating bugs.   9. Is it eating bugs?   10. It was eating bugs.   11. It was not (wasn't) eating bugs.   12. Was it eating bugs?   13. It will eat bugs.   14. It will not (won't) eat bugs.   15. Will it eat bugs?   16. It is going to eat bugs.   17. It is not (isn't) going to eat bugs.   18. Is it going to eat bugs?   19. It has eaten bugs.   20. It has not (hasn't) eaten bugs.   21. Has it eaten bugs?   22. It had eaten bugs.   23. It had not (hadn't) eaten bugs.   24. Had it eaten bugs?   25. It will have eaten bugs.   26. It will not (won't) have eaten bugs.   27. Will it have eaten bugs?

59-2   1. We live in an apartment.   2. We do not (don't) live in an apartment.   3. Do we live in an apartment?   4. We lived in an apartment.   5. We did not (didn't) live in an apartment.   6. Did we live in an apartment?   7. We are living in an apartment.   8. We are not (aren't) living in an apartment.   9. Are we living in an apartment?   10. We were living in an apartment.   11. We were not (weren't) living in an apartment.   12. Were we living in an apartment?   13. We will live in an apartment.   14. We will not (won't) live in an apartment.   15. Will we live in an apartment?   16. We are going to live in an apartment.   17. We are not (aren't) going to live in an apartment.   18. Are we going to live in an apartment?   19. We have lived in an apartment.   20. We have not (haven't) lived in an apartment.   21. Have we lived in an apartment?   22. We had lived in an apartment.   23. We had not (hadn't) lived in an apartment.   24. Had we lived in an apartment?   25. We will have lived in an apartment.   26. We will not (won't) have lived in an apartment.   27. Will we have lived in an apartment?

59-3   1. They go to college.   2. They do not (don't) go to college.   3. Do they go to college?   4. They went to college.   5. They did not (didn't) go to college.   6. Did they go to college?   7. They are going to college.

8. They are not (aren't) going to college.   9. Are they going to college?   10. They were going to college.
11. They were not (weren't) going to college.   12. Were they going to college?   13. They will go to college.
14. They will not (won't) go to college.   15. Will they go to college?   16. They are going to go to college.
17. They are not (aren't) going to go to college.   18. Are they going to go to college?   19. They have gone to college.   20. They have not (haven't) gone to college.   21. Have they gone to college?   22. They had gone to college.   23. They had not (hadn't) gone to college.   24. Had they gone to college?   25. They will have gone to college.   26. They will not (won't) have gone to college.   27. Will they have gone to college?

60   Regular and Irregular Verbs Review

60-1   1. did   2. screamed, saw   3. filled   4. fell   5. felt, failed   6. walked, talked   7. burned/burnt   8. put
9. broke, needed   10. painted   11. read   12. wore   13. forgot, brought   14. borrowed, lent   15. ran
16. climbed, dived/dove   17. lost   18. went   19. barked, growled   20. left, melted   21. blew, made
22. snored, annoyed   23. thanked   24. dreamed/dreamt   25. cost   26. owned, sold   27. followed,
kept   28. mailed   29. ordered   30. chewed   31. hurt, said   32. lasted   33. knitted/knit   34. thought
35. hid   36. woke, heard   37. sold, bought   38. forgot, froze   39. shined/shone   40. sewed
41. played   42. moved   43. spent   44. convinced   45. found   46. gave   47. typed   48. spilled/spilt
49. asked, said   50. flew

61   Grammar Review

61-1   1. OK.   2. She goes to the corner to wait for the bus.   3. Will she have talked to her mother by tonight?
4. OK.   5. They decided to leave before midnight last Wednesday night.   6. We lent them our sleeping
bags and tent last weekend.   7. Have you been to the museum?   8. We drove to Toronto for the weekend.
9. I already read that book.   10. OK.   11. We are going to see a play at the theater tonight.   12. OK.
13. OK.   14. Put it in the garbage can.   15. They won't have noticed the changes we made to the
document.   16. Will they publish your story?   17. We only stayed for an hour.   18. OK.   19. He went
to the store for milk and bread last night.   20. She broke my favorite glass yesterday morning.   21. Don't
walk in the puddle.   22. Are there enough toys for the kids to play with?   23. He is going to go to the
circus with his niece.

61-2   1. We like to look at the stars at night.   2. She goes to the library to study.   3. OK.   4. I talked to the
owner of the building.   5. Don't worry. They won't forget about it.   6. I have brought cookies for everyone
many times.   7. Our girls like strawberry ice cream.   8. Why did you do that?   9. Tracy has many new
friends at school.   10. We sent the package last week.   11. OK.   12. I have five gold rings on my fingers.
13. It wasn't raining yesterday.   14. The twins are 10 years old.   15. Janet tries to exercise every morning.
16. OK.   17. I am really cold. I will put on my slippers.   18. Are they your brothers?   19. Susan isn't very
tall for her age.   20. We flew to Boston for their wedding.   21. OK.   22. OK.   23. They met their friends
in Quebec City.

61-3   1. Mrs. Fletcher taught eighth grade last year.   2. OK.   3. There weren't enough chairs in the classroom
for all the students.   4. Did you answer the phone?   5. It is a very special birthday card.   6. I hope he
likes his gift.   7. OK.   8. You need a uniform to enter the building.   9. I haven't seen the results of the
tests.   10. Arnold likes black cats.   11. OK.   12. We want to go to Alaska next summer.   13. She will
hold the baby while I go in the bank.   14. There are a few foxes in the woods.   15. OK.   16. OK.
17. I sat next to Philip on the plane.   18. The baby cried all night last night.   19. Give the screwdriver to
Justin, please.   20. OK.   21. Did they watch the baseball game last night?   22. We eat at the restaurant
every Friday night.   23. There wasn't enough time.

62   Vocabulary Review

62-1   1. corkscrew   2. lawn mower   3. clothesline   4. pan   5. shirt   6. soap   7. kettle   8. watch
9. pond   10. appointment   11. noodles   12. recipe, dessert   13. butter   14. blush   15. pregnancy
16. noise   17. truth   18. housework   19. mall   20. plan   21. sing   22. ship   23. hangers
24. mouth   25. garden   26. nice   27. icing   28. lid   29. scar   30. snack   31. dew   32. reason
33. tusks   34. cheek   35. guests   36. wrist   37. bleachers   38. lend   39. beard   40. wrinkles
41. pancakes   42. window   43. silk   44. crown, crowd   45. everything   46. pie   47. mortgage
48. dizzy   49. kitchen   50. wig   51. elbow   52. ferry   53. wasp   54. oar   55. groom   56. ant
57. flour   58. pebble   59. leftovers   60. sunrise

63 Word Search Puzzles

63-1

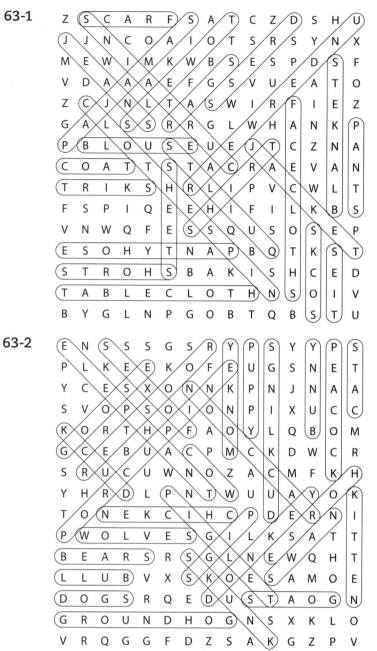

63-2

63-3

```
T S H E L L S D J G W H A L E
C R Z F T U O R T O W A V E S
L S E S L L R B C G D N A S W
A W H A P S Z G T G K I C W M
M O S H S S Y C O L O R F U L
S N I S G U E D E E W A E S S
X N F K O X R L J S G T H H W
S I T C L Q M E B E J S I H A
G M A O D Z Q S T B I P M E T
O L C R F S S L U F U P M A E
R O E U I I E N P Q B K T E R
F O X E S B L U S N O R K E L
D U B W H H S T L M A T W R L
N E M G O R F S E H R S C H H
S R E V I D G O S R K G P O A
```

63-4

```
V B H S E O H S Q R X E E Q A
M L N A B I K E A M T L O J Q
D A I Q I R S K I S Q Z I R N
M N S R V R E K D I E Z D K J
P K O K D A D M O M P U A A T
O E D J A O S R M O U P R M T
S T A Z Q T L Y Y A B S A S E
S S P U C R E L O E H L T L A
S E H T O L C S S T R R T C P
D I S H E S J E O R O T S R O
F U R N I T U R E L E T I I T
B O W L S P G Z L K O A K B C
K S A P R H A E L O H X S N R
I R L O Y A R N L C V F U M S
Y W U O P R G S S T F E T L X
```

64 Scrambled Sentences

64-1
1. Please call me next week if you have time.   2. She gave it to her daughter for her birthday.   3. I worked late last night, so I am very tired today.   4. There are many ships at the bottom of the ocean.   5. I need my crutches to walk from here to there.   6. It was a nice day, so I hung my sheets on the clothesline to dry.
7. Last night I burned my finger when I lit the match to light the fire in the fireplace.   8. Mary hopes that her mother makes a chocolate cake with vanilla icing for her birthday party next week.   9. I gave you a five dollar bill, so give me four one dollar coins, three quarters, two dimes, and a nickel.   10. We were making supper in the kitchen when the fire started in the basement.

64-2
1. My landlord raised the rent again, and he wants me to sign a new lease this year.   2. I am in trouble because my teacher wrote a note to my parents about my bad behavior in class.   3. When I arrived at work this morning, I realized that I was wearing my shirt inside out.   4. There is something wrong with that bird because it is flying upside down.   5. I lent my new car to my nephew, and when he brought it back, there was a dent in the door.   6. My brother wore a new suit and a black tie to work today because he had a very important meeting.   7. Martin is looking for a new job because he is making only the minimum wage.
8. I live in a quiet and friendly neighborhood very close to Montreal.

NOTES

Notes

NOTES

NOTES

NOTES

NOTES

NOTES

NOTES

NOTES

NOTES